THE COMPLETE VEGETABLE COOKBOOK

THE COMPLETE VEGETABLE COOKBOOK

JAMES STRAWBRIDGE

*A seasonal, zero-waste guide
to cooking with vegetables*

Art Direction and Food Photography James Strawbridge
Other Photography Simon Burt

Project Editor Holly Kyte
Art Editor Abi Read
Project Art Editor Harriet Yeomans
Editorial Assistant Lucy Philpott
Senior Editor Alastair Laing
Managing Editor Ruth O'Rourke
Managing Art Editor Christine Keilty
Production Editor Heather Blagden
US Editor Kayla Dugger
US Consultant Tom Hirschfeld
Production Controller Rebecca Parton
Jacket Designer Amy Cox
Jacket Co-ordinator Lucy Philpott
Art Director Maxine Pedliham
Publishing Director Katie Cowan

First American Edition, 2021
Published in the United States by DK Publishing
1450 Broadway, Suite 801, New York, NY 10018

A catalog record for this book
is available from the Library of Congress.
ISBN 978-0-7440-3673-2

Printed and bound in China

For the curious
www.dk.com

CONTENTS

Introduction

I started to really love veggie cooking when I left school and was living a self-sufficient lifestyle with my family in Cornwall. We were growing almost all our own food on a smallholding, and the responsibility to do the veggies justice once harvested was huge. Taking turns cooking our vegetables was a daily challenge and a source of great enjoyment, with a fun competitive edge. I learned many lessons along the way and was forced to become a creative chef by necessity—as keen gardeners will know, when faced with a surplus, you need to think outside the box and come up with fresh recipes each week to avoid veggie fatigue. The same challenge faces many of us who order a veggie box or try to eat seasonally.

Today, lots of people are aiming to improve their diet and reduce their impact on the planet by living more sustainably. And increasing the proportion of vegetables you eat is one of the most effective ways to do both. The health and eco benefits are matched by rewarding culinary experiences. Vegetables are utterly delicious, and whatever your motivation is for eating more of them, I hope this book provides you with plenty of creative ideas. My aim is to revitalize your vegetable cooking and broaden your repertoire of recipes, and also to share culinary tips and information about zero-waste cooking. Some dishes have been handed down through generations; others I've tasted when traveling and replicated at home, or invented out of necessity. They all enliven my senses. This book is not a vegetable manifesto. It's more a celebration of veggies intended to inspire and enthuse. If you're not smiling, you are doing it wrong!

RELAX AT THE DINNER TABLE

I've inherited an approach to food heavily inspired by my mom and dad, who fed our family good, home-cooked food when I was young, and I try to instill that same from-scratch approach in my children. I do feel that a strong awareness of the environmental impact of our food is essential to bring about change across our society. So we express gratitude for each meal and take the time to enjoy eating together whenever we can.

This slowing down at the table and the removal of processed foods from your diet makes a huge difference in how you feel after eating. Even the notion of taking time to digest, talk, and catch up over a meal is a ritual that has been lost from many family dinner tables. I hope that these dishes brighten your mealtimes and make them a welcoming, communal experience for your family and friends. Nowadays, the lines between vegan, vegetarian, and flexitarian have become more blurred, and I think that is a positive. We are less judgmental about who eats what, and therefore it's no longer an odd thing to say proudly, "I love eating vegetables." Good food should always be shared and appreciated with an open heart.

DEVELOP YOUR SKILLS

To create delicious recipes, you need great ingredients and a set of basic skills. I've provided a range of my favorite methods in the "Ways with Veggies" section. Try to reinforce your kitchen confidence by practicing lots, and once you have a good grip on a particular vegetable, never be shy about experimenting. To regain the love of cooking and eating veggies, which is especially important if you've been put off certain vegetables as a child due to soggy school meals or overcooked dinners, start with the basics and then gradually get more adventurous. Most veggies are extremely forgiving once you've mastered the basic preparation. Try unusual ingredients together and make up your own flavor combinations. Be innovative and brave— have fun and unleash your inner veggie chef!

EMBRACE ZERO WASTE

Often vegetables are sold with their roots and tops removed, wrapped in plastic, and sometimes even prechopped in a single-use bag. This disconnect from how veggies are pulled from the ground is tragic. We have lost so much knowledge of how to help raw veggies on their journey from fork to plate.

In a bid to get food that's quicker to prepare, easier to chop, or that simply fits in the fridge more compactly, we throw away and waste so many valuable parts of the plant. I hope that by looking at each vegetable closely and suggesting ways to cook the tops, peel, roots, and shoots, I can help you reduce food waste and make nutrient-packed meals in the process. Zero-waste cooking is a mindset, and once you embrace it, you will find yourself constantly seeking new ways to use all the edible parts. This is not a new style of cooking; it's inspired by the past.

Cooks used to be more thrifty with their food, making their own stocks and sauces and using all of the vegetable to deliver extra flavor. With greater convenience have come complacency and such horrendous waste. Together, we can reverse this culinary trend and all do our small part to achieve a zero-waste future. It'll take a long time and plenty of carrot-top pesto and root-peel chips, but I hope this approach will soon become standard kitchen practice again, a habit we have all formed rather than something we have to tell ourselves to do.

SEASONALITY

Eating food that's in season is a way of life rather than just a way of cooking. It involves a patient worldview that celebrates what we have in the moment rather than looking over the horizon and wanting more. We've grown accustomed to the global movement of ingredients, so we are sold asparagus in September or tomatoes in January, when they are not in season. This crazy availability of vegetables all year round has removed the simple joy you get from waiting for something to grow, mature, and ripen, ready to eat. We are all responsible for this lapse, having been suckered into the intoxicating array of veggies you can buy all year round, and it's going to take years of adapting back to a more seasonal way of cooking. But from my perspective, it is worth persevering with,

because the taste and flavor of local, seasonal vegetables cannot be beaten. I love eating braised cabbage in winter or spicy stuffed bell peppers in the summer. This outlook on food also represents a simpler way of cooking that's focused closer to home and feels more supportive of our local community and the wider environment. Fundamentally, seasonal vegetables taste better, are better for the planet, and give your body more of the nutrients you need to be healthy—it's a no-brainer.

> " "
>
> *As the soil warms up and the days lengthen, tender shoots and leaves arrive, bringing optimism, fresh flavors, and a great sense of well-being.*
>
> " "

SPRING

Asparagus
LOVE ME TENDER, COOK ME WELL

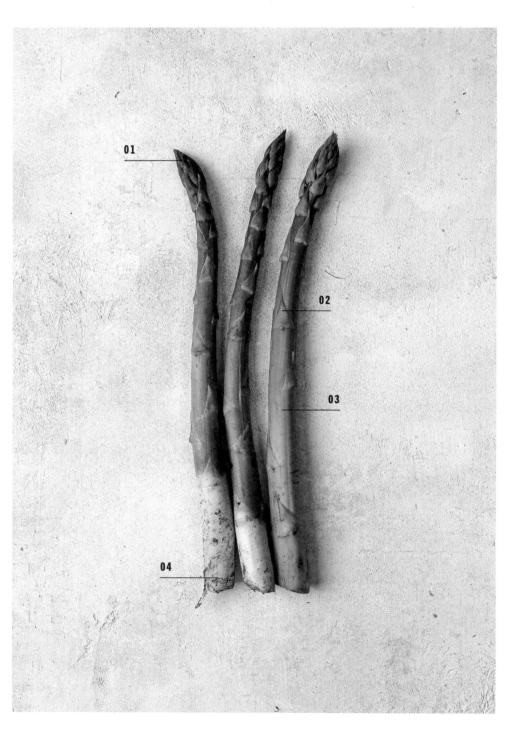

01

02

03

04

EDIBLE PARTS

01 CONICAL TIP

The tip is the most tender part of the plant and has a soft, buttery texture when gently steamed or sautéed. The flavor is often more intense in the tips, and they require less cooking.

02 LEAVES

These leaf scales are edible and don't need to be trimmed off. In many restaurant kitchens, asparagus is peeled, but there is huge flavor in the skin layer, so I always cook the stem whole.

03 STEM

From the base to the top, you will find a difference in texture and taste, but the whole stem is edible. The prized section is upward of the snapping point above the foot.

04 FOOT

Asparagus is harvested from just below the soil level, so often the foot of the stem will have traces of soil or sand on it and need cleaning. The foot is fibrous and woody but usually still edible.

The asparagus season is tantalizingly short and a time to rejoice that spring has arrived. Despite their delicate taste, the tender pistachio-green spears pair well with robust flavors, so cook them with ingredients that fortify their earthy notes.

PLANT

Asparagus grows best in temperate climates in well-drained, weed-free soil that needs plenty of conditioning to achieve the ideal neutral pH level of 6.5–7.5 before planting. It commands a high price due to its short growing season and the fact that it can't be harvested for the first two seasons while the crowns develop. It spends most of the year dormant and is actually a perennial herb that establishes an underground rhizome. The edible stems are either male or female, male being preferred for harvesting, as they produce better-quality spears. They are also rich in the antioxidant glutathione and the amino acid asparagine, which helps the body process excess salts.

COOKING TIPS

Asparagus can be steamed, sautéed, grilled over coals, or stir-fried. The tip and very top of the stem are so tender that I often treat them differently from the rest of the plant. Cut the conical tops into a risotto at the last minute or use them raw in a salad. For larger spears, cut through the center lengthwise for an even, faster cook or try peeling them into fine ribbons. The foot of the stem is woodier in texture, so braising, roasting, or chargrilling will soften it and bring out the sweetness. It also stands up to more robust sauces and glazing. You could purchase a special asparagus steaming pan, which works well but isn't essential.

PREPARATION

When choosing asparagus, make sure it is fresh for the best flavor. The stalks should be firm and the tips tightly closed. The purist will always snap the stem of an asparagus spear at its natural breaking point near the foot and keep the tender top section. This removes the end that's more fibrous, but it's also a waste of asparagus. Personally, I try to use every inch of my asparagus and will only discard a section if it's really too tough to cook (see *Cooking Tips*). Wash any soil from the stems just before cooking.

ZERO WASTE

Asparagus keeps for up to a week when stored unwashed in the fridge. It can help to place the foot of the spears upright in an inch of water or to wrap the ends in a wet sheet of paper towel. If you are lucky enough to have an asparagus surplus, try blanching and then freezing the spears for a treat later in the season. I rarely preserve asparagus because the season is so short and I enjoy cooking it fresh so much, but it does pickle extremely well. A bay leaf added to the brine along with pickling spices such as black peppercorns, yellow mustard, chili, and garlic helps retain some snappy texture to the stems.

TYPES

STANDARD

The favorite, producing green spears up to 9 in (23 cm) tall and harvested in temperate regions from March to late April.

JUMBO

Despite its larger size, jumbo asparagus, with its plump pale-green stalks, retains its quintessential texture and flavor. The larger the asparagus, the nuttier its flavor, though it's harder to discern the delicate notes. Withstands robust cooking.

WHITE

Hugely popular in Europe, white asparagus is forced, so it is grown without sunlight for a milder, refined flavor that has hints of bitterness. I find it tastes more like turnip or pea compared to the vegetal, grassy notes in green asparagus.

PURPLE

Similar in flavor to standard green asparagus though distinctly less fibrous, with a 20 percent higher sugar content, making it sweeter. The violet color is only skin deep—beneath, you will find the same pale-green, cream-colored flesh.

WILD

This delicious perennial is widely available globally but is rare and endangered in most of the UK. If you are foraging, be responsible and only take a small number of spears so the plant can continue to thrive. It grows later in spring and has thin stalks; a firm, crisp texture; and fernlike foliage.

MAIN MEAL

Teriyaki Asparagus Noodles and Pickled Eggs
SERVES 2

The beauty of a stir-fry is that it's fast, tasty, and convenient, and as there is next to no time in the pan, the subtler flavor notes of the asparagus are preserved. You can enjoy the individual flavors of your spring vegetables tied together with a simple soy dressing. The addition of a pickled egg, which will need to be prepared several hours in advance, provides some brightly colored sharpness to cut through the sweet and salty asparagus nest.

INGREDIENTS

Udon noodles (optional)

6 asparagus spears

1 tbsp sesame oil

1 tbsp finely sliced fresh ginger root

½ napa cabbage, finely sliced

2 tbsp teriyaki sauce

2 tbsp roughly chopped fresh cilantro

Pinch of shichimi togarashi (Japanese seven spice, see page 37)

For the pickled eggs

⅓ cup (75 ml) cider vinegar

1 beet, cooked and diced

1 tbsp granulated sugar

½ tsp sea salt

2 eggs, hard-boiled and peeled

Method

01 To make the pickled eggs, heat the vinegar and ¼ cup (50 ml) water in a saucepan, add the beet (this provides color and earthiness to the pickle), then add the sugar and salt and stir until dissolved. Next, submerge the peeled eggs in the solution and leave for 4–6 hours, turning occasionally. They will absorb the pink color from the beet and take on the sweet-and-sour pickle flavor.

02 If serving with udon noodles, prepare these ahead by boiling in salted water according to the package instructions. Drain under cold water to remove some of the surface starch.

03 Meanwhile, peel the asparagus spears with a potato peeler or mandoline so you have long, thin strips. Heat the sesame oil in a wok, then add the ginger, cabbage, and asparagus and cook for 2 minutes.

04 Add the teriyaki sauce and fresh cilantro. Stir well and mix in the udon noodles (if using).

05 Finish each dish with a pickled egg and a generous pinch of spicy shichimi, then serve immediately.

BRUNCH

Seaweed Hollandaise Asparagus Spears

SERVES 2

This is a sunny brunch recipe that after years of cooking is still one of my all-time favorites. It's mild-mannered and refined while simultaneously bold and in your face. Tender asparagus stems are simply cooked and dressed in a rich velvet coat. The seaweed hollandaise is my little twist on the classic butter-kissed sauce that pairs so effortlessly with them.

INGREDIENTS

1 tbsp olive oil

8–12 asparagus spears

Pinch of seaweed salt (found at Asian grocery stores or online)

Juice of 1 lemon

1 tbsp cider vinegar

4 eggs

Generous handful of watercress, to serve

For the seaweed hollandaise sauce

4 egg yolks, at room temperature

½ tsp Dijon mustard

1 garlic clove, finely chopped

1 tsp nori flakes

10 tbsp (150 g) butter, then left to cool slightly

1 tbsp lemon juice

Pinch of seaweed salt

Method

01 Start by making the hollandaise sauce in a large mixing bowl. Whisk the egg yolks and add in the mustard, garlic, and nori flakes. Then add the butter while continuing to whisk. Finish by stirring in the lemon juice and season to taste with the seaweed salt.

02 For the asparagus, heat the olive oil in a large frying pan and, once hot, add the spears. Cook for 2–3 minutes on each side, turning regularly. Finish with the seaweed salt and lemon juice.

03 Meanwhile, poach the eggs. Boil a pan of water and add the cider vinegar. Stir to create a whirlpool and crack the eggs one by one into the middle. Poach on a rolling boil for 2–3 minutes, then remove with a slotted spoon. Serve the eggs on a bed of asparagus, with the warm hollandaise and plenty of watercress on the side.

SIDE

Asparagus Tempura Spears

SERVES 2

There is a certain self-assured confidence that asparagus will always retain, even when surrounded by bold flavors. This recipe celebrates the punchy, nutty flavors by pairing the spears with the sweet and sour notes of the dipping sauce and generously seasoning with seaweed salt. When cooking tempura vegetables, I often blanch them first to soften them slightly before frying, but with asparagus, the few minutes of cooking in hot oil is enough to keep the light golden batter crisp and the asparagus beneath tender with just a bit of bite.

INGREDIENTS

Vegetable oil, for deep-frying
12 asparagus spears
1 tsp seaweed salt or kimchi powder

For the batter
¾ cup (100 g) cornstarch
1¼ cups (150 g) all-purpose flour
2 tsp (10 g) baking powder
¾ cup (180 ml) ice-cold sparkling water

For the dipping sauce
2 tbsp soy sauce
1 tbsp mirin or rice vinegar
1 tbsp finely diced cucumber
1 tsp honey
1 tsp sesame oil
1 tsp sesame seeds
½ tsp finely chopped fresh ginger root
½ tsp seeded and finely chopped red chili
½ tsp finely chopped garlic

Method

01 Preheat the vegetable oil to 350°F (180°C) in a large wok or frying pan. Make the batter by mixing the cornstarch, flour, and baking powder together in a bowl. Slowly add the iced sparkling water while whisking until the batter has a smooth consistency that coats your finger.

02 Next, make the dipping sauce by mixing all the ingredients together in a bowl.

03 Coat the asparagus in the batter, then fry in small batches for 3–4 minutes each. Lift from the oil with a slotted spoon and place on a sheet of paper towel to remove any excess oil. Season with the seaweed salt or kimchi powder and serve hot with the dipping sauce.

New Potatoes

HERALD OF SPRING

01

02

Charlotte

Red Duke
of York

Cornish
Earlies

Jersey
Royal

EDIBLE PARTS

01 SKIN

The skin is very thin and can be easily bruised, so wash off the soil carefully with a brush or cloth. Most of the nutrients are in the flesh, but the edible layer of skin is rich in potassium, so I tend to keep it on when cooking.

02 FLESH

The sweet white, yellow, or butter-colored flesh of new potatoes is the prized part of the plant. They can be cooked whole or sliced to speed up cooking.

When this humble vegetable arrives, it's time to get your hands dirty and dig for gold. Smell the sweet soil that coats the new potato and savor this earthy harbinger of spring. Whatever shape, size, or color, I am their loyal kitchen servant.

PLANT

New potatoes are specific varieties that are grown from seed potatoes for their early harvest and distinctive flavor. They are different from baby potatoes and are planted to provide fresh vegetables early in the season. Most types share a firm, waxy texture, but some are more floury. They have a thin skin that crisps up nicely when roasted. Unlike some more powdery, mature potatoes, they keep their shape well once cooked and cut. New potatoes are low in fat and high in vitamin C. Their sugars have not yet converted to starch, so they taste sweeter than fully grown potatoes. They are also known as salad potatoes, as they particularly suit cold dishes and lighter flavors and don't break apart when tossed in a salad.

PREPARATION

Start by choosing firm, dry, blemish-free potatoes. Don't peel new potatoes; instead, scrub them gently with a soft brush or cloth (**fig. a**). They may seem like more work than you're used to, especially in a plastic-wrapped age where no dirt is ever seen on our groceries. But that said, unwashed potatoes last longer, as the dirt protects them slightly from bruising and can easily be cleaned off.

TYPES

JERSEY ROYAL

The best known of the new potatoes, revered for its sweet flavor and waxy texture when boiled. It grows in the rich, fertile soil of Jersey and has PDO (Protected Designation of Origin) status. Tends to arrive early in the season and is one of my personal favorites.

RED DUKE OF YORK

This variety has a striking purple-pink skin that survives when cooked, a creamy white flesh, and a deep flavor. It is less waxy than most.

CHARLOTTE

My sister is called Charlotte, so out of simple family loyalty, we've always enjoyed cooking with this variety. I may be biased, but it's fantastic, with a white skin, oval shape, and a hint of sweetness. It makes an exceptionally good potato salad.

CORNISH EARLIES

Again, this one's special to me, as this is my local spud. Due to our warmer springs and mild maritime climate in Cornwall, farmers are able to plant in January and therefore harvest early. These are soft-skinned potatoes that can be cleaned by just rubbing off the wafer-thin skin with your thumb. Rich and sweet-tasting.

Figure a.

CONT.

Figure b.

COOKING TIPS

As an ingredient, new potatoes are highly versatile and have a subtle almond flavor. They are delicious boiled or roasted, hot or cold. To boil, simply put them in cold salted water and bring to a boil (rather than adding to boiling water, as you would with main-crop potatoes; as they are so small, this is to avoid overcooking the outside and undercooking the middle), then cook for 10–15 minutes. Chop larger new potatoes in half so they all cook in the same time frame. Once soft enough to easily slide in a knife tip, drain and then toss with salted butter and fresh herbs, such as parsley or chives.

Another go-to suggestion to try is adding some large sprigs of mint or rosemary to the water when boiling for an herby infusion—then serve with sea salt and olive oil. I have also been making a twist on the classic new potato salad for a few years, which uses the components of tarter sauce with freshly boiled potatoes. Try chopping in a tablespoon each of dill, parsley, chives, lemon zest, capers, diced gherkin, and mayonnaise. Toss while the potatoes are still warm for a fresh, zingy salad (**fig. b**).

New potatoes also work wonderfully in curries. My granny in Northern Ireland got us hooked on this growing up and would add boiled potatoes to rich, spiced tomato sauces. Also try a classic saag aloo (spinach potato curry) with cumin seeds, garam masala, and fenugreek. The buttery potatoes absorb flavor like a sponge and add wonderful sweetness to spicy recipes.

ZERO WASTE

The key to storing new potatoes is to keep them in a cool, dark, well-ventilated pantry. A perforated cardboard box or brown paper bag will help keep them fresh for longer. If you are growing your own, leave them in the ground for as long as possible. Once you've dug them up, eat them within a few days.

A favorite method of mine for preserving new potatoes for longer periods of time is to ferment them. Lacto-fermentation adds a tang to the sweetness before roasting, developing a greater flavor, and once fermented, you can store them for several months. My preference is to ferment for a relatively short period (see pages 282–283), no longer than 4–5 days, then transfer to the fridge to boil or roast. Remember to clean them well with a brush before fermenting with a 3 percent brine solution.

LIGHT LUNCH

Hasselback Potato and Watercress Soup
SERVES 4

This soup is extremely simple to make but offers something that, as a chef, I strive for every time I cook: it tastes just like you hoped it would when you read it on the menu. The balance of sweetness from the potato with light, metallic watercress is warming but not overwhelming. The Hasselback potatoes are my replacement for croutons but provide so much more than just a crunchy texture. Smooth, velvety, clean, and mildly peppery, this soup celebrates spring with understated splendor.

INGREDIENTS

2¼ lb (1 kg) new potatoes
2 tbsp olive oil
1 shallot, diced
1 tsp sea salt
1 tsp ground white pepper
1 tsp cracked black pepper
½ tsp nutmeg
2 cups (500 ml) vegetable stock
½ cup (100 ml) milk
7 oz (200 g) watercress
Mint oil, to serve
Plain yogurt, to serve

Method

01 Preheat the oven to 425°F (220°C). Carefully slice half of the potatoes into Hasselbacks—this means slicing thinly but not all the way through. Place in a roasting pan and coat with 1 tablespoon of the olive oil, drizzling it between the slices. Season with a pinch of salt and cracked black pepper and roast for 30–35 minutes.

02 Meanwhile, dice the remaining new potatoes. Add the rest of the olive oil to a saucepan and soften the diced potato over low heat with the shallot. After 10 minutes of sweating the onion and potato, add in the salt, ground white pepper, cracked black pepper, nutmeg, and vegetable stock. Bring to a boil and simmer for 10 minutes.

03 Check the potato to see if it's soft enough to squash between your fingers. If it is, add the milk and watercress and blend until smooth with a hand-held (immersion) blender.

04 Taste for seasoning and warm through. Serve with whole or segmented Hasselback potatoes and a drizzle of mint oil, and try it with a swirl of plain yogurt for contrast.

MAIN MEAL

New Potato Bake with Garlic Scapes, Fermented Chili, and Olives

SERVES 4

My wife Holly took initial inspiration from an Ottolenghi recipe a few years ago to create this adaptation, which is now a regular on our spring family menu. The potatoes are a perfect contradiction: crispy, chewy, soft, and waxy all at once. The olives and fermented chili add briny highs, while the garlic scapes provide the allium bass line. This is simple cooking at its best—no tricks or frills.

INGREDIENTS

2¼ lb (1 kg) new potatoes
1¾ oz (50 g) green olives
1 shallot, sliced
8 artichoke hearts, cooked
1 bunch of garlic scapes
2 sprigs of thyme
1 tbsp fermented chili
  (or 1 tsp chili flakes)
1 tsp sea salt
4 tbsp olive oil

Method

01 Preheat the oven to 400°F (200°C) and slice all the potatoes thinly— approximately ⅛–¼ in (2–5 mm) thick. Try using a mandoline for uniformity.

02 Mix all the ingredients except the oil in a roasting pan, then drizzle generously with the olive oil. Mix again to ensure an even coating of the oil, then spread the ingredients out in a thin layer.

03 Roast for 20–25 minutes, turning occasionally to coat again in the oil.

04 Serve once the potatoes are all cooked through and have crisped up in places.

SIDE

Roast Potato Salad with Elderflower and Lemon

SERVES 4

The emergence of the first elderflowers in late spring brings with it the desire to cook with a lighter touch, but our hearts still yearn for warming comfort. This remake of a potato salad bridges that gap between the seasons. My recipe roasts new potatoes with thinly sliced lemon and garlic for a bittersweet umami treat, tossed with crunchy flower heads that lift the nutty tubers with floral honey notes.

INGREDIENTS

2¼ lb (1 kg) new potatoes
1 lemon, finely sliced
2 garlic cloves, sliced
8–12 heads of elderflower
2 tbsp olive oil, plus extra
*   for drizzling*
Sea salt and cracked black
*   pepper*

Method

01 Preheat the oven to 425°F (220°C).

02 Parboil the potatoes in slightly salted water for 5–10 minutes, then drain.

03 In a roasting pan, mix the potatoes, lemon slices, garlic, elderflowers, and olive oil, then season well with salt and pepper.

04 Roast for 20 minutes, turning halfway through. Cook until the potatoes are crispy on the outside but soft and waxy in the middle. The lemon, garlic, and elderflowers should have caramelized nicely.

05 Drizzle with extra oil before serving and finish with another pinch of sea salt.

Spring Cabbages

EARLY GREENS, SOFT AT HEART

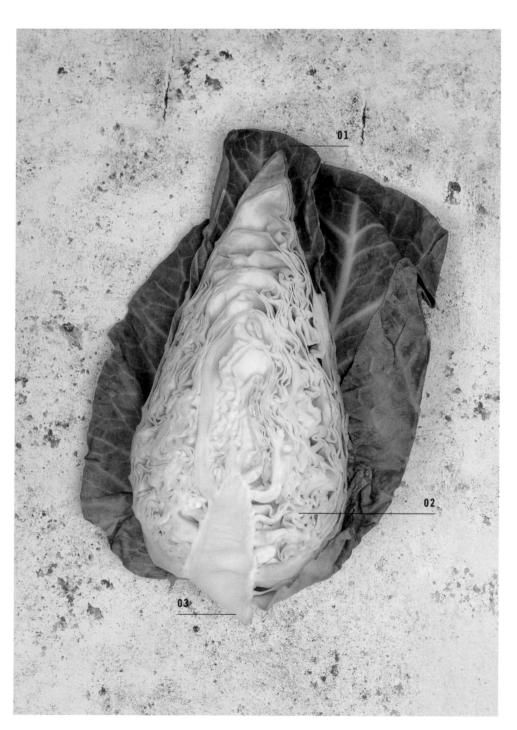

EDIBLE PARTS

01 OUTER LEAVES

The darker outer leaves have been exposed to more light when maturing and are therefore stronger in flavor. Many chefs will discard them, but they also contain the most vitamins and nutrients in the plant, so I suggest always using them.

02 INNER LEAVES

These closely packed leaves that grow into a point are sweet when cooked and very tender. They are gently flavored and can be eaten raw.

03 STEM/HEART

The stem of a spring cabbage will be more bitter than the leaves, but it's not as tough as a round cabbage heart.

The arrival of spring cabbages drives away the winter blues. These sweet, tender leaves yearn for a lashing of oil; melted butter and lemon; or rich, herby braising stock. They also work wonderfully cooked simply with just salt and pepper.

PLANT

Part of the brassica family, spring cabbages are rich in vitamins K and C and include varieties of early cabbage, but also the thinnings and tops from the wider brassica family, including turnips. They can be pointed in shape or looser leafed and are tender compared to their winter cousins, as their inner leaves form only a small heart or connect to the stem without a central heart at all. They are particularly popular in Northern Europe, where they are often the first leaves to be harvested. The cabbage is cut close to soil level, and the cut stem can then be sliced with a deep cross to get a second crop of mini cabbages.

COOKING TIPS

If it's your first time cooking spring cabbages, start by slicing the leaves and sweating them down with butter and lemon juice for a few minutes. Add the lemon near the end of cooking so that it doesn't cause bitterness and discoloration. The leaves also work well with nutmeg, white pepper, rosemary, and nuts. For the tougher stem, try slicing it lengthwise into quarters to expose more to heat. Baste when roasting or grilling to stop it from drying out. Treat it like a cauliflower or broccoli stalk for best results—it should retain some bite, but also a little give when pricked with a skewer or paring knife. Likewise, when cooking the hearts whole, baste with fats and marinades regularly to keep them moist.

PREPARATION

When choosing spring cabbages, opt for firm, bright-looking specimens that are not too dark and limp around the edges. The dark greens indicate a stronger flavor that can be overpowering for some palates. Try to treat the cuts distinctly from one another, like a meat eater would when roasting a large joint. The stem is like a bone that is full of flavor but needs time to soften and break down the connective tissue around the inner leaves. Remove and wash the darker outer leaves before processing and play around with shredding finely, splitting lengthwise to roast, or using the whole leaf.

ZERO WASTE

Once picked, spring cabbages will keep well in the fridge for about a week, but if you want to extend the shelf life, then try making sauerkraut or kimchi from the inner leaves (see pages 284–285). Ferment in a 3 percent sea-salt solution and try adding caraway or cumin seeds to the recipe—and lots of ginger and chili if you want to make a spring-green kimchi. Once cleaned, the stronger-tasting outer leaves can be used instead of parchment paper when fermenting. Cut out a sheet of leaf, place over the solution, and lay a fermentation weight on top to keep your kraut or kimchi beneath the level of brine.

TYPES

CONEHEAD OR POINTED

This is my personal favorite. It is tender and much loved for its medium-to-large head with a uniform point and sweet flavor. After braising, it retains a little lingering bite and is equally delectable in a raw slaw.

SPRING GREENS

Often known as collards, spring greens are the first young tender cabbages of the year, with loose green leaves that form without a hard heart.

TURNIP TOPS

These are often discarded, but the zesty leaf provides lots of vitamins C and A. Popular in southern US cooking and in regional dishes from Northern Europe, they are great for making kimchi. Best picked young for the tastiest leaves.

Spring Cabbage with Yellow Coconut Curry

SERVES 4

Cabbage doesn't have to feel monastic. Here, it's been given a zen makeover with lemongrass and ginger for the perfect Friday-night comfort food to brighten up still-lengthening evenings and to conjure up dreams of exotic shores. The conehead cabbage is a great alternative to noodles—the green shredded leaves shine with the rich turmeric glaze, and the bite remains just firm enough to be twirled around a fork or wrapped on chopsticks.

INGREDIENTS

1 tbsp coconut oil

1 tbsp ground turmeric

1 tbsp thinly sliced fresh ginger root

1 tsp yellow Thai curry paste

½ conehead cabbage, thinly sliced

1 red bell pepper, sliced

1 carrot, peeled and sliced

3½ oz (100 g) shiitake or oyster mushrooms, sliced

6 spring onions, sliced

2 lemongrass stalks, chopped

1 zucchini, sliced

4 makrut (kaffir) lime leaves

2 tbsp finely chopped cilantro

¾ cup (200 ml) coconut milk

1 tsp coconut sugar

Soy sauce, to season

Method

01 In a large wok, heat the coconut oil with the turmeric, ginger, and yellow curry paste for 1–2 minutes over high heat, then add all the other ingredients except the coconut milk, coconut sugar, and soy sauce.

02 Stir well and cook until the cabbage wilts and the vegetables soften, then add the coconut milk and sugar.

03 Bring to a boil and simmer for 3–4 minutes, season to taste with the soy sauce, then serve.

SIDE

Charred Cabbage with Rosemary and Orange

SERVES 2

This is one of my signature dishes—a highly personal one that I've put on a few restaurant menus—inspired by the widespread trend among chefs in recent years to grill spring greens over a fire. The vegetable itself is perfectly designed to knit together my love of aromatics, layers of flavor, and architectural simplicity. This may sound a bit over the top for a cabbage, but you really can taste the metamorphosis. The woven leaves of a conehead cabbage form perfect pockets to laminate with flavor and dress with silken butter.

INGREDIENTS

5 tbsp (75g) butter

4 garlic cloves, sliced

Zest and juice of 1 orange, retaining a little zest to garnish

2 sprigs of rosemary, leaves stripped and roughly chopped

1 conehead cabbage, such as Caraflex

Handful of garlic scapes or spring onions

Sea salt

Method

01   Melt the butter in a pan with the garlic, orange juice, and chopped rosemary leaves. Add the orange zest, then remove from heat and leave to infuse.

02   Preheat the oven to 400°F (200°C) or light the barbecue for roasting, then slice the cabbage in half and brush all sides with a little of the butter.

03   Roast the cabbage halves in a roasting pan or place directly on a grill over hot coals or charcoal, trying to avoid flare-ups from dripping butter. Turn regularly and baste each time with the garlic and rosemary butter.

04   Keep roasting and basting the garlic and greens for 20–25 minutes until the stems soften and the cabbage leaves char. (The more often you baste and the longer you roast, the softer the heart will become.) Add the garlic scapes to the roasting pan or grill after 15 minutes, cooking until softened.

05   Serve when the cabbage stem is tender enough to carve easily. Season to taste with sea salt and add a pinch of orange zest to lift the aroma with citrus oils.

SIDE

Chestnut and Cider Braised Cabbage

SERVES 2

This recipe hits all the senses even while being unashamedly beige. The pale-green heart of a conehead cabbage is ideal for gently braising in warm spiced cider to bring out its sweetness. I've gone the extra mile and added a decadent shaving of black summer truffle, because frankly the cabbage deserved it, but it works well with a little grated chestnut instead. The dish is a throwback to winter, but I keep some raw cabbage back to serve for a bit of the crunch and freshness that only spring cabbage can offer.

INGREDIENTS

1 conehead cabbage, such as Caraflex

3½ tbsp (50 g) butter

1 tsp ground nutmeg

Pinch of white pepper

3½ oz (100 g) chestnuts, peeled and cooked (plus extra, to garnish—optional)

1 cup (250 ml) hard cider

Sea salt

1 black summer truffle (optional)

Method

01 Start by slicing the cabbage into quarters. Then, using a mandoline, shave off some of the sides from each section and keep the shavings in ice water until later.

02 Prepare the braising liquid in a wide sauté pan by first melting the butter with the nutmeg and white pepper. Add the quarters of cabbage and the chestnuts and sear them in the butter on each side to build some umami depth of flavor and a roast profile to the dish.

03 Next, add the hard cider, then cover the pan with a lid. Cook for 15–20 minutes on a rolling boil until the cabbage softens and the liquid has reduced. Season well with a pinch of sea salt.

04 To serve, start with a layer of the drained raw cabbage shavings. Cover with the braised cabbage, chestnuts, flavored butter, and reduced cider juices. Finish with freshly grated truffle or some grated chestnut.

Radish

PEPPERY PUNK-ROCKER

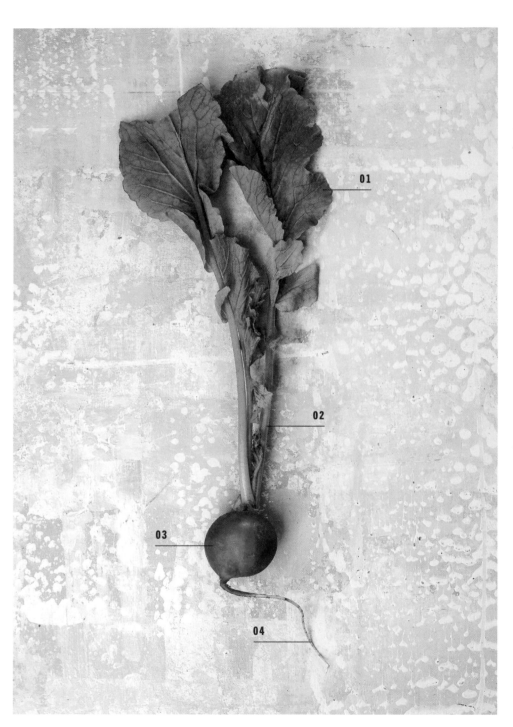

EDIBLE PARTS

01 LEAVES

When they are picked young the leaves are soft enough to eat raw, chopped into a peppery salad. As the radish grows, the leaves become tougher and small bristles make the texture spiky to eat. Sauté older leaves like spinach or nettle or try them grilled over coals. The radish tops also work well wilted in butter with napa cabbages.

02 STEMS

The radish stem is juicy and peppery like mustard. It can be eaten raw in a salad or chopped into stir-fries or vegetable bakes.

03 ROOT

The root bulb is the prime cut. Beneath the brightly colored skin, you will find white flesh. Often spicy, and crisp in texture, it can be eaten raw or cooked.

04 TAPROOT

The taproots can be eaten raw, or you can fry a bunch of them for a crispy garnish.

A bunch of radishes in the kitchen is a sight to behold, with their scarlet globes and bright green leaves growing out of the top like a radical punk hairdo. A real grassroots rebel, this is a small vegetable that makes a big statement on the plate.

PLANT

The radish is a member of the brassica family, and for years it has quietly gone about its job as one of the gardener's best catch crops, as it is fast-growing and easy to fit in between other rows in the vegetable patch. It has long divided cooks with its fiery, peppery flavor. Some people don't like the mustard heat, while others can't resist a spicy radish right from the garden. There is an array of different types available in various shapes, colors, and flavors, and the entire plant is edible and full of flavor. Sow them little and often from February to July to enjoy all season long.

PREPARATION

When working with radishes, remove any soil under a running tap and discard any older leaves that are damaged and might taste bitter. Try trimming off the leaves and submerging them in a large bowl of ice water. The cold helps keep the leaf crisp and is also a good way to firm up the roots before serving. The roots can be high maintenance, as they are so small and fiddly. Larger varieties, such as the hybrid 'Bluemoon', can be finely sliced with a sharp knife **(fig. a)**, while a Japanese mandoline (with a guard if you prefer) can be helpful to process smaller types to achieve translucent thin slices. Equally, don't be afraid of cooking radishes whole or slicing them in half to braise with other seasonal vegetables.

TYPES

RED RADISH
Also known as the table radish, this variety has a classic scarlet-colored globe shape with white flesh, a strong mustardy bite to the leaves, and a watercress flavor.

PURPLE PLUM
A small globe-shaped root with bright-purple skin and white flesh. Sweet with a pleasant sharp, spicy flavor, this radish remains crisp longer than most.

FRENCH BREAKFAST RADISH
Another violet-hued radish but with an elongated shape and leafy tops. The color fades to a bright-white tip and the flavor is semisweet and peppery.

MIRABEAU
A cylindrical, graduated, vivid red root with a pretty white tip; crunchy with a good, strong peppery flavor. Grilling or roasting brings out the inherent nutty and sweet flavors.

BLACK JAPANESE
Long and slender in shape with rough, dull brown or black skin and a dense, crisp white flesh. This one has a lower water content than most and a spicy, raw flavor. It is good pickled or cooked over coals.

MOOLI OR DAIKON
This is a hardy winter radish that's easy to grow and tastes mild, more like a turnip. It's robust to cook with and larger in size than others, growing up to 12 in (30 cm) long.

Figure a.

CONT.
_____

Figure b.

Figure c.

COOKING TIPS

Many people would never dream of cooking a radish, and I can understand why—they are fantastic eaten raw. That said, cooking radishes opens up so many exciting possibilities. Grilling or charring releases their sweetness, while pickling tempers the spicy warmth and is an ideal way of peppering a recipe with a bright crunch.

My key bit of advice is to start by trying a slice raw, then use this taste test as a guide to adjust the other flavor components of your dish. Radish pairs well with butter, so try it ice-cold with unsalted herb butter and sea salt flakes as an appetizer. Simply remove any tough leaves to cook separately later (see *Zero Waste*) and dunk the whole remaining plant in ice water to crisp further. Serve as a seasonal finger-food starter to get the party going **(fig. b)**.

Alternatively, white radish sweated in plenty of butter or braised in stock with spring greens and white pepper **(fig. c)** is a wonderful warming side dish to serve with a nut roast or fluffy champ (see page 54).

ZERO WASTE

The entire radish is edible, and there is no reason not to cook the whole plant. Try frying the leaves with olive oil, sea salt, and lemon juice the first time to understand how they cook and to enjoy the peppery flavor profile. They are robust and work with other bold flavors.

If you want to preserve radishes, for me, the only way is to pickle them in vinegar. My go-to pickles for this are either a rice vinegar with white miso, nori, and star anise or a more conventional combination of mustard seeds, black peppercorn, chili flakes, and dill in a sweetened cider vinegar. I also recommend pickling them with heritage beets and pink onions or fennel shavings. Add some citrus and spice to the pickling jar, then serve with butter, cheese, and rich vegetable dishes.

Charred Radish and Labneh

SERVES 2

The first time I cooked radishes, it was right from a garden on a rocket stove; I blistered and charred them, then loaded them onto a flatbread with the rest of my harvest. Since then, my eyes have been opened to the black magic of introducing radishes to a naked flame and a hot pan. The flavor change is dynamic—you get a vivid contrast of color that seems almost sacrilegious. This is a wonderful recipe that leaves you both shocked and in a quiet reverie.

INGREDIENTS

8–12 radishes, with tops
1 tbsp olive oil
Sea salt
Mint leaves, to garnish

For the labneh
2 tbsp labneh or strained yogurt
½ tsp pink peppercorns
½ tsp sumac
½ tsp za'atar

Method

01 If cooking indoors, heat a sturdy frying pan—ideally a cast-iron skillet, as it can withstand a searing high heat that can char the radishes. Otherwise, prepare a charcoal fire under the grate on the grill. In a bowl, dress the radishes in the olive oil, then lay them on the hot grill. Cook over high heat or above hot coals until they start to char. Turn regularly with some tongs. Don't worry about the leaves wilting—they taste delicious cooked, too.

02 Remove from the grill and season well with a good pinch of sea salt flakes.

03 Prepare the labneh by sprinkling over the pink peppercorns, sumac, and za'atar. Finish the dish with some fresh mint leaves and serve the radishes still warm.

BREAKFAST OR LIGHT LUNCH

Radish Top Frittata

SERVES 2

If you're like me, no matter how hard you try, you'll still be left with excess radish tops. I always fall prey to temptation and eat the scarlet root bulbs before they make it into the safety of the fridge. So this recipe is born out of necessity— a great way to cook radish leaves for a quick, nourishing breakfast or light lunch. This frittata celebrates the peppery radish tops as a star ingredient in their own right.

INGREDIENTS

3 large free-range eggs

Sea salt and cracked black pepper

1 tbsp grated cheese (mature Cheddar, Gouda, or Gruyère—optional)

2 tbsp (25 g) salted butter

6–8 radish tops

Method

01 Preheat the oven to 400°F (200°C) and warm an oven-safe frying pan on the stove.

02 Beat the eggs and season the mixture with salt and pepper to taste. Add in grated cheese if you want a richer frittata.

03 Melt the butter in the frying pan and before it browns and starts to bubble, add the radish tops followed by the egg mixture, then stir for a moment or two over high heat.

04 Reduce heat to medium and allow the mixture to settle in the pan. Cook for a further 2 minutes, then transfer the pan to the oven and cook for 5–10 minutes until the frittata is golden on top.

Crispy Radish Tops and Shichimi Togarashi

SERVES 2

This is one of those quick ideas that redefines how you perceive a radish. When fried, the leaf takes on a peppery, umami, seaweedlike depth of flavor and yet at the same time a lightness. It's so translucent that, when held up to the sun, the leaf appears like a stained-glass window. As you eat it, the shards smash with a delightfully delicate crunch, and I find that the wafer-thin leaves are extra moreish when served with some sea salt and Japanese seven spice.

INGREDIENTS

2 tbsp vegetable oil

12 radish tops

Sea salt

Lime mayo (1 tsp lime juice to 1 tbsp mayo), to serve

Chive flowers, to garnish (optional)

For the shichimi togarashi

1 tsp chili flakes

1 tsp poppy seeds

1 tsp Sichuan peppercorns

1 tsp nori flakes

1 tsp white sesame seeds

1 tsp black sesame seeds

1 tsp ground ginger

Method

01 To make your own shichimi spice mix, blend all the ingredients together in a spice grinder or work into a fine dust with a pestle and mortar.

02 Heat the vegetable oil in a frying pan and fry 2–3 large radish leaves at time. Cook for 2–3 minutes until rigid, bright green, and extremely crispy.

03 Place the fried leaves on a sheet of paper towel to absorb any excess oil, then season while still warm with the shichimi spices and sea salt to taste.

04 Try serving the fried leaves with some lime mayo on the side and garnish with chive flowers, if you have them.

Peas

INSIDE THE POD LIES INNER PEACE

Snow pea

Garden pea

01

02

03

EDIBLE PARTS

01 PEA

The pea itself is the sweet green fruit or berry hidden in the pod. They are delicious raw and are best used soon after harvesting, as they immediately begin to lose their sweetness.

02 PODS

All pea pods are edible, but the shells of some varieties (notably the garden pea) are not as pleasant to eat raw. With this type, you may want to snap it and pull off the fibrous string to reveal the sweet peas within. For sugar snap and snow peas, the entire pod can be eaten.

03 SHOOTS

Pea shoots—tendrils, leaves, and stems—make delicious salads and if picked young are tasty eaten raw.

FLOWERS

The pretty, delicate flowers are edible, but, along with mature shoots and leaves, they will benefit from being given some heat for a minute in a hot pan with a drizzle of oil.

The magic of peas is revealed when you pluck the plump pods from the plant, break into them with a snap, and carefully tease out the sweet peas as a prize. They are a family favorite, raw or cooked—simple bright-green joy.

PLANT

Peas are part of the *Fabaceae* (legume) family and are particularly rich in vitamins A and B, calcium, and zinc. They are also a great source of protein and carbohydrates. The plant grows well in a sunny position and can reach up to 4 ft (1.2 m), so it needs support with a trellis or pea sticks for the tendrils to curl around. It takes up a lot of space in the veggie plot for a limited return, but, like potatoes, there are early-crop and main-crop varieties and, as they don't all crop at once, you can enjoy a handful of fresh podded peas from the garden each day. To provide a longer harvest season, try to succession sow every couple of weeks. Remember to enjoy the shoots, as well as the mature pods, and that planting over winter under cover provides an early burst of green in the garden as spring arrives.

PREPARATION

Depending on the variety of pea, there is very little kitchen prep needed other than shelling, and almost all peas are tastiest eaten raw, so the cooking is basic, too. If you are shelling a variety with a tougher pod, try blanching it in boiling water for 2 minutes before refreshing it in ice water (**fig. b**), which stops it from cooking any further. Next, pull back the fibrous string that runs down the side of the pod. Snap the shell open to remove the peas, then freeze or cook them. Always process peas soon after picking, before the sugars convert to starch, to keep them at their sweetest.

TYPES

GARDEN PEA

Large green pods encase sweet, plump peas that are crunchy, making them great to eat raw or cooked. The pods are fibrous but can be cooked down and blended into a soup or dip or used to fortify stocks and sauces.

SNOW PEA

Also known as Chinese peas or mangetout, these pods produce much smaller peas. The flat pod is cooked and eaten whole.

YELLOW SNOW PEA

*This variety is slightly slower to mature but tastes sweet and nutty, with golden-yellow pods (**fig. a**). Yellow snow peas are hardy and may be sown over winter for early-spring picking, when the peas are hardly visible inside. The flowers are a striking purple color.*

SUGAR SNAP PEA

This stringless variety of pea offers a crisp, juicy pod and six to eight peas within that are lovely and sweet. They are a cross between garden peas and snow peas. They don't need to be shelled before cooking.

Figure a.

Figure b.

CONT.

Figure c.

COOKING TIPS

Peas are extremely versatile and can be
used in all sorts of recipes, including curries,
colorful purées, sauces, soups, and stews. I
usually opt for minimal cooking—either
steaming or adding to water already at a
rolling boil for just 2–3 minutes—so they
retain their color, sweetness, crunchy texture,
and fresh appeal. I also love to cook them
whole in their pods so that they steam in
the shell. Or try drizzling with a little oil and
cooking in a metal sieve held over a hot grill
or blistering in a hot frying pan with some
flaked almonds and mint leaves. The pods
char while the peas within soften but retain
their sweetness. Peas also create a tasty
snack when roasted. Season the blanched
peas well with sea salt, then roast in the
oven for 35 minutes or fry in oil. Try adding
wasabi powder for a spicy flavor combo.

ZERO WASTE

My granny used to make champion pea-pod
wine for the Women's Institute in Ireland
and, inspired by this, I always try to use the
pods rather than compost them. You can
blanch and purée them with peas for a
rustic hummus or roast the shells for added
umami depth in stocks and gravies. Also
try making a zero-waste garden pea soup
(fig. c). Use the pods and peas and sauté
with a chopped shallot and fresh mint.
Blend until smooth and serve with charred
pods instead of croutons and a swirl of tart
plain yogurt for a rustic springtime soup.

If you are planning on preserving peas, do
so as close as you can to harvesting for the
best-tasting vegetable. Freezing is the most
common method. Always blanch first in
boiling water for 1–2 minutes, then drain
and submerge in ice water to halt the
cooking process. Try to freeze them in a
single layer on a baking sheet first so they
don't clump together. This makes it easier to
then transfer them to a bag or container—
to aid removal when you want them later.

MAIN MEAL

Pea and Mint Bulgur Wheat Risotto with Preserved Lemon

SERVES 4

This was one of the first dishes my wife and I agreed must be served at our wedding. Pea and mint are still a timeless combo, but I've given my version a small update. The salty cured lemon and floral bee pollen complement the sweet peas, while plenty of pepper keeps the flavor grounded. This dish is close to my heart, and I will always keep working on it.

INGREDIENTS

1 shallot, finely diced

2 garlic cloves, finely diced

2 tbsp olive oil

1¾ cups (250g) bulgur wheat

⅓ cup (75 ml) white wine

7 oz (200 g) fresh peas, shelled

2 tbsp finely chopped mint

2 small preserved lemons, coarsely chopped

4 cups (1 liter) vegetable stock (add the pea pods if making your own; see pages 266–267)

1 tsp sea salt

1 tsp cracked black pepper

2 tsp bee pollen

Grated Parmesan cheese, pea shoots, and a blanched sugar snap pea, to garnish

Method

01 Start by softening the diced shallot and garlic in the olive oil over low heat for 4–5 minutes.

02 Next, stir in the bulgur wheat and coat with the oil. Add in the white wine to deglaze the pan and leave to reduce for 2–3 minutes.

03 Add the peas, mint, preserved lemon, and stock. Simmer over medium heat for 10–15 minutes, stirring regularly so that the risotto doesn't stick. Cook until the stock is absorbed.

04 Before serving, season with the salt, pepper, and bee pollen. Garnish with grated Parmesan, pea shoots, and a blanched sugar snap pea.

LIGHT LUNCH OR SIDE

Pea Shoot Salad with Edible Flowers and Lemon Oil

SERVES 2

Pea shoots make a fantastic salad—I like that they've been universally accepted in kitchens as an edible part of the pea plant. The same goes for flowers in my cooking. They encourage you to explore an ingredient and celebrate all its component parts. The flowers I've used here work wonderfully with the sweet pea shoots and peppery radishes to provide pops of color and unusual flavors. If you can't find them all fresh, use as many as you can, or use dried petals instead for a summery floral seasoning.

INGREDIENTS

4 radishes
2 large handfuls of pea shoots
Sea salt
1 tbsp fresh rose petals
1 tbsp fresh marigold flowers
1 tbsp chive flowers
1 tbsp fennel flowers

For the lemon oil
Grated zest of 1 lemon
3 tbsp (50 ml) olive oil

Method

01 Make the lemon oil by heating very gently the lemon zest and oil in a small saucepan for 10–15 minutes, but do not allow it to simmer. Then remove from heat and leave to infuse until cool. Strain and set the infused oil aside for drizzling over your salad.

02 Prepare the radishes by slicing thinly on a mandoline or with a sharp paring knife.

03 Dress the pea shoots and radish slices with a little lemon oil and a pinch of sea salt.

04 Transfer into bowls and garnish with rose, marigold, chive, fennel, and seasonal flowers of your choice.

Smashed Peas on Pumpernickel

SERVES 2

This is another recipe that serves peas with their springtime partner in crime: the radish. Full of Jazz Age swagger, these flavors veer between sweet and peppery. It's a wonderful improvised recipe that is raw, easy, and mouth-wateringly fresh. Pumpernickel provides a strong, nutty profile that complements the subtle bitter notes from the blended shells. I also include lots of zingy lemon zest to finish in full swing.

INGREDIENTS

5½ oz (150 g) peas, shelled and pods retained, with any tough strings removed

1 tbsp olive oil

1 tbsp pine nuts

2 tbsp lemon zest

1 tbsp lemon juice

1 tbsp grated Parmesan cheese

1 tbsp finely chopped mint

1 tsp smoked sea salt

2 slices of pumpernickel or dark rye bread, toasted

4 radishes, finely sliced

Pea shoots, to garnish

Method

01 Place the pea pods in a food processor with the olive oil and pine nuts and blend until smooth.

02 Next, smash the peas, lemon zest, lemon juice, Parmesan, and mint in the same food processor, pulsing a few times until you get a very roughly blended texture. Season the coarse pea pâté with the smoked sea salt.

03 Toast the pumpernickel or rye bread, then layer with the thin radish slices. Top with a generous dollop of smashed peas and garnish with some pea shoots.

Lettuce

COMEBACK SALAD STAR

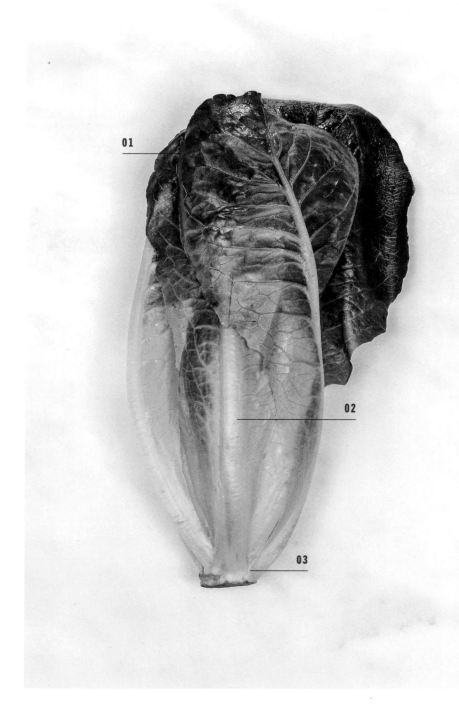

EDIBLE PARTS

01 LOOSE OUTER LEAVES

The outer lettuce leaves tend to have a more pronounced bitter flavor. They are more likely to bruise and can wilt if dressed too early before serving. I love the cupped shape, which can be used as a soft-shell taco to cradle other ingredients.

02 INNER HEART

The tighter inner leaves can be crunchy and crisp. They also taste sweeter and can be charred to bring out more flavor. I find that the inner lettuce leaf takes on stronger dressing flavors and is more robust for cooking.

03 STALK

The stalk is edible but can be devoid of flavor. It is still worth using, however, and can be sliced thinly across the grain and added to slaw or used as a crunchy topping in a salad. The stalks work well with high levels of citrus.

Lettuce spent a long time out in the wilderness but has come back with a chart-busting concept album. Growers and chefs are now experimenting with all shapes and sizes of exotic leaf to provide a festival of flavor that has something for everyone.

PLANT

There are several basic types of lettuce and plenty of other popular greens that you can use in a similar way for salads. Overall, lettuce is very nutrient rich, although the high water content makes it less nutritionally dense than darker leaves like kale or spinach. Lettuce is generally best in spring, as it is really a cool-weather crop that often bolts (quickly runs to seed) in summer. Some types can be harvested a few leaves at a time, while others provide a dense head to pick all at once. Baby leaf is extremely popular for salads and is a term that refers to lettuce leaves that have been harvested when immature and more tender.

PREPARATION

Give lettuce a rinse under cold running water to clean it **(fig. a)**, then submerge in ice water to crisp up the leaves before serving. I like to divide lettuce into parts for cooking. Many varieties are loose-leafed and can be used as a single ingredient, but others—personally, my favorite types— have a different taste from tip to stalk and from outer to inner leaf. These can be divided into sections for dressing and cooking separately to bring out these subtle flavor changes.

TYPES

ROMAINE
An iconic lettuce with lime-green leaves growing from a pale stem. Has slightly bitter leaves and a crisp, tight center that is sweeter.

ICEBERG
This dense lettuce goes in and out of fashion. It is super crisp but not as flavorful as others.

BUTTERHEAD
A delicate variety with a crisp head and cupped leaves. The Boston type is larger and sweet, with a fluffy texture.

RADICCHIO
Also called Italian chicory, this striking magenta or speckled leaf is bitter when fresh and sweeter when grilled.

FRISÉE
Also called curly endive, this lettuce tastes fantastic tossed in vinaigrette. It is frizzled and curly and has a delicious crunch.

COS
Cos has a gentle crunch and a delicate flavor. Often known as Little Gem, it can be thinly sliced or charred in sections.

LAMB'S LETTUCE
Has a sweet, succulent flavor and good body, with four or five succulent leaves attached to the root. Clean to remove grit.

LEAF LETTUCE
Grows as a loose-leaf salad from a single stalk in shades of red, green, and bronze. Dress just before serving to avoid wilting.

Figure a.

CONT.

Figure c.

COOKING TIPS

As an example of how a single lettuce can be used in various ways, a common romaine can be split into multiple components. The lush green outer leaves with their stronger flavors are perfect for serving in a leafy salad bowl dressed with a honey mustard dressing, while the tighter inner cream leaves may suit a thinly sliced yuzu and cilantro dressing, to be used with barbecued tofu as a fresh, zingy slaw. The stem, meanwhile, can be sautéed and then blended into a chilled gazpacho or delicate watercress velouté. Alternatively, you can keep it simple—for me, a taco isn't complete without a bed of shredded lettuce (**fig. c**). It adds crunch and bite to the softer ingredients and also serves as a palate cleanser against heavy spices and complex citrus flavors. Shredded lettuce is also fantastic under grilled halloumi to cut through the rich grilled cheese.

ZERO WASTE

To me, the notion of preserving lettuce goes against its inherent freshness. It's a bit like preserving edible flowers. You could freeze it to make a lettuce soup later (see below), but it does destroy the beautiful frills and leafy curves. If you want to keep it fresh for longer, try wrapping it in a damp paper towel and sealing it in a plastic storage bag or glass jar.

If you have reached salad overload and want to try something different to avoid wasting leftovers, you could try making the aforementioned lettuce soup with either fresh or frozen leaves. Sauté the leaves with onion and add potato for a creamy body. Season well and try with chopped parsley for extra flavor and a brighter green color. This silky, fresh-tasting soup can be eaten hot or cold or frozen to eat later. A sprinkle of julienned radish also adds a peppery garnish and a pop of color.

LIGHT LUNCH

Charred Caesar Salad

SERVES 2

The original Caesar is a classic; my charred version is a more rebellious twist. When I first started to serve it in restaurants, I had trouble explaining why the lettuce was grilled—it seemed odd at the time to burn a lettuce. Nowadays, it's accepted that this enhances the sweetness and tames the bitter profiles of a Little Gem or romaine. The caramelized pears, salty caper berries, and crunchy croutons work well with the glossy dressing, so it's worth a try if you secretly want to topple the old vegetable regime and have some fun on the grill.

Method

01 First, make the Caesar dressing by blending all the ingredients except the salt in a food processor until smooth. Then season to taste with a pinch of salt.

02 To make the croutons, first preheat the oven to 400°F (200°C). Cut the bread into cubes, coat in the olive oil, and sprinkle with a pinch of salt and the thyme. Fry until crisp and golden, then transfer to a baking sheet and finish in the oven for 10 minutes to dry out.

03 Carve the heads of lettuce through the core lengthwise into quarters or eighths and brush with oil. Preheat the grill or a ridged griddle pan and char the lettuce segments for 2–3 minutes on each side. Brush with more oil while cooking and finish with a generous squeeze of lemon.

04 Brush the pear slices with a little oil and grill them and the capers on the grill or in the pan alongside the lettuce.

05 Build the salad with all the elements overlapping and pour over plenty of Caesar dressing. Enjoy warm, topped with the Parmesan, the pickled onion slices (see page 287), and some grated lemon zest.

INGREDIENTS

2 heads of Little Gem or 1 romaine lettuce
2 tbsp olive oil
Zest and juice of 1 lemon
1 pear, sliced
2 tbsp caper berries
1 tbsp grated Parmesan cheese
1 tsp sliced pickled onions

For the croutons
2 slices of stale bread
2 tbsp olive oil
Sea salt
1 tsp chopped fresh thyme

For the Caesar dressing
1 egg yolk
1 garlic clove, grated
2 tbsp grated Parmesan cheese
2 tbsp mayonnaise
2 tbsp olive oil
1 tsp Dijon mustard
1 tsp white wine vinegar
Sea salt

Cobb Salad

SERVES 2–4

With the right dressing, lettuce can steal the show, even when you pack lots of other loud ingredients around it. The crisp lettuce leaf cuts through all the noise with precision and pitch-perfect clarity of flavor. My playful Cobb salad is exuberant and punchy, with mature Cheddar, raw red onion, and crunchy baby zucchini assaulting the senses. But it's the Bronze Arrowhead lettuce that conducts the recipe with elegance and brings the salad together.

INGREDIENTS

12 large Bronze Arrowhead lettuce leaves
3½oz (100g) mature Cheddar cheese, diced
½ red onion, thinly sliced
½ red bell pepper, roughly chopped
2 baby zucchini, finely sliced
2 tbsp sprouting seeds
4 soft-boiled eggs

For the dressing
2 tbsp olive oil
1 tbsp cider vinegar
1 tbsp lemon juice
1 tsp finely chopped chives
1 tsp whole-grain mustard
1 tsp honey
Sea salt and cracked black pepper

Method

01 First, mix all the ingredients for the dressing except the seasoning in a bowl with a whisk until smooth, then season to taste with the salt and pepper.

02 Wash the lettuce leaves, then submerge them in a large bowl of ice water. Leave to crisp up for 5–10 minutes, while you chop the other salad ingredients and peel the eggs.

03 Remove the lettuce, shake dry, and place on a sheet of paper towel to absorb the extra moisture.

04 Place the leaves in a salad bowl to cover the base and sides, then add all the other Cobb ingredients, halving the boiled eggs and placing them on top.

05 Drizzle the salad dressing generously from above rather than tossing the leaves in it as is more common. I find that this allows the lettuce to stay crisp, lightly dressed, and refreshingly simple when served.

Soft-shell Taco with Lentil Caviar

MAKES 12

When canapés are passed around at a garden party, the vegetarian option feels often like an afterthought—some limp asparagus spears or tired-looking olives. I want to readjust the balance, and this recipe will certainly catch people's eyes as it weaves around your guests. It's always rewarding when the vegetarian option is the talk of all your friends and family, and this one is simple and elegant, bite-sized and fun. The mixture of bitter and sweet leaves provides real interest and bursts of flavor.

INGREDIENTS

3½oz (100g) black beluga lentils

1 tsp sea salt

12 chive leaves

Handful of small lettuce leaves—Little Gem and baby leaf

1¾oz (50g) crème fraîche

Zest and juice of 1 lemon

White truffle oil, for drizzling

Method

01 Cook the black beluga lentils in a saucepan of water for 20–25 minutes or until cooked through, then drain and rinse. Season with the sea salt, then allow to cool.

02 Prepare the lettuce boats by blanching the chives in boiling water for 30 seconds and then refreshing them under cold water. Tie a bundle of mixed lettuce leaves together at the base with a couple of chives to form a shallow boat that you can fill.

03 Mix the crème fraîche with the lemon juice and place a teaspoon of the mixture into the base of each lettuce boat. Top each one with a spoonful of seasoned beluga lentils and finish with a sprinkling of grated lemon zest and a drizzle of white truffle oil.

Spring Onions
SPRIGHTLY AND BRIGHT

EDIBLE PARTS

01 GREEN LEAVES

The tips of a spring onion are sweet and tangy with a strong flavor. I use these raw or thrown into a dish at the last moment to serve as an herb. They are also delicious sweated in butter with spring greens.

02 STEM

The middle section of the elongated leaves is probably my favorite part of the spring onion. It combines the best elements from both the juicy, crisp bulb and the bright-green tips. Ideal for cooking or finely slicing raw into a soy dressing or potato salad.

03 BULB

The slender bulbs are where you will find the strongest allium hit. These can withstand grilling, roasting, and stir-frying. Personally, I find the bulb rather harsh to serve raw, but it can make a pleasant addition to the humble grilled cheese.

04 ROOTS

The fine roots are really delicious. They crisp up nicely when fried but keep their more delicate onion flavor.

Fantastic raw or cooked, spring onions are incredibly versatile. Compared to mature onions, they are lighter on the palate and have a high note that offers a grassy heat to finish a dish without masking the other flavors with heavy pungency.

PLANT

The spring onion is part of the *Allium cepa* group and is essentially an onion that's harvested early, before the bulb has had a chance to swell. It is often referred to interchangeably with scallions or green onions, but they are different: the former develops a bulb, while the latter grow in less bulbous clusters, known as "bunching." The spring onion is small, at around 6 in (15 cm) tall, with straight tubular leaves that are darker green at the tip, leading to a slender white bulbous base. The entire plant is edible, can be grown all year round, and is also available in striking red varieties. It has a much milder flavor than mature onions.

COOKING TIPS

Spring onions can be used raw or cooked in anything from fresh salads and grain bowls to barbecued foods or stir-fries. The bulbs always get cooked first to infuse the other ingredients with a subtle peppery flavor and sweetness, then I tend to toss the sliced greens in near the end of cooking or add them to a finished dish. Spring onions are often paired with ginger in Asian cooking. They also add a lightly pungent background to salsas and dipping sauces and can be great in ranch dressing. Try wilting the crunchy tops like leeks with oil and lemon or finely chopping alongside parsley and mint for a twist on a tabbouleh. Also try dredging the roots in flour and then frying, as a garnish on top of soups or hot salads.

PREPARATION

Start by cleaning the roots under cold running water, then strip off any dry outer leaves. I normally separate the plant into piles—the green leaves, the white bulb, and the roots—before proceeding (**fig. a**). I then slice the greens and whites in one of three ways: vertically into long ribbons for tacos and rice pancakes (these long, thin strips are also good fried for an allium crisp nest with the roots); across the bulb into thin circular slices that have a good bite to them; or diagonally as a Chinese cut. This adds attractive flecks of green to dishes and maximizes the onion's surface area, making it a particularly good cut for a spiced sauce.

ZERO WASTE

Don't trim off and discard the green ends unless they are damaged. Enjoy the difference in taste between the various parts of a spring onion, and you will find that you don't waste any of it. Essentially, you are getting a vegetable and herb all in one plant.

Spring onions will keep in the fridge for around 5–7 days—or longer, if you wrap them in a damp sheet of paper towel. They certainly don't last as long as mature onions, as they have much more moisture in them. If you aim to preserve them for longer than a couple of weeks, blanching and freezing works well. If you have a surplus, the best bet is to pickle them, whole or sliced, in a strong solution of 2:2:1 cider or white wine vinegar, water, and sugar (see page 55).

TYPES

GREEN

Also known as scallions, green onions are less bulbous than spring onions and are closer to chives. They have a dense, succulent base and are sweet and pungent. Very popular in Asian and Mexican cooking, they are excellent finely chopped into curries and rice dishes.

CALÇOT

Juicy and tender with a slight smoky sweetness when cooked. This onion is crossed with a leek, resulting in a larger variety, and is also available as red calçot. Similar in taste to green spring onions but juicier in texture, it's fantastic when flash-blanched and then grilled to develop a charred caramelization with a distinctive sweet flavor.

RED TIP SCALLION

A bunching onion with elongated leaves, a thin base, and bright-red hues. It has a crisp, grassy flavor. I find it mildly sweet and, again, all parts of the immature onion are edible.

Figure a.

SNACK OR SIDE

Charred Calçot with Romesco Sauce
SERVES 2

Cooking freshly harvested calçot over the fire is traditional in Catalonia. They even use the soil they are grown in to provide a barrier from the fierce flames. The onions are then peeled to remove the muddy outer layers and dipped in chilled romesco sauce. For my version, I've fried the roots as a crispy garnish and roasted the red pepper for the sauce to serve warm.

INGREDIENTS

6–8 calçot onions, roots trimmed off and reserved
1 tbsp olive oil

For the romesco sauce
1 red bell pepper
3 tbsp olive oil, plus extra for drizzling
1¾ oz (50 g) blanched almonds
1 garlic clove
1 tbsp sherry vinegar
1 tsp smoked paprika
Sea salt

Method

01 For the romesco sauce, first roast the red pepper on a baking sheet. Preheat the oven to 400°F (200°C) and drizzle the pepper with a little olive oil, then roast for 25–30 minutes. Allow to cool slightly before using for the sauce.

02 Toast the blanched almonds in a dry pan for 3–4 minutes, then blend in a food processor with the roasted red pepper, garlic, vinegar, and paprika into a coarse sauce.

03 Slowly drizzle the olive oil into the processor and pulse to form a glossy dip. Season to taste with the sea salt.

04 Cook the whole onions over a grill, barbecue, or hot embers until charred and wilted.

05 In a frying pan, fry the calçot roots in the olive oil until crisp and serve on top of the charred onions with a generous spoonful of sauce.

SIDE

Champ
SERVES 4

Coming from a large Irish family, it was part of my early kitchen education to learn how to cook champ. It's extremely basic, but it's a classic that tastes super comforting and works well with veggie sausages, wilted greens, or a nut roast. Like many of the best Irish meals, you need to start with some good potatoes and plenty of butter. The spring onions steal the show with their pungent, sweet flavor, but they only work so well with the rich, fluffy mash as a contrast.

INGREDIENTS

12 vegetarian sausages

1 lb 10 oz (750 g) potatoes (Yukon Gold, King Edward, or Maris Piper), peeled

⅔ cup (150 ml) whole milk

3½ oz (100 g) green spring onions, sliced and separated into white bulb and green stem

7 tbsp (100 g) butter, plus extra if needed

Sea salt and ground white pepper

Method

01 Preheat the oven to 400°F (200°C) and cook the veggie sausages for 25 minutes.

02 At the same time, boil the potatoes in salted water for 20 minutes until soft.

03 Meanwhile, warm the milk with the white part of the chopped spring onions added. Bring to a boil, then remove from heat to infuse.

04 Drain the potatoes, then return them to the pan and add the butter. Mash until fairly smooth and creamy. Personally, I like a coarse champ, so I don't overmash.

05 Add the milk and white spring onion bulbs and mix together well.

06 Finish by mixing in the remaining green tips of the spring onions and season to taste with the sea salt and white pepper. Add extra butter if required, then serve the mash topped with the veggie sausages. You can also try adding wilted cabbage and turnips cooked in butter on the side.

Pickled Spring Onions

MAKES 1 16 FL OZ (500 ML) JAR

I love pickled onions, but it's fair to say they can have an overpowering flavor and be eye-wateringly hot to eat. I love this milder recipe for crunchy pickled spring onions. The hint of red chili, garlic, and dill provides extra piquancy and anise back notes. They are delicious served with cheese and crackers for a twist on a traditional meat and cheese platter, taking the whole meal up a notch.

INGREDIENTS

12 spring onions
¾ cup (200 ml) cider vinegar
6 tbsp (75 g) granulated sugar
2 garlic cloves
1 tsp black peppercorns
1 tsp chili flakes
1 tsp Aleppo pepper flakes
1 tsp yellow mustard seeds
2 allspice berries
Sea salt
1 tbsp chopped dill

Method

01   Remove any dry or yellowing outer leaves from the spring onions and wash the roots to remove any soil under cold running water. Sterilize a 16 fl oz (500 ml) jar by baking in the oven at 175°F (100°C) for 15 minutes, then pack the spring onions into it.

02   Next, add all the other ingredients except the salt and dill to a large saucepan with ½ cup (100 ml) water. Add a pinch of salt, then heat until the solution reaches boiling point.

03   Pour the hot pickling solution, including the aromatics, into the jar and, once it has cooled for 5 minutes, add the dill.

04   Seal the lid and leave for at least 2 days to allow the flavors to develop before opening. This pickle can be stored unopened in a cool pantry for up to 6 months, although the spring onions will become less crunchy over time. Once opened, store in the fridge for 1–2 weeks.

Watercress

THE COOK'S SUPERFOOD

01

02

03

EDIBLE PARTS

01 LEAVES

The leaflets grow off the stems and from the roots. The smaller leaves are tender and succulent, with a gentle mustard flavor. Larger leaves build in peppery heat and are often better cooked.

02 FLOWERS

The spicy-scented small white flowers are edible and make a stunning decoration for salads, although watercress with too many flowers may have more bitter-tasting leaves.

03 STEMS

The hollow stems carry sap and are therefore moist and crisp. They are not woody like the stems of many brassicas but do still provide bite when cooked, retaining a pleasant texture in soups or pesto.

One of the earliest leaves eaten by humans, with a sharp, mustardy flavor, peppery aroma, and bags of vitamins and minerals, watercress is the original superfood. Prized by cooks and nutritionists alike, it should be bottled as a miracle cure.

PLANT

Part of the brassica family, watercress is an aquatic perennial plant that forms a dense mat of foliage with hollow floating stems. It is full of vitamins C, K, and A; calcium; iron; and folate. Watercress also contains bioactive plant compounds, or phytochemicals, plus antioxidants such as beta-carotene and quercetin, which lower the risk of chronic diseases, neutralize free radicals, and possess anti-inflammatory qualities. As watercress is 95 percent water but still nutritious, it's often suggested for dieting, but for me, it is not about denial. It really is a taste of the good life, and I count watercress as one of my favorite ingredients to cook with. It is undoubtedly good for your health, can be foraged for free in the wild or bought year-round when grown commercially, and tastes less bitter than many spring cabbages and some lettuces. There is a mustard heat and metallic bitterness to it that I adore.

PREPARATION

You can generally find fresh bunches of watercress all year round. Commercially grown watercress will still need to be trimmed and prepared before cooking. Start by separating into larger leaves that may require cooking and the fresh young shoots and leaves that will suit a salad. Then wash any roots to remove soil and sand. Discard damaged leaves and wash the plant gently under cold running water. If you are foraging, do so with care—fool's watercress (*see right*) can easily be mistaken for true watercress, and although both are edible, they may both carry a risk of liver fluke, a parasite that can pollute waterways, caused by livestock grazing upstream. It's extremely dangerous, so be very sure the location is safe when foraging for wild watercress and ensure it is always cooked before eating.

TYPES

WATERCRESS

Despite being commercially grown on a large scale, watercress doesn't have a long shelf life, so find a local supplier for the freshest plants. The flavor should be peppery and sweet with a metallic tang.

RED WATERCRESS

This variety has leaves deeply veined with a striking red-to-purple color with a strong pepper flavor and mustard notes. It's often sold as a microgreen for chefs.

FOOL'S WATERCRESS

Not in the true family of watercress but a similar edible variety that can be foraged wild, although be aware that there may be a risk of liver fluke if it's growing near polluted waterways. Gather with care and ensure it is always cooked. It has a strong carrot flavor and aroma, with more serrated leaves than watercress.

UPLAND CRESS

This herb, also known as winter cress, resembles watercress but tends to have a stronger peppery flavor and is from a different family. It grows well both in the wild and commercially and is often sold with the roots attached to prolong its storage life.

GARDEN CRESS

Sometimes called pepperwort, this is a leafy annual herb, often harvested when immature. It has succulent young leaves, and the flavor is less spicy than many other mustard greens. It's easy to grow as a microgreen.

CONT.

Figure a.

Figure b.

COOKING TIPS

Raw, watercress is my go-to spring garnish, adding mustardy heat and a splash of color to many dishes, while in everyday cooking it's a fantastic alternative to spinach—in omelets, quiches, or soups. It adds a complex peppery edge to pesto and bright-green color to purées and sauces. The flavor weakens slightly when cooked, and it shrinks down as it wilts, so don't be afraid to use large quantities. At the end of its storage life, try mixing it with potato for a refreshing spring soup (see page 23). Alternatively, try sautéing it with young nettle tips (**fig. a**), which can be foraged in spring, then blend with cold vegetable stock and chill for a green gazpacho. Add nutmeg for a classic match and cushion the heat with cream, crème fraîche, or yogurt. If making fresh pasta, add blended watercress for bright green flecks of color and a gently peppery flavor. Partner with a fava bean and mint filling for a delicious ravioli (**fig. b**). Other flavors that work well with watercress include nuts, mold-ripened cheese, apple, and shallot.

ZERO WASTE

The entire watercress plant is edible, so it's easy to avoid food waste by blending it into a paste and combining it into butters and pesto. I often use it as a natural green food dye, the added benefit being that it has a metallic tang and pungent aroma. For breads, quiches, soups, or pastas, it can boost the color and supercharge the flavor with a mustard hit.

Leaves and stems are very perishable and will only keep for a few days in the fridge. Store the stems upright in a glass of water and cover with a bag in the fridge to extend their freshness after harvesting. To preserve, try blanching, squeezing out the water in a sifter, and freezing in ice cube trays for easy-to-use portions.

STARTER OR LIGHT MEAL

Watercress and Saffron Arancini

SERVES 2

When I want to make a statement with my food, I source fresh, seasonal ingredients, then convert them into something new, with splashes of natural color, contrasting shapes, and strong aromas. This recipe is a prime example: it pairs bright-green watercress with Cornish saffron and charcoal breadcrumbs for a visual treat and a dramatic flavor bomb.

INGREDIENTS

1 shallot, finely diced

1 tbsp olive oil

Pinch of saffron

3½ oz (100 g) risotto rice

⅓ cup (75 ml) white wine

3 cups (750 ml) vegetable stock

2 tbsp all-purpose flour

Sea salt and cracked black pepper

2 eggs, beaten

4 tbsp panko breadcrumbs

1 tbsp charcoal powder

Vegetable oil, for frying

Fennel fronds and flowers, to garnish (optional)

Lemon oil, to serve (see page 42)

For the watercress purée

1 shallot, diced

3½ tbsp (50 g) butter

7 oz (200 g) watercress, plus extra to garnish

1 tbsp lemon juice

Method

01 In a large pan, make a saffron risotto. Sauté the finely diced shallot in the olive oil for 3–4 minutes, then add the saffron and risotto rice. Coat in the oil, then deglaze the pan with the white wine.

02 Start adding the stock one ladleful at a time. Allow the rice to soak up the stock and infuse with the saffron spice and color. After 15–20 minutes, remove from heat and allow to cool.

03 Once cool enough to handle, roll the risotto mixture into 6 large balls. Season the flour with a pinch of salt and pepper, then roll each risotto ball in the seasoned flour, the beaten eggs, the breadcrumbs, and finally the charcoal powder. Shallow fry in hot oil for 4–5 minutes until the breadcrumbs are crispy and black. Keep warm in the oven at 400°F (200°C) for 5–10 minutes while you make the watercress purée.

04 For the purée, in a frying pan, sauté the diced shallot in the butter to soften. Then blanch the watercress in boiling water for 1 minute. Remove from the water, squeeze to remove excess water, then add to the pan with the sweated shallot. Add in a splash of lemon juice, then blend the mixture into a purée in a food processor. You can pass the mixture through a sieve at this stage if you like, but I don't mind a coarser texture and don't like the waste.

05 Remove the arancini from the oven and serve with a spoonful of the purée. Season to taste with sea salt, then garnish with watercress, fennel fronds and flowers (if using), and a drizzle of lemon oil.

LIGHT LUNCH

Melon, Watercress, and Fig Salad

SERVES 4

Watercress has been cultivated since Roman times, and this dish is inspired by my trips to Italy and the many wonderful antipasti and Venetian salads I've eaten over the years. For me, this plate displays how versatile and commanding watercress can be. When you pair the delicate younger leaves with raw figs, bitter melon, and crumbled rich blue cheese, the result is a sensation. Alternatively, you can try this salad with roasted figs and melted blue cheese. Either way, it's a salty, peppery, sweet treat.

INGREDIENTS

½ cantaloupe melon, diced

4 figs, finely diced

Sea salt

1 tbsp olive oil

2 bunches of watercress (about 7 oz/200 g)

12 mint leaves

3½ oz (100 g) blue cheese, crumbled

4 crackers or crispbreads

2 tbsp balsamic glaze

Handful of chive flowers

Method

01 Put the diced melon and figs in a bowl, season with a pinch of salt, and gently mix together with the olive oil.

02 If you have them, place a large forming ring on each plate and another smaller one inside it. Fill the space between the two rings with the fig and melon mix. This is how I would build the dish for an impressive restaurant-level finish, but it's fine to assemble it as a rustic salad with all the components layered instead.

03 Next, start filling the center ring (if using) with leaflets of watercress, sprigs of mint, and crumbled blue cheese.

04 Remove the forming rings and finish each individual salad with some broken cracker shards sticking around the crown and a drizzle of balsamic glaze. Garnish with chive flowers, then serve.

Watercress, Pear, and Walnut Tart

SERVES 4

I've made all sorts of pastry products over the years to sell in supermarkets, restaurants, and delis around the UK. With all that experience, I have yet to find a springtime savory tart that I enjoy as much as this recipe. It has it all: fruity sweetness, nutty notes, a peppery background, and creamy cheese—and it's no secret that the star is the watercress. Try serving this tart with some pickled cabbage and a lentil and watercress salad on the side.

INGREDIENTS

For the pastry

1 lb 2 oz (500 g) all-purpose flour

1 cup (250 g) cold salted butter, diced

For the filling

2 eggs

½ cup (100 ml) heavy cream

3½ oz (100 g) mature Cheddar cheese, grated

½ tsp grated nutmeg

Sea salt and cracked black pepper

1 bunch of watercress (about 5½ oz/150 g), roughly chopped

1 pear, thinly sliced

2 tbsp walnuts

Method

01 Make the pastry in advance by rubbing the flour and cold butter together between your fingers into a breadcrumb texture. Then gradually mix in around ½ cup (100 ml) of cold water until you have a dough that can be formed into a ball. Leave in the fridge to chill for 1–2 hours.

02 Preheat the oven to 400°F (200°C) and roll out the pastry on a floured surface. Press into a greased tart pan, about 12 × 5 in (30 × 12 cm), and gently prick the base with a fork. Line the pastry crust with parchment paper and baking beans and blind bake for 15 minutes. Remove the beans and parchment and bake for a further 10 minutes, then remove and allow to cool.

03 While the pastry crust is cooling, make the tart filling. Beat the eggs in a bowl and stir in the cream, Cheddar, and nutmeg, then season with a pinch of salt and pepper.

04 Place the chopped watercress, pear slices, and walnuts in the pastry crust and spread out evenly, then pour over the egg mixture. Bake in the oven for 20–25 minutes until just set, then remove. Cool in the pan for 10 minutes before turning out onto a wire rack. Serve at room temperature.

Fava Beans

PLUMP PODS OF JOY

EDIBLE PARTS

01 BEANS

Within the cottony interior of the pod, you will usually find 2–7 lime-green-colored beans. They are best harvested young when they are tender, with a pleasant grassy flavor. The skin's texture ranges between crisp and firm when picked young to creamy and starchy as they get older.

02 TOPS

The sage-green leaves, shoots, and tendrils are all edible. They can be cooked in a tempura batter, blended into a pesto, or eaten raw in a salad.

FLOWERS

Fava bean flowers are black and white with a splash of purple and have a mild, sweet flavor and soft texture. They can be cooked along with the shoots and leaves, or they make a lovely garnish for a salad.

As a family, we relish the time spent together preparing fava beans. It's the tactile quality of their duvet-lined pods and the delicious emeralds that lie beneath the pale-green skins. Cooking with fava beans isn't a chore—it's a culinary treat.

PLANT

A member of the legume family, fava beans are a good source of both protein and carbohydrates. Their season runs from around June to September and they are very easy to grow, so they frequently appear in vegetable plots and allotments. They are also often used in crop rotation to counter nutrient depletion—nitrogen-fixing nodules on their roots are good for keeping your soil balanced. At the end of the growing season, when you have finished harvesting, it's a good idea to pull the plant up, but leave the roots lying on the soil for a few days so that the nutrients can wash back into the earth.

COOKING TIPS

When cooking fava beans, season well to bring out the grassy flavor in older, large beans. They also tend to absorb plenty of olive oil, so you may need to use more than usual when cooking them to make up for this. A simple recipe is to blanch the beans, then toss in a frying pan for 2–3 minutes with olive oil, lemon juice, and a pinch of cracked black pepper and sea salt. Alternatively, if cooking them in a rustic stew or chunky soup, add the beans for the last 10 minutes of cooking.

PREPARATION

Fava beans are at their best when picked while young and fresh, with a snappy crisp texture and more sweetness. If they are left to grow on the plant for too long, they lose some of their vibrancy, often tasting slightly bitter, but they are still delicious if prepared correctly. To shell fava beans, first snap the pod from the plant cleanly and remove the sinew that runs down the length of the bean. Then slide a finger into the jacket and remove the beans. If the beans are small, start cooking them right away. If they are large, first blanch them in boiling water for 2 minutes, then cool them in ice water before cooking (**fig. a**). The final step is to pop the beans from their pale-gray skins to reveal the green "inner" bean.

ZERO WASTE

Young fava bean leaves can be eaten as a salad, like pea shoots; try thickly sowing whole dried beans in a tray of shallow compost, and snip the leaves at 3 in (6 cm). The outer pods are edible, but I avoid eating larger ones, as they have a fibrous texture. They taste best young; chargrill them to bring out the sweetness, or try making bean-pod ash by roasting for 1–2 hours, then cooling and blending with sea salt to season dishes. To preserve, blanch and freeze for up to 3 months, or dehydrate for authentic hummus or to add to soups and stews.

TYPES

LONG PODS

A hardy variety of fava bean that grows to about 3 ft (1 m) tall and is well suited to fall and early-spring sowing. Support them with canes when they get taller. Each pod bears 8–10 large, flat, kidney-shaped beans.

DWARF FAVA BEANS

Shorter than long pods, therefore more suited to exposed plots or container growing on a patio.

WINDSOR

Also known as short pods, this variety produces 4–7 rounder beans that are in shorter, broader pods. I find that these are the fullest in flavor.

Figure a.

Fava Bean Buddha Bowl

SERVES 2

For a bright springtime brunch, a Buddha bowl is hard to beat. My version uses smashed fava bean hummus and some chili salt. Fava beans govern the competing flavors with creamy poise and bittersweet balance. They hold everything else in the bowl together like a good hug. Try serving with a warm poached egg for a rich, creamy topping.

INGREDIENTS

For the fava bean hummus
5½ oz (150 g) fava beans in their pods
2 tbsp lemon juice
1 tbsp grated Parmesan cheese
1 tbsp olive oil
1 tbsp tahini
1 garlic clove, grated
1 tbsp chopped mint leaves
½ tsp sea salt

For the vinaigrette
2 tbsp olive oil
1 tbsp cider vinegar
1 tsp lemon juice
1 tsp chopped chive leaves
½ tsp honey
½ tsp Dijon mustard
Sea salt

For the Buddha bowl
1 tbsp cider vinegar
2 eggs
2 large handfuls of mixed salad leaves
   (watercress, arugula, and baby lettuce)
2 tomatoes, chopped
2 tbsp sprouted seeds
1 avocado, sliced
1 tsp chili sea salt
Olive oil, for drizzling

Method

01 Blanch the fava bean pods, then blend in a food processor with the lemon juice, Parmesan, olive oil, tahini, and garlic, pulsing until you have a coarse hummus texture. Then fold in the chopped mint and season with the sea salt.

02 Make the vinaigrette by simply whisking all the ingredients together except the salt in a small bowl. Season to taste with a pinch of salt.

03 Next, poach the eggs. Boil a pan of water and add the cider vinegar. Stir to create a whirlpool and crack the eggs one by one into the middle. Poach on a rolling boil for 2–3 minutes, then remove with a slotted spoon.

04 Now begin to build your Buddha bowls. Add the salad leaves to the bowls and dress them with the vinaigrette, then add the chopped tomatoes, the sprouted seeds for texture, and the avocado. Serve each bowl with a generous dollop of fava bean hummus and top with a poached egg. To finish, season with the chili sea salt and a drizzle of oil.

Habas Fritas with Smoked Sea Salt

SERVES 4

Traditionally eaten with a small glass of wine or a cold beer, this Spanish-inspired snack is a delicious wake-up for your taste buds before a meal—the smoked sea salt and paprika are perfect with the sweet fava beans. You can fry or bake these in the oven and play around with different seasonings to make your own creations.

INGREDIENTS

1 tbsp all-purpose flour
1 tsp smoked paprika
2 tsp smoked sea salt flakes
7 oz (200 g) fava beans, shelled, blanched, and peeled (see page 63)
4 tbsp olive oil

Method

01 First, season the flour by adding the smoked paprika and 1 teaspoon of the smoked sea salt, then dredge the peeled fava beans in the seasoned flour.

02 Heat the olive oil in a frying pan and cook the beans for 5–6 minutes, turning occasionally.

03 Remove the beans from the pan and lay on a sheet of paper towel to soak up the excess oil. Season while still warm with the remaining smoked sea salt. Enjoy warm or allow to cool first. For similar end results but using less oil, you can bake the beans in a hot oven. Drizzle a lined baking sheet with just enough oil to grease the surface and lightly coat the beans, then bake at 425°F (220°C) for 10–15 minutes. Serve warm.

Bean Salad with Fava Bean Pesto

SERVES 2

This pesto can be enjoyed cold or warm and is a fantastic way to finish a dish with a fresh burst of color. For my version, I temper the slight bitterness of the fava beans with extra zing, so I use lemon and fresh sorrel complemented by mint. I like it best served with a verdant explosion of steamed peas and shelled beans.

INGREDIENTS

For the pesto

3½oz (100g) fava beans, shelled, blanched, and peeled (see page 63)

¼ cup (50g) olive oil

scant 1oz (25g) sorrel leaves or baby spinach

1 tbsp chopped mint leaves

1 garlic clove, finely diced

Juice of 1 lemon

½ tsp cumin seeds

Sea salt

For the bean salad

1¾oz (50g) frozen peas

1¾oz (50g) frozen edamame beans

1¾oz (50g) fava beans, shelled, blanched, and peeled (see page 63)

1 tbsp olive oil

Sea salt

4 tbsp kefir or strained yogurt, to serve

Mint, wood sorrel, and chervil, to garnish

Method

01 To make the pesto, blend the fava beans in a food processor with the olive oil, sorrel or baby spinach, mint, garlic, lemon juice, and cumin seeds until smooth. Season to taste with a pinch of sea salt.

02 Allow the frozen peas and edamame beans to defrost, then prepare the bean salad. Toss the fava beans, peas, and edamame beans in olive oil over medium heat for 2–3 minutes, then finish with a pinch of sea salt.

03 Serve the beans warm with cold kefir, a swirl of fava bean pesto, and some more fresh mint, with wood sorrel and chervil leaves, to garnish.

Spinach
LEAVES FIT FOR SUPERHEROES, SORT OF

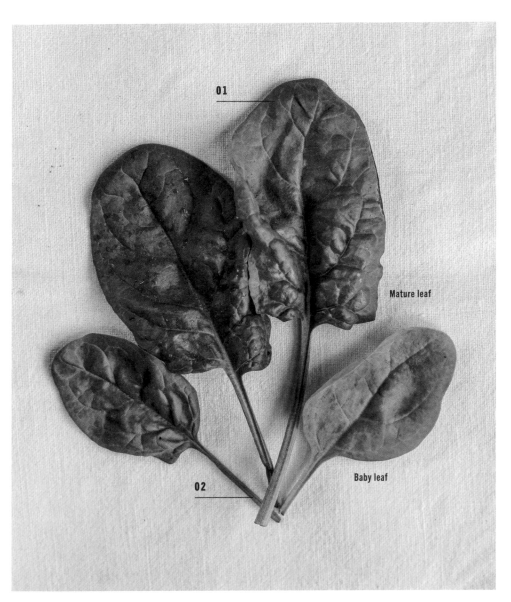

01

02

Mature leaf

Baby leaf

EDIBLE PARTS

01 LEAF

The spinach leaf is delicious raw or cooked. Mature, darker leaves taste stronger than the more melt-in-the-mouth baby leaves and provide more bite when cooked. Try to reserve baby leaf spinach for salad, as it loses much of its flavor when cooked.

02 STEM

The stems are more fibrous than the leaves but still relatively juicy. I tend to cook them along with the leaf (except if baby leaf, which is best raw), as they provide a fantastic bite to any spinach dish. If a recipe calls for stems to be removed, chop them finely before cooking with the rest of the leaves rather than wasting them.

Many of us grew up watching Popeye, which showed how eating lots of spinach gives you superhuman strength. And it's almost true. Spinach is a powerhouse: it's good for you, has an iron-tasting strength, and wears a bright-green superhero cape.

PLANT

Spinach has spoon-shaped leaves, which can be flat-leafed or partially crinkled. It's a superb source of antioxidants and beta-carotene, which is converted by the body into vitamin A or retinol, helping promote good vision and healthy organs. To get the best nutritional value, it is best eaten raw or gently cooked. An excellent cut-and-come-again crop, the plant produces more leaves to replace those you cut, allowing for several crops in one season. There is a big difference between the popular baby leaf spinach sold in supermarkets, which tends to taste rather bland, and the more robust perennial spinach and mature heirloom types, which withstand cooking and are worth seeking out.

PREPARATION

Always wash spinach before use, as it can be notoriously gritty. Rinse gently in a colander with cold running water, then pat dry **(fig. a)**. The leaves can bruise easily and deteriorate fast, so save the washing until the last minute and don't store wet in the fridge. I sort the baby leaves for salads from the larger mature leaves for cooking. I rarely trim off the stems to cook separately—I love to wilt the leaves whole—but if you have leaves with thick stems, you can remove them at this point. Make clean cuts while holding a bunch lightly so it doesn't bruise. Before cooking, taste the leaf and gauge the flavor and texture. I do this to decide if the leaves should be cooked or left raw. It also helps assess how much acid and seasoning to include in the recipe to offset the stronger vegetal bitterness of mature spinach.

Figure a.

TYPES

FLAT-LEAF SPINACH

A strong variety growing all year round, with deep-green glossy leaves. This classic spinach is popular the world over. All parts of the plant are edible, and it can be eaten raw or cooked.

PERPETUAL SPINACH

This is actually a type of chard but incredibly similar to spinach in flavor. A hardy biennial winter green that keeps on giving as a cut-and-come-again crop, it has a tannic flavor and cooks extremely well.

BABY SPOON

This is the immature leaf of the classic flat-leaf spinach. Very popular in salad mixes, it is prolific, with round bright-green leaves and a chewy yet juicy texture. Harvested as small, crisp leaves, it is sweeter than mature spinach, with a delicate flavor and edible stems. Not worth cooking, as it loses flavor.

BLOOMSDALE SPINACH

This is a heritage spinach with darker-green leaves that are harvested at the base of the stem. Sweet and moist, it is more robust than most spinach, with a strong winter green taste and a substantial texture when cooked.

RED SPINACH

A striking variety with scarlet veins and stems and a mild sweetness to the leaf. It's often cut as a microgreen or used to add color to a baby leaf salad. If left to mature, the red veins become more pronounced. If cooked, they lose some of their vibrant color.

CONT.

COOKING TIPS

Spinach responds well when paired with aromatic spices, especially ginger, fenugreek, cumin, garlic, and chili. Raw spinach is good with vinaigrettes, sharp citrus dressings, herbs, and mellow olive oil. Wilt gently in a pan with a little butter or oil for a bright side dish and add cream and nutmeg for a richer version.

To enjoy baby leaf spinach, I recommend using it raw in a sandwich or salad. For more mature leaves, try a large bunch wilted in 1 tablespoon of melted coconut oil with sliced garlic and red chili, then finish by creaming with coconut milk. This makes a wonderful exotic side dish for vegetable curries or served with boiled cassava.

One of my favorite recipes for spinach is by my mom's husband and is affectionately known as "Rob's Spinach Quiche" **(fig. b)**. He makes a pastry crust (see page 61) using brown spelt flour instead of all-purpose, then blind bakes it in a flan pan for 15–20 minutes at 350°F (180°C). He gets a small shopping bag stuffed with spinach, wilts it in a huge pan, squeezes out as much moisture as possible, then blends it in a food processor with a little milk, 5 eggs, and some seasoning to make the filling. He pours the mix into the blind-baked pastry crust, adds in half a block of diced feta, then bakes at 375°F (190°C) for about 30 minutes.

Figure b.

ZERO WASTE

If you have a serious surplus of spinach, a fun method to try is dehydrating it, then turning it into a powder for smoothies, pastry, and pasta. For this process, clean the leaves and remove any stems. (Keep these for use in a curry or pasta sauce.) Lay the leaves in a dehydrator at 120°F (50°C) for 6–8 hours, then grind or blend into a powder. This is a good method to try with other winter green vegetables and can provide a nutritional superfood powder to play with. The added benefit is that spinach powder takes up far less space than the bulky leaves in the fridge.

You can also preserve spinach by freezing. Blanch it first, but for no longer than 1 minute, then immediately submerge in ice water to stop it from cooking and further leaching the flavor, vitamins, and nutrients. Squeeze out any excess water to make it as dry as possible and to improve the texture, then pack in ice cube trays, label, and freeze.

BREAKFAST OR LUNCH

Spinach and Feta Parcels

MAKES 8

Every Saturday when we lived in London, my wife and I used to walk, bleary-eyed in the early-morning sun, down deserted streets with our eldest son cradled in a sling. Our mission was the first coffee of the day, croissants, and a spinach and feta roll each for second breakfast. I never did get the Spence Bakery's recipe, but after much trial and error, I found the winning formula. We now enjoy these treats with our bigger family—and they taste just as good as they did then.

INGREDIENTS

Large colander of washed spinach—about 1 lb 2 oz (500 g)

1 shallot, finely diced

1 tbsp olive oil

2 tbsp pine nuts

Zest and juice of 1 lemon

1 tsp nutmeg

2 tbsp chopped mint

½ tsp dried wild thyme

½ tsp oregano

5½ oz (150 g) feta cheese, crumbled

Sea salt and cracked black pepper

10 oz (275 g) package of phyllo pastry sheets

7 tbsp (100 g) butter, melted

Method

01 Preheat the oven to 400°F (200°C). In a large pan, sauté the spinach with the finely diced shallot and olive oil. Cook for 3–4 minutes or until the leaves have wilted and the shallot has started to soften.

02 Allow to cool for a couple of minutes, then use a sieve to squeeze most of the moisture from the spinach. When the spinach is still warm, combine in a large mixing bowl with the pine nuts, lemon zest and juice, nutmeg, herbs, and feta. Use your hands to mix the ingredients together and season to taste with a pinch of salt and pepper.

03 While the spinach filling continues to cool, cut the phyllo sheets into 8 strips about 4 in (10 cm) wide. Place a generous spoonful of filling in the center of each strip.

04 Fold the corner of the pastry diagonally over the spinach filling so it makes a triangle, then brush the outside with melted butter. Fold the triangle over on itself 4–6 times, brushing with butter after each fold, and continue until you have a sealed triangular parcel. Repeat for each parcel.

05 Place on a lined baking sheet and bake for 25 minutes until golden. Serve warm.

Saag Paneer

SERVES 4

Several months spent living in the Himalayas building cooking stoves gave me some insight into how spinach can be used with spices, rice, and a cilantro chutney to knit together a complex, satisfying meal. Spinach is like a silk fabric that can be embroidered and adorned with sequins and splashes of intoxicating color, elevating it to suit any occasion. The wilted stems curve and illuminate the dish, sending earthy aromas up off the plate.

INGREDIENTS

1 tsp fenugreek seeds

1 tsp dried fenugreek leaves

1 tsp turmeric

1 tsp garam masala

1 tsp Kashmiri (mild) chili powder

3½ tbsp (50 g) ghee or butter

9 oz (250 g) paneer, diced

1 onion, diced

1 tbsp grated fresh ginger root

1 red chili, halved, seeded, and chopped, plus extra to garnish (optional)

3 garlic cloves, finely diced

1 lb 2 oz (500 g) mature spinach

½ cup (100 ml) coconut milk

1 tbsp lemon juice

1 tsp sea salt

Pinch of coconut flakes, to garnish (optional)

Method

01 Toast the spices in a dry saucepan for 1–2 minutes, then add in the ghee or butter and stir into a smooth paste.

02 Next, add the diced paneer, onion, ginger, chili, and garlic. Cook for 4–5 minutes until the cheese is golden and the onion has softened.

03 Mix in all the spinach and wilt for 5–10 minutes, stirring well to prevent the cheese from sticking to the pan.

04 Finish with the coconut milk and lemon juice. Bring to a boil and simmer for 10–15 minutes to develop all the flavors. Season with the salt and serve hot, garnished with chili rings and coconut flakes (if using). I like to accompany the saag with roti, steamed rice, and spicy green chili and cilantro chutney.

BREAKFAST

Green Super Smoothie

SERVES 2

Food envy is the curse of a family chef. Often, I will be quietly making a snack at home, when suddenly the seagulls descend. My children love smoothies if they're purple, pink, or orange, but when they see this super-green number, they tend to stand down—and long may it continue. My wake-up smoothie is a great kick-start to the day—fresh, nutrient-rich, and perfect for not sharing. When you blend spinach with lime, kiwi, avocado, and apple juice, it's packed with vitamins and tastes supreme. Consider also trying a green lassi version by adding plain yogurt, grated turmeric root, and fresh mint.

INGREDIENTS

2 large handfuls of baby leaf spinach

2 ripe kiwis, peeled

½ cup (100 ml) apple juice

½ avocado or ½ banana

Juice of 1 lime

1 tsp grated fresh ginger root

Crushed ice (optional)

Method

01 Add all the raw ingredients to a blender and blend for 1–2 minutes until smooth. Personally, I enjoy ice-cold smoothies, so I always include a handful of crushed ice when blending. I also love a zingy breakfast smoothie, but this recipe can be toned down a bit to taste, with less lime for a gentler wake-up call.

Arugula

PEPPERY FIRECRACKER

EDIBLE PARTS

01 FLOWERS AND SEED PODS

The bright yellow or white flowers are edible and very decorative. It's no disaster if the plant bolts, as the flowers and seeds are a tasty garnish.

02 LEAF

The leaves are all edible and the younger ones will be sweeter and more tender. As they mature, they tend to get darker and more peppery.

03 STEM

The stems can be a little tough and woody, but they are edible. Try sautéing them like asparagus in a little oil with lemon juice to soften. They are also good in stocks along with a mirepoix for a peppery flavor (see page 266). The flower stems are less woody but can still be tough.

When I started my first job as a kitchen porter at 15, arugula was a taste I didn't enjoy or understand. As I grew up and my cooking skills grew, arugula was a revelation—wonderfully sweet, bitter, and peppery, with edgy leaves like green flames.

PLANTS

For me, arugula wears the crown among all cut-and-come-again leaves. Also known as rucola or rocket, it is prolific, doesn't shy away from flavor, and is packed with nutrients, including high levels of vitamin C, folic acid, and potassium. The unique taste can be hot, peppery, and sweet, depending on the genotype and phytochemical composition. It is fast and easy to grow in sunny positions—in as little as six weeks, you can start cropping—and has a long harvest period. Provide some shade for the plant—otherwise, in hot weather, the leaves become tough and almost unpalatable—and remove flowers to prolong leaf production.

COOKING TIPS

Young leaves are tender and have the milder flavor. Older leaves are more peppery, so I often separate them to add to a sauce, sauté with olive oil, or throw into stir-fries. The woody stems can be used in stocks or blanched and blended into pesto and soup; they are not as pleasant to eat raw. Also try grilling thick, fibrous stalks over embers to serve with asparagus, burrata, and chili oil.

Arugula can also be added to smashed peas to add a spicy note or extra heat to a watercress soup or sorrel velouté. Try it wilted and cooked in stir-fries or with cumin, red chili, and lime juice for a refreshing Indian-inspired achar pickle.

PREPARATION

The plant is a cut-and-come-again vegetable, so pick a few leaves at a time from different stems rather than harvesting large bunches, which will weaken the plant. When preparing arugula, separate the mature leaves from the delicate baby leaves, as they may need to be treated differently. Larger shoots and broad leaves will have a spicier flavor and may be better cooked rather than served raw. For smaller leaves, especially salad arugula, wash gently and pat dry before dressing. Do not store washed arugula, as it can degrade quickly in the fridge.

ZERO WASTE

Arugula is best eaten soon after harvesting. If you do want to store it, keep it in a zipper-lock bag or sealed container for up to a week in the fridge. Older fibrous leaves can be blanched and frozen. These leaves are delicious added to a pearl barley stew or mixed with roasted vegetables as a peppery seasoning. Also try pickling the stems and serving on a cheeseboard with figs or scattering on a pizza with melted blue cheese.

If you have a large bag of arugula, consider making a pesto with grated pecorino, pumpkin seeds, lemon juice, and olive oil, or try incorporating a handful of arugula leaves into other dishes to avoid waste.

TYPES

WILD ARUGULA

This is my favorite variety of arugula, as it has the strongest peppery profile, with more serrated leaves and a much stronger, spicier taste. It's often called perennial arugula, as it will thrive year after year in milder climates.

SALAD ARUGULA

Quick growing and more delicate than wild arugula, salad arugula is still peppery but also sweeter. I hardly ever cook with salad arugula, but if you do have a surplus, then try making a pesto. The flowers of salad arugula are edible and have a distinctive sesame flavor. Leaves are best in spring and fall; in summer, it is likely to bolt.

DRAGON'S TONGUE

With purplish-veined leaves that are bolt resistant, this variety has a good, strong flavor and looks very attractive in salads.

WASABI

A very hot variety that has a spicy horseradishlike flavor and is also fast growing.

LIGHT LUNCH OR SIDE

Miso-glazed Carrot, Pecans, and Arugula

SERVES 2

Arugula rarely plays the leading role in recipes, but in many ways it deserves its own lifetime achievement award for best supporting artist. In this recipe, there is real chemistry between the peppery arugula salad and sweet roasted carrots. The complex flavors of both are magnetic in the bowl, and I've added pecans for an acclaimed box-office hit. I'm lucky to spend much of my working life cooking, directing, and writing the scripts for my food. It's a creative process, and every so often you find a recipe that will stay with you forever. This is one of those. It's an action-packed, riveting dish that I hope you enjoy eating as much as I do.

INGREDIENTS

3½ tbsp (50 g) butter

6 baby carrots, whole or halved

7 oz (200 g) French green lentils

1 tbsp red miso paste

2 tbsp honey

2 sprigs of thyme, plus extra to garnish

⅔ cup (150 ml) vegetable stock

1¾ oz (50 g) pecans

2 handfuls of wild arugula, woody stalks removed

Sea salt

Arugula flowers, to garnish

Method

01 Melt the butter in a frying pan, add the baby carrots, and pan sear on all sides until they start to char. Meanwhile, rinse the lentils, then simmer in plenty of boiling water until tender but not falling apart, usually 30–40 minutes.

02 After 5–10 minutes, add the miso, honey, and thyme to the pan. Turn regularly and allow the carrots to caramelize and absorb all the sweet, charred umami flavor.

03 Add the stock to deglaze the pan, then reduce the heat to a simmer.

04 Cook for a further 10–15 minutes until the stock reduces and the carrots are soft when you insert a paring knife. Add in the pecans for the final couple of minutes of cooking, until they and the carrots are sticky.

05 Prepare the salad by laying a generous nest of arugula in each bowl. Cover with hot cooked lentils and finish with the carrots and pecans. Season with a pinch of sea salt, and garnish with extra thyme leaves and a few arugula flowers.

LUNCH

Arugula and Orzo Salad
SERVES 4

I've taken the comforting and nostalgic elements of a pasta salad and made my own version here, which is packed with flavor and would brighten up any early-summer barbecue or springtime feast. This recipe works well with wild or salad arugula, as you use the residual warmth of the freshly boiled pasta to wilt the leaves, then toss them in generous amounts of fruity olive oil and lemon juice for a silky dressing. The secret with my twist is a surprising amount of lemon zest. The arugula can really take the extra citrus and makes this pasta salad bright, lively, and fresh.

INGREDIENTS

7 oz (200 g) orzo pasta

2 tbsp olive oil

4 large handfuls of arugula

2 tbsp sliced green olives

2 marinated artichoke hearts, sliced

1 tbsp cornichons, diced

Zest and juice of 1 lemon, plus extra zest to garnish

Sea salt

Method

01 Start by boiling the orzo pasta in salted water for 15 minutes. Drain, then put into a large bowl and coat the pasta in the olive oil.

02 Next, mix in all the other ingredients. Turn the arugula, olives, sliced artichoke, cornichons, and lemon zest and juice together in the bowl with the pasta while it is still steaming hot.

03 Finish with a generous pinch of sea salt and garnish with extra lemon zest.

LIGHT LUNCH

Arugula and Fig Salad
SERVES 2

Sometimes, as a chef, you need to put your hands up, your knives down, and stop trying to reinvent the wheel. This recipe is a classic flavor combination that covers all the main taste profiles of sweet, bitter, sour, salty, and umami. It is bright, colorful, and satisfying and will remain unchanged in my repertoire for many years to come. The key is to use the more delicate salad arugula variety that can be eaten in large forkfuls without building levels of peppery heat. The addition of the arugula flowers is my simple gardener's twist on this much-loved salad.

INGREDIENTS

2 large handfuls of salad arugula

1 tbsp lemon oil (see page 42)

Sea salt

4 fresh figs

1¾oz (50g) Parmesan cheese

1 tbsp balsamic glaze

Arugula flowers, to garnish

Method

01   Start by dressing the arugula in a dish or bowl with the lemon oil and seasoning lightly with a pinch of sea salt.

02   Next, slice the figs in half and place in the bowl with your peppery salad leaves.

03   Peel Parmesan shavings into the salad and drizzle with the tangy balsamic glaze.

04   Garnish with edible arugula flowers and serve before the lemon oil starts to wilt the delicate arugula leaves.

"

*The summer harvest fills
me with joy. With more
sunshine, vegetables develop
a heightened sweetness and
rich layers of flavor.*

"

SUMMER

Artichoke

HEART OF GOLD

EDIBLE PARTS

01 LEAVES

Also known as bracts or scales, the outer leaves are bitter and more fibrous, so I often remove and compost them. At the base of the inner leaves around the heart is a sweet layer of flesh that is delicious when boiled or fried. Many varieties have tiny needlelike tips on the leaves that are inedible even when cooked, so these should be removed.

02 STEM

The stem is also edible. It is more tender closer to the base of the flower bud. The upper section can be peeled to remove the woody exterior, revealing the tender stem beneath.

FLOWER HEAD

When immature, the flower can be prepared for eating, but once they bloom with their bright-purple flowers, they are best left for the bees. The smaller flower buds can be eaten whole raw, but as they grow, they require preparation before cooking.

CHOKE

In the center of the flower is a mass of purple florets, sometimes called the beard. These are edible but only in smaller, immature artichokes that are closer to a golf ball in size rather than a tennis ball.

HEART

This is the prized edible part of the artichoke and has a delicate, buttery taste. The flesh is found at the base of the petals and blends into the stem. It is grassy and nutty in flavor and meaty in texture.

Make it past the architectural, ornamental exterior of an artichoke and you are rewarded with the delicate flavor and Mediterranean elegance within. This is a classy vegetable, and it is worth the effort to master the cooking it requires.

PLANT

Growing up to 6½ft (2m) in height, the artichoke plant is a perennial thistle with an edible flower bud. Feed it with compost in summer for larger flower heads and water well for a good crop. Harvest when the buds are tight and feel dense to the touch to ensure tenderness. When buying, if it squeaks when you squeeze it, then it is fresh. The heart is the prized cut of an artichoke plant and, once prepared, makes a fantastic ingredient. Hidden beneath layers of thorny leaves, it takes a great deal of preparation to get to it, but it is definitely worth the effort. Artichokes are at their best when the hearts are soft and tender, and they have a wonderful green-lemon taste.

Figure a.

PREPARATION

Artichokes require some skill to prepare. The key is to work in a speedy, calm manner and to have a bowl of lemon ice water on hand to prevent browning **(fig. a)**. Trim the stem to around 2in (5cm) and snap off the outer leaves until the paler ones are revealed. Next, slice off the tips of the leaves with scissors to remove the thorns and rub the exposed tips with a cut lemon. Turn the artichoke in your hand, trimming off the leaves from the base with a sharp paring knife as you go, and peel the stem back, too. Cut across the top of the exposed flower head to reveal the hairy choke in the middle. Use a teaspoon to remove the choke and quickly submerge the heart in cold lemon water to avoid discoloration.

TYPES

GLOBE

These range in size but can reach 6in (15cm) in diameter, with heavy and densely packed leaves around a compact floret and pale-green colors throughout. The prized hearts are large and tender.

COCKTAIL

Also known as baby artichokes, these are simply harvested from the globe artichoke when they are smaller. They are more conical in shape than older artichokes, with very little choke. Every part of trimmed baby artichokes is edible and can be cooked.

PURPLE

Petit Violet and purple globes are striking artichokes with deep-purple buds. Excellent eaten raw when young.

CARDOON

This type of artichoke has a celery stick appearance but needs cooking before eating. It is blanched to reduce the bitterness for a sweeter and more tender plant and is heavy and moist to eat, with a beautiful pale-pistachio color. The leaves are not tasty, but the suedelike stalks are nutty and sweet.

SPINE

Also known as Peruvian artichokes, these have spiky, triangular leaves. When peeled, the leaves blend to a yellow-purple floret core. They are versatile and tangy in flavor, with a grassy taste.

CONT.

Figure b.

Figure c.

COOKING TIPS

When cooking artichoke hearts, it is a good rule to boil them for 10–15 minutes in acidulated water with herbs for added flavor. You then can marinate, grill, roast, or fry to add extra pizzazz. They can be cooked robustly over fire or in hot oil and also work well in tray bakes with chickpeas, sun-dried tomatoes, and olives. Marinated roasted hearts with rose harissa oil is one of my favorite recipes. To make this, prepare the hearts and boil for 10–15 minutes before roasting at 400°F (200°C) with olive oil and 1 tablespoon of harissa for 25 minutes. Store submerged in olive oil with rose petals, pink peppercorns, and fennel seeds for a wonderful pizza topping or rustic tapas dish **(fig. b)**.

The stems can also be used if you peel and cook them like a root vegetable. Try boiling first in water with some lemon and herbs, then either roast with thyme and sea salt; stew in garlic, parsley, and olive oil; or slowly braise with butter and white wine.

ZERO WASTE

There is inevitably some waste when preparing a larger artichoke, but there are ways to use the tougher inner leaves instead of throwing them away. Rinse and scrub well to remove the bitter film that coats the leaves before cooking. Try frying as chips and serving with tarragon aioli or tomato salsa. Or boil them for 10 minutes and serve with melted butter or a deviled hollandaise sauce for an elegant appetizer **(fig. c)**.

After cutting, artichokes stay fresh for about 1 week. To extend shelf life, keep the stem moist in a small bowl of water or in wet paper towel and store in the fridge. If you want to preserve them for longer, boil the hearts for 10–15 minutes in salted lemon water, then pack loosely into a sterilized jar with a brine of 2½ tsp (15 g) salt to 4 cups (1 liter) boiling water, seasoned with white wine vinegar or lemon juice. Submerge the jar up to its neck in a pot of boiling water for 1 hour 45 minutes. Alternatively, store the boiled hearts under oil and refrigerate for 2–3 weeks.

SIDE OR SNACK

Fried Hearts and Hot and Blue Cheese Sauces

SERVES 2–4

Fried artichoke has a toasted-nut flavor that can handle both a Louisiana-style hot sauce and a strong blue cheese sauce. This dish reminds me of a country food festival I once went to where lovestruck sweethearts strolled around the rides, playing ring toss and balloon darts. It's fun, loud, and memorable. The hot sauce could be basted over the fried artichokes, but I prefer dipping rather than finger-licking.

INGREDIENTS

4 artichokes, peeled and choke removed

1 lemon, sliced

4 sprigs of thyme

2 tbsp all-purpose flour

1 tbsp ground paprika

1 tsp sea salt

4 tbsp vegetable oil, for deep-frying

For the hot sauce

3½ tbsp (50 g) butter

1 tbsp brown sugar

2 tsp cayenne pepper (less if you don't like spice)

½ tsp paprika

½ tsp garlic powder

½ tsp white pepper

Sea salt

2 tbsp Louisiana-style hot sauce

For the blue cheese sauce

scant 2 tbsp (25 g) butter

1 tsp all-purpose flour

¼ cup (50 ml) whole milk

2½ oz (75 g) blue cheese, crumbled

Method

01 Start by slicing the artichoke hearts into quarters and cook the segments for 15 minutes in boiling water flavored with the sliced lemon and thyme.

02 Season the flour with paprika and salt, then drain the artichokes and dredge them in the seasoned flour until they are evenly coated.

03 Next, make the hot sauce by melting the butter with the sugar, spices, and a pinch of salt, then stir in the hot sauce. Simmer for 3–4 minutes until glossy and smooth.

04 For the blue cheese sauce, melt the butter, then add the flour and stir to make a roux. Slacken with the milk as needed and stir in the crumbled cheese. Cook over low heat for 4–5 minutes until smooth. Allow both sauces to cool.

05 Finally, heat the vegetable oil to 350°F (180°C) in a frying pan and cook the artichoke hearts until golden and crispy. Serve while still hot alongside the dipping sauces.

Grilled Artichokes with Smoked Hollandaise Sauce

SERVES 2

My passion for this rustic dish stems from its simplicity. It tastes best cooked outdoors over an open flame, and alfresco food is a great leveler, stripping an ingredient back to its roots. There's no formal training required—anyone can grill and serve this at their next barbecue. So kick any concerns you might have about cooking artichokes out of the window and light a fire under this revered vegetable.

INGREDIENTS

1 lemon, halved

6 small artichokes, peeled and choke removed

3½ tbsp (50g) smoked butter (either cold smoke salted butter for 6 hours over oak chips or add smoked sea salt to unsalted butter)

1 tbsp chopped parsley

For the smoked hollandaise

7 tbsp (100g) smoked butter

4 egg yolks

1 tsp Dijon mustard

1 garlic clove, grated

Squeeze of lemon juice

Sea salt

Method

01 Squeeze the juice of 1 lemon half into a bowl of ice water. Slice the artichoke hearts in half and store them in the lemon water to avoid discoloration.

02 Bring a pot of water to a boil and add the juice of the other lemon half. Simmer the hearts for 10–15 minutes until a knife inserted into the flesh goes through easily. Cool by returning the hearts to the lemon ice water.

03 Light a grill or heat a griddle pan on the stove. Melt the butter in a pan, add the parsley, then brush the blanched artichokes hearts with the herb butter.

04 Grill or griddle the hearts for 15–20 minutes, turning regularly and basting at intervals with more herb butter.

05 To make the hollandaise, melt the smoked butter in a pan on the stove. Whisk the egg yolks in a bowl, then add the mustard and garlic. Slowly pour in the melted butter, whisking constantly until the sauce is glossy and thick. Finish with lemon juice and season to taste with salt.

06 Serve the artichokes drizzled with the hollandaise sauce.

Artichoke and Truffle Dip

SERVES 2

Sophisticated and elegant, an artichoke dip is the ultimate intrigue before a meal. My version uses minced black truffles for a gentle kiss of luxury, but a drizzle of truffle oil works just as well. The artichoke flesh has a buttery texture when blended—perfect with the snappy crunch of olive breadsticks and marinated artichoke hearts for a refined platter.

INGREDIENTS

5½oz (150g) artichoke hearts, plus marinated hearts, to serve

3½oz (100g) cream cheese

1¾oz (50g) Parmesan cheese, grated

½ shallot, finely diced

2 tbsp olive oil, plus extra to cover

1 tsp grated black truffle or 2 tbsp black truffle oil

Sea salt

Caper berries, olives, and breadsticks, to serve

Method

01 First, boil the artichoke hearts in lemon water for 10–15 minutes as on page 86, opposite, then drain well to remove any excess water.

02 Roughly chop the cooled artichokes and blend with all the other ingredients except the sea salt in a food processor until smooth.

03 Season to taste with a pinch of salt and either eat right away or store in the fridge, covered with a layer of olive oil to stop it from drying out. Consume within 4–5 days. Serve on a platter with more marinated artichoke hearts, caper berries, olives, and breadsticks.

Zucchini

VERSATILITY IN ABUNDANCE

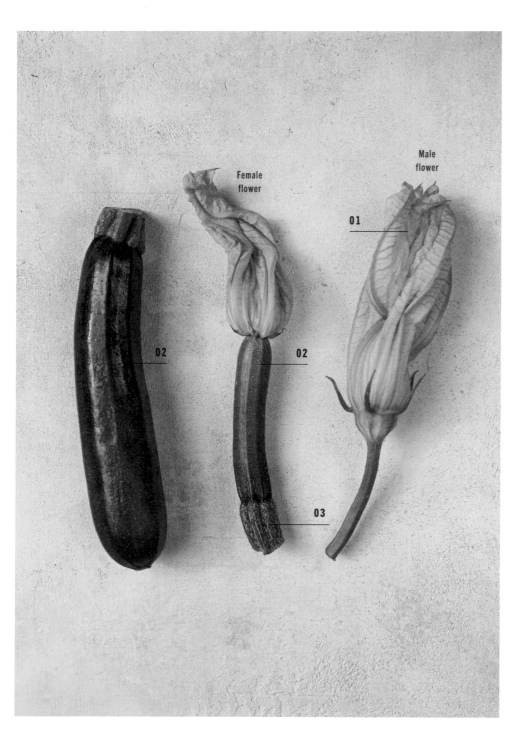

Female flower

Male flower

01

02

02

03

EDIBLE PARTS

01 FLOWERS

The tissue-paper-thin flowers are yellow-green outside with a vibrant orange interior. They are all edible, but I try to only use the male flowers, which will not develop a fruit at the base. Delicious stuffed, battered, and lightly fried.

02 FRUITS

The skin, flesh, and tiny seeds of zucchini fruits are all edible. Younger fruits tend to lack flavor but are extremely succulent and have a soft, moist, glossy skin. Crisp and light with underdeveloped seed cavities, they can be eaten raw, with their mild peppery taste and bright, grassy notes. The high water content makes them perfect in salads dressed with olive oil, lemon, oregano, and toasted pine nuts. Mature fruits have a tougher skin and a more robust flavor, making them better suited to cooking.

03 STEMS

The crisp, hollow stems are also edible and are particularly tender on baby zucchini, where they can be cooked or fried along with the fruit. They can be eaten raw but are often a little spiky and benefit from time in the pan.

Both the vegetable plot and vegetable box can be heaving with zucchini in summer, which may leave you out of ideas for how to cook them. The solution? Embrace their versatility and explore their vast potential—the rewards are well worth it.

PLANT

Known as courgettes in the UK, zucchini are a type of summer squash. There are many varieties in all sorts of shapes, colors, and sizes that are growing in popularity, but green zucchini is still the most common. All zucchini produce fruits and edible flowers and are highly productive, fruiting for a few months at a time. Regular picking when small ensures a longer harvest season. They are also thirsty plants that need watering regularly. I tend not to pick the leaves to eat, as they provide shade and keep the soil from drying out. That said, all parts of the plant are edible and can be eaten raw or cooked.

COOKING TIPS

I prefer to cook zucchini over extreme heat with oil or butter rather than boiling or slow cooking. Try them roasted, grilled, or sautéed in oil. They're also great chargrilled or fried in a tempura batter. For something different, salt sliced zucchini for a couple of hours, then pickle in a sweet cider vinegar solution. Coat in a beer batter and fry, then serve with pickled mustard seeds. Zucchini ribbons make a great substitute for pasta if you blanch them before gently frying. They can also be used instead of noodles in a stir-fry. Soften with baby corn, coat with teriyaki sauce, and serve with flowers and lime juice for a colorful bowl.

PREPARATION

When processing zucchini, I tend only to trim off the base stem, as this can be spiky and less sweet than the fruit, although this can be cooked and eaten, too, if you wish. The tips at the flowering end are edible and can be cooked with the rest of the zucchini. The fruits themselves can be prepared in a multitude of ways. They are robust enough to grate, peel, spiralize, chop, or dice.

Store the flowers wrapped in a damp sheet of paper towel in the fridge and use within 1–2 days. The stamen and anther inside the flowers are edible but are often removed to make more room for stuffing.

ZERO WASTE

Once picked, zucchini will stay firm and crisp in the fridge for 1–2 weeks. Because they have an extremely high water content, I rarely dehydrate them, but you can preserve them as a spiced chutney with vinegar and sugar. I find that garlic, cumin, and chili work well with zucchini in both pickles and chutneys to boost the subtle flavor. Also consider fermenting baby zucchini with caraway seeds and dill, as you would when making gherkins.

If faced with a surplus, use them as the star vegetable. Try making a moist zucchini polenta cake with lemon zest and poppy seeds, or grate them into breads or slaws.

TYPES

GREEN ZUCCHINI

The most popular variety of zucchini, with a mild flavor and smooth texture. If left to mature, it will grow into a big, woody marrow. It's extremely versatile, with an almondy, sweet flavor and firm texture. Avoid boiling, as it can become mushy.

PALE-GREEN RIBBED ZUCCHINI

An early zucchini with pale-green fruit and gentle ridges with distinctive flecks. Tender and delicately flavored, it can be slightly bland when cooked, so it needs citrus or aromatic herbs to bring out the taste.

YELLOW ZUCCHINI

Cylindrical with a glossy yellow body and bright-green stem, this variety retains its color when cooked. The fruits have a crisp skin and creamy seed cavity.

ROUND ZUCCHINI

These yellow, dark green, or light green zucchini can grow to about the size of a grapefruit and can be watery. They are particularly well suited to stuffing.

CROOKNECK SUMMER SQUASH

Ranges from bright daisy yellow to pale sapling green in color, with a narrow tip and a curved, bulbous bottom. When immature, it has a delicate skin, but some varieties become bumpier.

PATTYPAN SQUASH

These resemble UFOs and are best picked young, when the skin is still moist and soft. They are small and versatile and grow in yellow, white, and dark green.

LIGHT LUNCH

Stuffed Zucchini Flowers
SERVES 2

Social media was designed for sharing photos of zucchini flowers. They are ostentatious and never shy from taking a selfie, and they continue to grow in popularity in kitchens from New York to Tokyo, Milan to London. This classic Italian-inspired recipe makes good use of them and is elegant, eye-catching, and fundamentally tasty. Pair it with a burnt tomato salsa and extra black garlic for added zing.

INGREDIENTS

6 zucchini flowers

½ tsp sea salt

½ tsp cracked black pepper

2 tbsp all-purpose flour

Vegetable oil, for deep-frying

Mint leaves, to garnish (optional)

For the batter

½ cup (50 g) all-purpose flour

⅓ cup (50 g) cornstarch

½ tsp baking powder

½ cup (100 ml) sparkling water, with ice

For the filling

3½ oz (100 g) crumbled feta cheese

½ shallot, finely diced

1 tbsp chopped mint

1 tbsp roughly chopped black garlic cloves

1 tbsp grated lemon zest

1 tsp cracked black pepper

Sea salt

Method

01 First, make the filling by combining all the ingredients except the salt in a large mixing bowl, then season to taste with the salt.

02 For the batter, start by sifting the flours together, then add the baking powder. Whisk in the ice fizzy water until you have a smooth, bubbly batter that runs off the whisk without lumps.

03 Stuff the zucchini flowers with 1–2 teaspoons of filling and gently pinch closed. Add the salt and pepper to the flour, then dredge the stuffed flowers in the seasoned flour before dipping in the batter.

04 Deep-fry the flowers in hot oil at 350°F (180°C) for 3–4 minutes until the batter is golden and crispy. Drain on a sheet of paper towel before serving with a few mint leaves scattered over the top, if you like.

BREAKFAST OR MAIN MEAL

Zucchini Fritters
SERVES 1

A fritter can work just as well for breakfast, lunch, or dinner. They can be served with eggs, salad, in a burger bun, or as a snack and are a superb way to use up a spare zucchini. My recipe has taken several years to perfect. I've started adding sprouted seeds and plenty of nuts for extra flavor and bite, while the subtle zucchini is intensified with lemon zest.

INGREDIENTS

1 zucchini, grated

Sea salt

2 tbsp sprouted seeds

1 tbsp grated lemon zest

1 tsp pine nuts

1 tsp dried oregano

1 egg, beaten

2–4 tbsp all-purpose flour, plus extra for dusting

2 tbsp canola oil, for frying

Handful of salad leaves, to serve (optional)

Hummus, to serve (optional)

4–6 mint leaves, to garnish (optional)

Method

01 In a sieve, sprinkle the grated zucchini with a pinch of sea salt and leave to drain for 5–10 minutes while you prepare the other ingredients.

02 Combine the zucchini, sprouted seeds, lemon zest, pine nuts, and oregano, and season with salt. Then whisk the beaten egg into the fritter mix.

03 Add a sprinkle of flour 1 tablespoon at a time, mix it in, then squeeze the mixture together with your hands until it just holds without falling apart. Form 2–4 patties and dust with a little flour.

04 Heat the oil in a frying pan and gently place each zucchini fritter in the pan and avoid moving them for 2–3 minutes. Once one side has crisped up, carefully flip each fritter over and cook on the other side for another 2–3 minutes or until golden.

05 Try serving with salad and a dollop of hummus and garnishing with mint, then finish with a pinch of sea salt flakes.

MAIN MEAL

Zucchaghetti with Pea and Lemon Pepper

SERVES 2

I firmly believe you should enjoy everything you eat—so this recipe is my go-to when I'm on a health kick. Zucchini is ideal as a substitute for spaghetti. You can try it with all sorts of sauces, but it's particularly fresh and healthy with protein-rich peas.

INGREDIENTS

2 zucchini

2 tbsp olive oil

2 garlic cloves, finely chopped

1 tbsp pumpkin seeds

3½oz (100g) peas

1 tsp lemon pepper

½ tsp sea salt

Squeeze of lemon juice, to serve (optional)

Grated Parmesan cheese, to serve (optional)

Method

01 Spiralize the zucchini into thin lengths, then boil some water in a large saucepan. Blanch the zucchaghetti for 2 minutes, then remove from the pan and drain well.

02 Heat the oil in a pan and cook the garlic over a gentle heat for 2–3 minutes to soften, stirring often so that it doesn't burn.

03 Add in the pumpkin seeds and peas. Cook for 3–4 more minutes before adding in the zucchaghetti. Quickly toss with the other ingredients and season well with the lemon pepper and sea salt.

04 Serve immediately and finish with a squeeze of lemon juice or some grated Parmesan.

Eggplant
PURPLE PRINCE

EDIBLE PARTS

01 FLESH

The spongy, cream-colored flesh has a slightly bitter taste and a subtle sweet profile as well. It is fantastic at soaking up flavors and can be roasted, grilled, or used as a meat substitute due to its firm texture.

02 SKIN

The edible skin can be eaten raw, but I recommend cooking it. In larger eggplants, it can be tough and may require longer cooking. The skin can be charred without breaking to provide a protective barrier for the flesh inside, allowing it to soften more slowly. This also adds a deep, smoky flavor to roasted eggplant.

03 SEEDS

The small, soft seeds are bitter and provide some texture when roasted. The subtle bitterness is more concentrated in the seeds, as they contain nicotinoid alkaloids. Eggplant is a relative of the tobacco plant, but there are no associated health risks.

This is the vegetable that started my love affair with food writing. To me, the humble eggplant—with its glossy purple-black skin, creamy flesh, bitter seeds, and subtle nuances—is vegetable royalty, and its stately beauty should be celebrated.

PLANT

Also known as an aubergine, eggplant is a member of the nightshade family. It is actually a perennial, but most gardeners grow it as an annual crop. The fruit has tender cream-colored flesh that is subtly sweet, with seeds inside the fruit and a lovely mild flavor. They can be slightly bitter depending on the type—older heirloom eggplants, for example, tend to require salting before cooking. All types are an excellent source of fiber, vitamin C, potassium, and antioxidants.

COOKING TIPS

The spongy flesh makes eggplant perfect for soaking up sauces and seasoning, as well as for grilling, as this accentuates its natural smoky quality. Try my version of bruschetta: marinate the eggplant in olive oil with dried oregano, lemon juice, and salt, then grill it until it has grill marks and is soft. Rub black garlic on toasted sourdough, then top with the eggplant and some basil.

Cooking eggplant whole over coals or in a wood oven will also bring out that sought-after charred flavor. The inside will soften, so you can scoop it out with a spoon. A faster option is to hold the eggplant over an open flame on the stove with some tongs.

PREPARATION

A ripe eggplant will feel firm and plump. It should have a glossy skin without blemishes and feel heavy to hold. If it feels lighter, it is probably older and may have a woodier texture when cooked. Eggplants bruise easily, so store them carefully in a cool, dark place or in the fridge. Don't keep them in a sealed container, as they can spoil faster.

Salting sliced eggplant before cooking reduces any bitterness and draws out some of the moisture. Many modern varieties have had the bitterness bred out of them, however, so this isn't always necessary. Salting also makes the flesh firmer and helps it absorb less fat when cooking.

ZERO WASTE

If you have some eggplant that is starting to look a little sad, try making eggplant "bacon": slice thinly; drizzle with oil; sprinkle with salt, pepper, and a pinch of paprika; and roast until crispy. Alternatively, barbecue or flame-grill the whole fruit so that it blackens. The smoky flavor adds an extra dimension to older eggplant.

I tend to use eggplant fresh, but my favorite options for preserving it include freezing it diced, ready to roast or add to curry and stews, or making a spiced cumin pickle or harissa chutney. Also try grilling slices and then preserving them under olive oil with garlic, thyme, and preserved lemon.

TYPES

GLOBE

The most common variety in the UK, with a shiny black-purple skin and a tough, meaty texture; fruits can grow 4–6 in (10–15 cm). They have been bred to be less bitter than older varieties and are very versatile.

ITALIAN

Similar to globes but smaller. These still have a thick, spongy texture but are slightly sweeter.

WHITE

One bulbous end tapers up to a green calyx. The marble-white skin contains fruit that is mild and slightly sweet.

THAI

Botanically classified as berries, these are small green pea-shaped eggplants that are superb for providing bursts of crunchy texture in a Thai green curry.

STRIPED

Also called a graffiti eggplant, this striking variety grows in a small teardrop shape. The outer skin is ivory white and speckled violet. Bred to be less bitter, they are well known for their unique shape, color, and sweet flavor.

JAPANESE

A slender eggplant variety that can be purple, almost black, variegated, or white. They are long and thin, with few seeds and thin skins, and are great stuffed with miso or paired with chili and garlic in a stir-fry.

APPETIZER OR SIDE

Baba and Zhoug

SERVES 2

Eggplant has the unique ability to withstand fierce heat—it absorbs smoky tones like other vegetables soak up a marinade. The flesh softens, sweetens, and develops dark umami tones while the skin burns, making for an enchanting baba ganoush. Here, the bitter eggplant and tahini are spellbinding with the sharp lemon juice, nutty oil, and spicy zhoug—and they are particularly tasty served with flatbread.

INGREDIENTS

For the baba ganoush
1 ripe eggplant
1 tsp tahini
1 garlic clove, crushed
2 tbsp lemon juice
1 tbsp olive oil
1 tbsp finely chopped mint
Sea salt
Pinch of za'atar

For the zhoug
Large bunch of cilantro
Small bunch of parsley, plus extra to garnish
4 black garlic cloves, chopped
½ cup (100 ml) olive oil
2 green jalapeño peppers, seeded and finely sliced
2 tbsp lemon juice
1 tsp ground cardamom
½ tsp red chili flakes
½ ground cumin
Sea salt

Method

01 Start by baking or charring the eggplant for the baba ganoush using either the oven, the grill, or a naked flame until the skin blackens and it softens inside. This can take between 20–30 minutes, depending on the method. Bake for 25 minutes in a preheated oven at 425°F (220°C) or for closer to 10 minutes in a wood-fired oven. Alternatively, hold the eggplant over a flame on the stove with some tongs and turn until charred on all sides and starting to collapse in on itself.

02 Once cooked, slice the eggplant in half and scoop out the flesh. Set the skins aside and slice the flesh into strips, then leave to drain in a sieve for 30 minutes.

03 Next, make the zhoug by blending all the ingredients except the sea salt in a food processor until smooth. Then season to taste with the sea salt.

04 Combine the eggplant flesh in a bowl with the tahini, garlic, lemon juice, and oil. Blend in a food processor until smooth, then stir in the mint.

05 Fill the eggplant skins with the baba ganoush mix and season to taste with the salt. Top with a tablespoon of zhoug and a pinch of za'atar and garnish with a few extra parsley leaves.

MAIN MEAL

Stuffed Eggplant Tagine

SERVES 2

While the finished dish looks complex, this recipe is in fact very easy. First, you'll need to roast the eggplants to tame the bitterness, infusing the flesh with smoke and sweetness. Then, for the show-stopping finale, simply mix in the spiced roasted vegetables and, like pulling a rabbit out of a hat, you've plated up a twist on a tagine that is as lively and colorful as a circus.

INGREDIENTS

2 eggplants

3 tbsp olive oil

5½ oz (150 g) cooked chickpeas, drained

3½ oz (100 g) mixed peppers, sliced

1 red onion, sliced

1¾ oz (50 g) dried apricots, chopped

1 tbsp ras el hanout

1 tsp sea salt

7 oz (200 g) cooked quinoa, to serve

1 tbsp chopped parsley

Method

01 Preheat the oven to 400°F (200°C). Brush the eggplants with 1 tablespoon of the oil and roast whole in a roasting pan for 25 minutes.

02 In a second roasting pan, mix the chickpeas, mixed peppers, sliced red onion, and apricots. Drizzle with the rest of the olive oil and sprinkle over the ras el hanout and salt, then roast simultaneously for 35 minutes.

03 When the eggplant has finished cooking, remove it from the oven. As soon as it is cool enough to handle, make a shallow incision along the length. Carefully scoop out the flesh, dice it, then place it back in the roasting pan with the other ingredients that are still cooking for the final 10 minutes or so. Set the eggplant skins aside.

04 Finish the dish by stuffing the combined eggplant and spiced vegetables back into the eggplant skins. Serve on a bed of quinoa and chopped parsley.

MAIN MEAL

Korean Barbecue Eggplant Steaks

SERVES 2

It's no surprise that eggplant is popular in faux-meat recipes. It has a firm bite and robust structure that can take on bold flavors. This dish makes good use of that. It is sweet, spicy, and smoky, with charred leeks for underground allium scenery, while the peppery white radishes illuminate the star of the show: the sticky, edgy, charred eggplant steaks, brushed with a Korean-barbecue-inspired sauce. For a twist on this dish, try it served with kimchi or finely diced in a bao bun with crushed peanuts.

INGREDIENTS

1 eggplant

1 tbsp sesame oil

6–8 spring onions

Sea salt

1 tbsp lime juice

2 white radishes, thinly sliced

1 tsp sesame seeds

For the sauce

1 tbsp honey

3 tbsp soy sauce

1 tsp gochujang sauce

1 tsp rice vinegar

1 tbsp sesame oil

Method

01 First, carefully slice the eggplant into steaks about ½ in (1 cm) thick. Score with a criss-cross pattern on both sides without cutting all the way through the flesh, then rub both sides with sesame oil and sear in a hot skillet.

02 Cook the spring onions at the same time on the other side of the pan. After 3–4 minutes, turn the spring onions and flip over the eggplant steaks to cook the other side of both for another 3–4 minutes. Once the spring onions are charred, remove them from the pan, season with a pinch of salt, and drizzle with the lime juice.

03 Once the eggplant steaks are charred on both sides, whisk the ingredients for the sauce in a bowl. Brush the sauce liberally onto both sides of the eggplant and cook in the skillet for 1–2 more minutes on each side.

04 Brush the eggplant steaks a final time before serving with the charred spring onions and radish slices. To finish, sprinkle the eggplant steaks with the sesame seeds.

Cucumber

KEEPING IT COOL

01

02

03

04

EDIBLE PARTS

01 FLESH

Over 90 percent water, the flesh is juicy and crisp and slightly bitter in flavor. The color ranges from pale green to straw.

02 SKIN

Cucumber skin is edible and has a delicate grassy flavor that becomes more bitter as it matures. The skin can be ridged or bumpy (some varieties can even be spiky and require trimming) and ranges in color from dark green to pale yellow. It's also the most nutrient-dense part of the cucumber, containing beta-carotene and vitamin K.

03 FLOWERS

The lemon-yellow edible flowers are great in salads or fried. For indoor plants, pick off the male flowers once a week to prevent pollination of female flowers, which leads to fruit with a more bitter aftertaste. A female flower has a swelling beneath it that will become a cucumber.

04 SEEDS

The small fleshy seeds are edible and do not need to be removed. They are a good source of fiber, with a mild sweetness.

Over the summer, my family lives off cucumbers. We put slices in our water pitcher, garnish almost every salad with them, and regularly pickle batches with dill and aromatics. The cucumber may not talk the loudest, but it's the coolest dude at the party.

PLANT

Cucumbers have enclosed seeds like tomatoes, which means that botanically speaking they are a fruit, but they are treated as vegetables. They grow as a bush or creeping vine with spiraling tendrils that usually need support, and their large leaves form a canopy above the fruit. They can grow in the ground or in pots and provide prolific crops, with a surprisingly long harvest. They range in size, growing up to 20 in (50 cm) long, and have a wonderfully aqueous yet crisp texture. They are also surprisingly nutritious, providing a good source of vitamins, potassium, and silica.

COOKING TIPS

Cucumbers are mostly eaten raw, but you can cook them in various ways: try braising, stewing, or blending into a stock for a delicate broth to poach other vegetables. They pair very well with mint, garlic, and lemon, as well as bold Asian flavors such as ginger, coconut, chili, and spring onion.

Cucumbers are also the ultimate cocktail garnish. They provide a sweet and bitter pairing with gin botanicals, sparkling elderflower, or summer Pimm's. Also try making a cooling cucumber sorbet to serve with strawberries or combining cucumber juice with mint, sherry vinegar, and cilantro for a fresh salad dressing.

PREPARATION

Choose cucumbers that are firm and have a strong color. They become bitter and pale if left on the vine too long to ripen, and it stunts the growth of other fruits. When preparing cucumber, a way to enhance the flavor is to grate or chop it, then sprinkle with salt and allow to drain in a sieve or colander. This process reduces bitterness and enhances the umami flavor; it means the cucumber loses some of its moisture and therefore intensifies the flavors. Try to avoid peeling cucumbers, as the skin is rich in nutrients and flavor.

ZERO WASTE

Don't store cut cucumbers in the fridge, as this can dehydrate them and lead to rot. Instead, place them in a storage bag or sealed container to help retain moisture. To preserve them, try pickling in a vinegar solution or fermenting (see page 103). Another option includes freezing—as cucumber has a high water content, this works extremely well. I've also tried dehydrating slices at 120°F (50°C) for 6–8 hours and found they make tasty chips. Once dried, also try blending into a powder and combining with granulated sugar and elderflowers to rim a cocktail glass or sprinkle on a strawberry fruit salad.

TYPES

COMMON

Broadly divided into two varieties: pickling cucumbers are smaller, oblong, and shorter at 4–6 in (10–15 cm), and slicing cucumbers are long and thin, up to 6–8 in (15–20 cm), and often more bitter.

CORNICHON

Also known as a gherkin, this is a very small, narrow cucumber with rounded ends and slightly bumpy skin. It has a tart, juicy flavor, perfect for pickles.

LEMON

Has a golden yellow skin and is similar in size to a lemon. The flesh is pale green with a sweet, cool taste and crisp texture. There is almost no bitterness.

JAPANESE

Cylindrical in shape and measuring up to 12 in (30 cm) long, these have a crisp, melonlike flavor.

ARMENIAN

Long, slender, and often curved, with longitudinal furrows and green stripes. These are crisp, sweet, and succulent with mild seeds, similar in aroma to melon.

PERSIAN

A fairly squat cucumber with thin, dark skin and shallow ridges. It has a mild, sweet taste and a good crunch.

CUCAMELON

An easy-to-grow perennial vine with grape-sized fruit that has grown in popularity due to its crunch and sourness. Excellent pickled or as a cocktail garnish.

Lactofermented Dill Pickles

MAKES 1 × 1¾-PINT (1-LITER) JAR

Sour pickles are an essential tool when building recipes that cover all the principal flavors: sweet, sour, bitter, salty, and umami. And fermenting cucumbers is also vital if you end up with an abundant crop. It preserves them and enhances their flavor with tried-and-true aromatics. I love these crunchy dill pickles as a snack, in a burger, or as a garnish.

INGREDIENTS

5–6 small cucumbers
3¼ tsp (9 g) sea salt
3 bay leaves
4 garlic cloves
1 red chili
1 tsp yellow mustard seeds
1 tsp black peppercorns
½ tsp chili flakes
½ tsp fennel seeds
2 allspice berries
2 tbsp chopped dill

Method

01 Wash the cucumbers under cold running water, then place in a bowl of ice water to firm up while you prepare the herbs and spices.

02 Make a 3 percent brine of ¾ tsp (3 g) sea salt for every ½ cup (100 ml) water to cover the cucumbers—for this recipe, I'd recommend approximately 3¼ tsp (9 g) salt to 1¼ cups (300 ml) water. Whisk until the salt has dissolved.

03 Place the cucumbers and the other ingredients into a sterilized 1¾-pint (1-liter) jar and cover with the brine. Weigh down the cucumbers with a fermentation weight or small zipper-lock bag filled with water to ensure they are submerged under the brine.

04 Cover with the jar lid but don't seal. Leave in a cool, dark place to ferment. After the first few days, you will see signs of fermentation, with bubbles and cloudy water in the jar. After 7–10 days (or 3–5 days in warmer climates), seal the jar and transfer to the fridge to slow the fermentation process, opening it every couple of days to release the gases. If you prefer a more sour, complex flavor, leave the jar at room temperature for longer.

05 Keep your pickles sealed in the fridge, burping the jar once a week to release any build-up of bubbles. Eat within 1 month.

DRINK

Cucumber-peel Gin

MAKES 1¾ PINTS (1 LITER)

I'm a self-confessed fashion victim when it comes to the latest artisan fad. The gin craze was no exception. I loved how every micro-distillery was creating unique botanical blends using everything from sea buckthorn to coffee. This recipe pays tribute to a classic G&T with a cucumber garnish. You can make it with a cheaper, less complex gin and the cucumber will still add sweetness, grassy notes, and subtle bitterness—not bad from what is sometimes seen as a waste ingredient.

INGREDIENTS

1 tbsp sea salt
Peel of 2 large cucumbers
1¾ pints (1 liter) good-quality gin, such as Hendrick's

Method

01 Start by sprinkling the salt evenly over the cucumber peel in a sieve or colander—this will remove some moisture and reduce the bitterness.

02 Leave for 30 minutes, then wash off the salt under cold running water. Pat the peel dry and add to a sterilized 1¾-pint (1-liter) bottle.

03 Pour in the gin to cover the cucumber peel, then seal and leave to cold infuse for 1–2 months. Turn and shake the bottle to mix daily for the first week, then reduce to once a week.

04 Once infused, strain the gin through a muslin-lined sieve to remove the peel. Serve with tonic, ice, and a slice of cucumber. It also tastes fantastic with elderflower cordial and soda for a summer cocktail.

Tzatziki and Greek Salad

SERVES 4

I've been lucky enough to spend some time exploring the Greek islands and the area around Athens. As a development chef, it was formative for me; the traditional, rustic recipes from around Greece are a thing of pure wonder—cooling, succulent, and fresh. This tzatziki is no exception. The combination of yogurt, mint, and cucumber with garlic is bold and bright. It's the ultimate cucumber test— prepared with the knowledge of thousands of years of civilization and eaten in minutes.

INGREDIENTS

For the tzatziki
½ cucumber
1 tsp sea salt
7 fl oz (200 ml) Greek yogurt
2 tbsp chopped mint
1 garlic clove, crushed
1 tbsp olive oil
1 tsp lemon juice

For the Greek salad
4 ripe tomatoes, chopped
½ cucumber, sliced
½ red onion, thinly sliced
½ red bell pepper, roughly chopped
2 tbsp green and black olives
2 tbsp caper berries
9 oz (250 g) block of feta cheese
1 tbsp olive oil
2 tsp red wine vinegar
Sea salt and cracked black pepper
1 tbsp chopped mint
Pita bread, to serve

Method

01 First, make the tzatziki. Grate the cucumber into a sieve, then sprinkle with the sea salt. Leave to drain for 15–20 minutes, then pat dry.

02 Mix the grated cucumber with the Greek yogurt, mint (reserving a few leaves as a garnish), and garlic, then finish by drizzling with the olive oil and lemon juice and sprinkling with the reserved mint leaves.

03 Make the Greek salad by combining the tomatoes, cucumber, red onion, red pepper, olives, and caper berries and arranging around the block of feta, then dress with the olive oil and red wine vinegar. Season with a pinch of salt and pepper, sprinkle with the chopped mint, then serve with the tzatziki and warm pita bread.

Chilies

PLAYING WITH FIRE

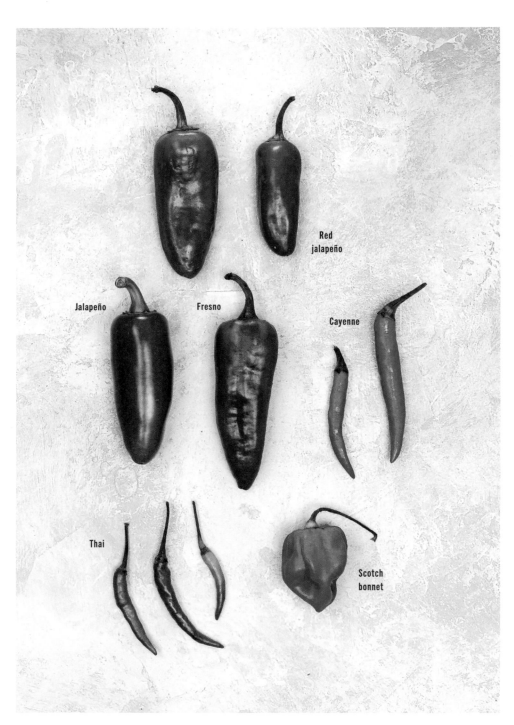

Red
jalapeño

Jalapeño

Fresno

Cayenne

Thai

Scotch
bonnet

EDIBLE PARTS

FLESH

The chili flesh can be sweet and juicy or crisp and tart in flavor. The heat gets more intense toward the shoulder. Be aware that if it seems mild at the blossom end, the rest of the chili might be hotter.

SEEDS

The seeds are one of the hottest parts of a chili with higher capsaicin levels. They are often removed (known as seeding) to reduce the heat and pungency of chilies. They retain their texture when cooked and are slightly bitter.

PITH

The pale membrane that connects the seeds to the flesh contains a concentrated amount of capsaicin, so it is often removed before cooking. It is edible, just extra spicy and bitter tasting, with a cottonlike texture.

LEAVES

I have not eaten chili leaves, but they are commonly cooked in Hong Kong, Korea, and the Philippines. Never eat them raw, as they are toxic unless cooked; try stir-fried with garlic or boiled.

I grew up almost obsessed with chilies, collecting new seeds like vinyl melody samples and always searching for that spicy next level. Now I've tamed that fire, I use chili for rounded flavor and warmth and occasionally to set the mouth alight.

PLANT

There are literally hundreds of different types of chilies to try. They are highly versatile and full of flavor and range in heat and color. Chilies are measured on the Scoville Scale according to their heat and spice levels. A sweet pepper scores zero, while some can range to over a million. Despite this general guide, each individual chili will contain different levels of capsaicin—the compound responsible for their pungency. They contain antioxidants, vitamin C, iron, and potassium, while chili seeds help lower cholesterol and blood pressure. It's also accepted that chilies help improve digestion and immune function.

COOKING TIPS

I use raw, finely sliced chili as a garnish to add fresh heat to a finished dish. It also works wonderfully when added early with garlic, onion or ginger as a warming base for stews, sauces, and curries. Try adding whole chilies to slow-cooked dishes, as they can gently suffuse them with flavor without overpowering them. For a fresh summer salad, combine raw chili rings with thin fennel shavings, fried sage leaves, fresh peas, pine nuts, and torn mozzarella. The milky cheese and piquant chili is a scintillating combination. Also try using chili in sweet dishes, as well as savory dishes to cut through the richness of chocolate and sauces.

PREPARATION

Prepare chilies with care and always wash your hands well under cold water after working with them (hot water can rub the chili traces into your skin further), as it can be very uncomfortable touching your eyes afterward. With a sharp paring knife, prepare a chili by first removing the paler pith and, if you want a less spicy meal, discard the seeds, too. Generally, I use the entire chili, seeds and all, to avoid waste— then I only need to use half a chili instead of the entire thing for the same levels of heat. If you are seeding, I find that, after slicing in half lengthwise, a teaspoon is a really easy way to scoop out the pith and seeds.

ZERO WASTE

If you need to use up what's in the fridge, chilies can come to the rescue. Sauté any sad-looking vegetables; add chili, paprika, garlic, and a can of beans; and cook for 1 hour for a zero-waste bean chili.

Alternatively, all chilies can be preserved. Air-dry for a few weeks or dry in an oven or dehydrator at 120°F (50°C) for 6–8 hours, then blend into flakes or a powder. Lacto-fermented chili is also a revelation in sauces, stir-fries, and curries. Blend 1 lb 2 oz (500g) fresh chilies and pulse into a coarse paste, then in a sterilized jar, mix with 2½ tsp (15g) salt. Leave open to ferment for 4–7 days, then seal and store in the fridge for 1–2 months.

TYPES

JALAPEÑO

Curved-to-straight chili pods in green, red, yellow, and purple, with glossy, taut skin and crisp flesh. One of the most popular chilies, it is moderately spicy, measuring 2,500–8,000 Scoville Heat Units (SHU).

THAI

Varying from green to red, with a waxy, bright skin, these are small at ¾–2¾ in (2–7cm) but pack a punch at about 100,000 SHU.

GHOST

Crinkled conical pods, 2–3 in (5–8cm), with thin skin and a waxy sheen. They have a slightly tangy, acidic flavor with fruity notes. The heat builds and ranges 850,000–1,000,000 SHU.

CAYENNE

Longer pods with glossy, rippled skin. They are sweet, acidic, spicy (at 30,000–50,000 SHU), and usually dried or powdered.

HABANERO

Small lantern-shaped pods with thin, crisp flesh. Sweet habanero is fruity and mild at 850 SHU, while orange habanero is much hotter at up to 350,000 SHU.

POBLANO

Mexico's most popular pepper, with a thick wall and meaty texture and a heat range of 1,000–15,000 SHU.

SCOTCH BONNET

Stubby, crinkled pods with a firm, waxy skin; a sweet fragrance; and intense heat— averaging 100,000–350,000 SHU.

Stuffed Jalapeño Poppers

MAKES 12

When I worked in a busy Mexican-style restaurant, I always made time for a casual plate of stuffed jalapeños—a simple mishmash of creamy soft cheese with sweet, spicy chili peppers. I've added some rosemary, lemon, and pepper to the crumb for my version. It's a dirty snack with a clean, sophisticated profile—what's not to like?

INGREDIENTS

12 jalapeño peppers
Vegetable oil, for deep-frying
1 lime, to serve
Hot sauce, to serve

For the filling
1¾ oz (50 g) grated mozzarella cheese
3½ oz (100 g) cream cheese
½ tsp paprika
Sea salt and cracked black pepper

For the breadcrumb coating
3½ oz (100 g) panko breadcrumbs
1 tbsp chopped rosemary
1 tbsp grated lemon zest
½ tsp sea salt
½ tsp cracked black pepper
2 tbsp all-purpose flour
2 eggs, beaten

Method

01 First, blanch the jalapeños in boiling water for 30 seconds to soften them. Once cool, use a small knife to slice from the shoulder close to the tip. Then use a small spoon or your finger to cut away the seeds and membrane. Repeat for all the peppers.

02 To make the filling, mix the mozzarella, cream cheese, and paprika in a large bowl, then season with a pinch of salt and pepper. Carefully stuff each pepper with the filling, then close up the cavity and wipe off any excess.

03 For the coating, mix the breadcrumbs, rosemary, lemon zest, salt, and pepper in a shallow bowl. Dust the stuffed peppers in the flour, then dip in the beaten egg and roll them in the herby breadcrumbs. Repeat with a double coating if you want them extra crunchy.

04 Deep-fry the coated peppers in vegetable oil at 320°F (160°C) for 3–4 minutes until golden brown. Drain on a sheet of paper towel to soak up the excess oil and serve with a squeeze of lime juice and some hot sauce.

Chili and White Bean Soup

SERVES 4

Soup need not only be enjoyed in the colder months. This combo is sunshine in a bowl, yet comforting and hearty at the same time, adding a fresh flash of color to the weekly routine. The red chili punctuates the dish with hot exclamation marks of bright, sweet surprise. Try serving with a soda bread and unsalted butter to mop up the rich chili broth.

INGREDIENTS

2 tbsp olive oil

2 garlic cloves, sliced

1 sweet potato, peeled and diced

Pinch of saffron

2¾ pints (1.5 liters) vegetable stock

2 red chilies, roughly sliced into rings

2 bay leaves

Large bunch of rainbow chard stalks

7 oz (200 g) can of lima beans, drained

1 tsp sea salt

1 tsp cracked black pepper

2 tbsp torn cilantro

Method

01 Heat the olive oil in a saucepan, then soften the garlic and diced sweet potato over medium heat for 10 minutes. Meanwhile, add the saffron to the vegetable stock and leave to infuse while you cook.

02 Next, add the chili rings, bay leaves, and chard stalks to the saucepan. Gently stir and sauté for 4–5 minutes over low heat to wilt the stalks and soften the chili, then add the lima beans, salt, and pepper.

03 Pour in the saffron-infused stock, then simmer for 5–10 minutes. Add the torn cilantro leaves and serve hot.

MAIN MEAL

Chili Nachos

SERVES 2–4

For a feel-good fiesta recipe, look no further than Mexican-inspired chili nachos. They are bright and comforting and celebrate chili with a familiar party kick. This recipe uses pickled, powdered, and fresh chili, so it also provides a good opportunity to try out at a few kitchen skills. Eat this with your hands and dig for hidden layers of chili heat.

INGREDIENTS

For the pickled jalapeños

6–8 green jalapeño peppers

⅔ cup (150 ml) distilled
     vinegar

3 tbsp granulated sugar

2 garlic cloves, sliced

2 tsp salt

For the bean chili

2 tbsp olive oil

½ white onion, diced

4 garlic cloves, finely sliced

1 red chili, finely diced

1 tsp paprika

1 tsp cayenne pepper

7 oz (200 g) vegetarian
     ground "meat"

5½ oz (150 g) black beans,
     drained

⅓ cup (75 ml) red wine

14 oz (400 g) can of chopped
     tomatoes

1 tsp oregano

1 tsp sea salt

1 tsp cracked black pepper

For the guacamole

1 avocado, peeled and stoned

1 tbsp chopped cilantro

1 garlic clove, finely diced

½ red chili, finely diced

2 tbsp fresh lime juice

For the nachos

1 large bag of tortilla chips

3½ oz (100 g) grated
     Cheddar cheese

1 tbsp sour cream

Hot sauce, to serve
     (optional)

Method

01   First, pickle the jalapeños. Slice them into rings about ¼–½ in (8–10 mm) thick. Heat the vinegar and sugar with ⅔ cup (150 ml) water in a pan. Add the garlic; salt; and, once boiling, the chili rings. Remove from heat and allow to cool; this should take about 30 minutes, so either do this in advance or while you make the other elements.

02   To make the bean chili, heat the oil in a frying pan and sauté the onion and garlic until soft. After 3–4 minutes, add the chili, spices, ground "meat," and beans. Cook for 2–3 minutes, then add the red wine to deglaze the pan.

03   Add the tomatoes and oregano, then reduce the heat. Simmer for 20–30 minutes, then add the seasoning.

04   Mash all the ingredients for the guacamole together.

05   Preheat the oven to 400°F (200°C). Layer the tortilla chips on a baking sheet and cover with half the grated Cheddar and the bean chili. Cover with the remaining Cheddar and bake for 10–15 minutes. To serve, top with the guacamole, sour cream, and pickled jalapeños, and finish with hot sauce if you like it super spicy.

Peppers

SWEET WITHOUT HEAT

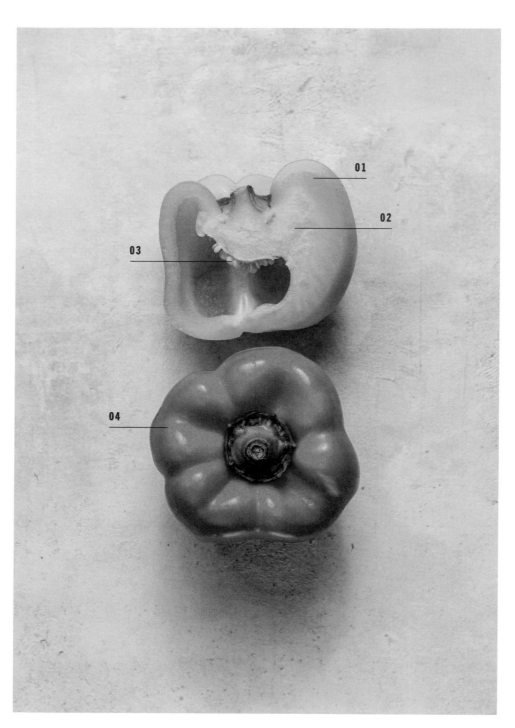

EDIBLE PARTS

01 FLESH

Compared to chilies, peppers are juicier, with a sweet flavor and a crisp yet slightly spongy texture. They can be eaten raw or cooked.

02 PITH

The inner white pith that connects the cavity to the seeds is rich in flavonoids and can be eaten. It is often removed out of habit, but it doesn't need to be.

03 SEEDS

Found in the core cavity of the pepper, the seeds are usually discarded after the stem is removed. They are edible and nutrient-rich like the rest of the vegetable but taste slightly bitter. I tend to include them in my recipes rather than wasting them. They retain their crunch even after prolonged cooking.

04 SKIN

The fine, waxy skin is often removed before the pepper is preserved in oil and can be easily peeled off if you want to make a really smooth sauce. That said, it is edible, and I usually cook the pepper whole, skin and all.

Peppers herald the longer light of summer. Their scent rises in the warm air while your eyes feast on their miraculous color. Eaten raw, they are clean and crisp, but once charred, roasted, or grilled, peppers are reborn as scorched sweets.

PLANT

Peppers belong to the nightshade family of plants along with chili peppers, tomatoes, potatoes, and eggplants. Growing on the vine, peppers defy sense, erupting from delicate, spindly branches and waxy, paper-thin leaves. They crop generously, with bright bulbous lanterns that can make a vegetable plot look like the busy store windows of Chinatown. Often referred to as bell or sweet peppers to differentiate them from their spicy chili cousins, they contain a decent amount of sugar and small amounts of capsaicinoids—the compounds that give chilies their heat—so they only rate 0 on the Scoville Scale.

Peppers come in a vast array of colors, from deep purple to yellow, green to chocolate red. This is due to the varying levels of carotenoid color pigments that change as they mature. There are subtle differences in flavor, depending on the color: green tend to be more bitter in profile, while orange and yellow are sweet, and red peppers are the sweetest. Bell peppers are exceptionally high in vitamin C—one serving contains approximately 97 percent of your daily intake—and also provide plenty of vitamin B6, vitamin A (in the form of the carotenoids), and vitamin E.

PREPARATION

Choose peppers with deep, vivid-colored skin. Four-lobed, block-shaped peppers are the most common type to work with in a kitchen, but many others are longer and have three lobes. The stems should be green and fresh-looking, and the pepper should feel heavy for its size and firm to the touch, with taut skin. Overripe peppers will feel slightly spongy and start to appear slack and wrinkly. If they feel overly firm, they may have been picked before ripening.

If you are removing the seeds because you want to create a cavity for stuffing or slice into julienne strips, for example, there is a simple way to do this that speeds up the butchering process. Using a sharp paring knife, slice off the top of the pepper, then pull out the green stem. Keep the circular top to chop later. The green stalk is inedible, so compost it. Then use a spoon to scoop out the seeds and inner pulp. Slice cleanly down the sides so that you have your desired sections plus a smaller base piece. From this point, it's extremely easy to stuff, dice, slice, or roast the sections.

TYPES

BELL

Also called sweet pepper or capsicum, these are large, crunchy sweet peppers that come in bright colors, including green, red, orange, yellow, and purple. They have a high water content and are great for adding color to any dish.

MINI SWEET PEPPER

These are not simply immature peppers; they are a variety that taste similar to bell peppers but are smaller and have fewer seeds. They often taste sweeter, too, and are lovely raw in salads. Available in many colors.

PADRÓN

I've included these here rather than with chilies, as only some of them are spicy. Cooking them is a little like playing Russian roulette, as only 1 in 10 is hot. The others are typically sweet and mild. Very popular in northwestern Spain grilled and served as tapas.

ROMANO

These elongated sweet peppers are low in water content, with a fleshy texture. They are particularly sweet and wonderful roasted or stuffed. Favorite varieties of mine include Marconi Rosso or Corno di Toro Rosso.

CONT.

Figure a.

COOKING TIPS

Peppers retain their bright colors when cooked. They work well in quick stir-fries, finely diced in a soffritto, or even grated raw over a salad. For curries, I use large chopped pieces of pepper to provide color and sweetness to balance out the rich spices.

Red pepper pesto is quick and easy to make for a sweet pasta dish or to enrich a sauce. Blend raw red pepper with garlic, pine nuts, olive oil, Parmesan, lemon, and basil leaves, then season to taste; store in a jar in the fridge and use within 2 weeks. You can also try a roasted red pepper version with smoked paprika, sherry vinegar, garlic, and plenty of olive oil. This is wonderful with charred vegetables or mixed with a hummus.

I also recommend trying to toast the pepper seeds for 10–15 minutes in the oven, then adding to a dukkah or homemade za'atar for some bitter crunch—it's very similar to using hemp seeds. Another interesting thing to try with a pepper is to grate it finely as a sweet garnish to lift a dish with a fresh burst of color.

ZERO WASTE

Store peppers in the fridge for 7–10 days unless they are green, in which case allow them to ripen at room temperature for a few days first. If you have a surplus, there are various things you can do to preserve them. If you simply want to freeze them, it's better to do so without blanching. Alternatively, try making DIY paprika. Remove the stalks and open up the peppers to allow airflow. Then dry either at 200°F (100°C) for 6–8 hours in the oven or at 130°F (55°C) in a dehydrator for 12 hours. Once dry, use a spice grinder to blend into a fine powder and store in an airtight container. Dried pepper flakes are also an excellent addition to all sorts of recipes, including soups, stir-fries, pickles, dips, and stews.

Also try chargrilling large slices of pepper and submerging them in olive oil with fennel seeds, grilled halloumi, and pink peppercorns (**fig. a**). These are perfect with salads, sandwiches, or as a tapas starter and can store in the fridge for up to 1 month.

MAIN MEAL

Stuffed Peppers with Feta and Olives

SERVES 2

Romano peppers have a thinner, sweeter flesh than plump bell peppers and are less watery. When roasted, they caramelize exceptionally well and make the best choice for stuffing. Being less rigid than a bell pepper, they will collapse slightly once roasted, but make no mistake: this is a heavyweight stuffed pepper. The preserved lemon and salty olives accentuate the peppers' sweetness, with the tart crumbled feta providing an extravagant topping. It works a treat served with couscous or tabbouleh.

INGREDIENTS

2 Romano peppers

5½ oz (150 g) black and green pitted olives

1¾ oz (50 g) sun-dried tomatoes in oil, roughly chopped

1¾ oz (50 g) sprouted seeds

1 preserved lemon, sliced

2 tbsp olive oil

2 tbsp flaked almonds

2 tbsp pomegranate seeds

1 tbsp finely chopped mint

½ tsp sea salt

3½ oz (100 g) feta cheese

Method

01 Preheat the oven to 400°F (200°C). Slice the peppers in half lengthwise and scoop out the pith and seeds if you want to. Personally, I leave them in for roasting to release extra flavor.

02 Combine all the remaining ingredients except the feta in a bowl to make the stuffing mix.

03 Carefully spoon a quarter of the stuffing mix into each pepper half, then push a quarter of the crumbled feta evenly into each pepper half.

04 Place the stuffed peppers in a roasting pan and roast in the oven for 25 minutes until the peppers start to char and the feta softens, then serve.

Roasted Pepper Soup with Charcoal Salt and Croutons

SERVES 4

This rustic soup tries to do justice to the intense brightness of peppers. It is easy to make and tastes wonderfully comforting. The sherry vinegar gastrique (caramelized sugar deglazed with vinegar), swirled in at the last moment, adds an acidic tang to balance the sweetness. Serve with nutty croutons for an aerated crunch and charcoal salt for a graphic color contrast.

INGREDIENTS

6 bell peppers (orange, red, or yellow)

6 garlic cloves

1 onion, roughly chopped

2 tbsp olive oil, plus extra for frying

2 sprigs of thyme

1 tsp sea salt

1 tsp black pepper

2 tbsp paprika

1¾ pints (1 liter) vegetable stock

2–4 slices of yesterday's sourdough bread

Charcoal salt, to serve

Fennel fronds, to garnish (optional)

For the gastrique

½ cup (100 ml) sherry vinegar

4 tbsp (50 g) granulated sugar

½ tsp sea salt

Method

01 Preheat the oven to 400°F (200°C), then prepare the peppers. Remove the stalks and slice the flesh into rough sections so they cook more quickly. Place on a baking sheet with the whole garlic cloves and chopped onion and drizzle with olive oil. Strip the thyme leaves off the sprigs and sprinkle them over the vegetables. Season with the salt and pepper, then dust with the paprika. Roast for 20–25 minutes.

02 Meanwhile, make the gastrique. Add the sherry vinegar, sugar, and salt to a small pan and stir to dissolve; reduce over low heat for 10 minutes. Remove from heat and allow to cool for 15 minutes.

03 When the roasted vegetables are nicely charred and softened, transfer them to a large saucepan and add the vegetable stock. Bring to a boil and simmer for 15 minutes. Remove from heat and blend until smooth.

04 To make croutons, tear the bread into large chunks and fry in olive oil for 3–4 minutes until golden and crispy. Serve the soup with a swirl of the gastrique and a pinch of charcoal salt flakes in each bowl, then garnish with the croutons and some fennel fronds if you like.

SIDE OR STARTER

Padrón Peppers with Yuzu Salsa Verde

SERVES 4

To cook Padrón peppers, you only need olive oil, sea salt, and a squeeze of lemon. But for this recipe, I've replaced the lemon juice with a yuzu salsa and chosen to use shichimi and smoked sea salt for the seasoning. Try serving with wilted cabbage for a more substantial starter.

INGREDIENTS

1 tbsp sesame oil
24 Padrón peppers
1 tsp smoked sea salt
1 tbsp shichimi

For the yuzu salsa
12 tomatillos or green tomatoes
½ onion, finely diced
2 tbsp chopped cilantro
1 garlic clove, grated
1 tbsp yuzu juice or 1 tsp yuzu paste
1 jalapeño pepper, finely chopped
½ tsp sea salt

Method

01 First, make the yuzu salsa. Blend all the ingredients except the salt together in a food processor until smooth, then season to taste with the salt.

02 Next, heat the sesame oil in a large frying pan and add the peppers. Cook over high heat for 3–4 minutes, turning the peppers every minute or two with a set of tongs, until they are blistered on all sides, are soft to the touch, and have started to collapse. Use a blow torch if you want to char them further.

03 While they are still hot, season the peppers with the smoked salt and shichimi.

04 Serve with the yuzu salsa on the side.

Sea Bean

FROM THE SEASHORE

EDIBLE PARTS

01 LEAVES

Small, fingerlike leaves sprout off the main stem and stretch upward as the sea bean grows. These are salty and delicate, requiring minimal cooking.

02 STEMS

The sea bean stem is edible, but near the base, it can become woody and tough to eat. Trim off any tougher sections and compost them. The stems, like baby asparagus, are tenderest at the tips. For tougher stems, you can hold them by the roots and strip off the flesh with your teeth.

Also known as "samphire" after Saint Peter the patron saint of fishermen, the sea bean is special to all sailors—and Cornish chefs. More than a seafood garnish, this marsh grass is a star in its own right, worthy of sea shanties and celebration.

PLANT

The sea bean is a halophyte—a plant that grows in salt water—so it can be found around coastal areas, estuaries, rock pools, and tidal marshland and has an immense oceanic flavor. On the rise in recent years, alongside other sea vegetables such as sea purslane and sea aster (**fig. a**), it is now available in many supermarkets.

Rock sea beans (**fig. b**) are so high in vitamin C, they were used by sailors to ward off scurvy. They prefer clinging to cliffs and rocky coastal paths, so are risky to forage. Marsh sea beans often grow near the tide line, so are more readily available. They grow like thin green reeds poking up out of muddy ground, tidal creeks, and sandy flats.

PREPARATION

You can find sea beans at fish counters, or you can forage for them yourself along the tide line. Avoid limp or dull-looking specimens and instead choose bright-green stems that have a snappy texture. Always wash it before cooking to remove any sand, grit, and excess salt and trim the plant to remove the roots, which are inedible, and woody stems. Also chop larger stems down so it all cooks in the same amount of time. As the sea bean reaches the end of its season, the flavor diminishes, and it can get tougher, even after cooking.

TYPES

MARSH

The most popular type of sea bean, with succulent green stalks; bumpy, fingerlike tips; and a crisp, salty flavor.

ROCK

Also known as sea fennel, this is a very decorative but bitter-tasting sea herb with a pungent carrot taste that challenges modern tastes. It's rich in aromatic oils and has edible umbels of white-and-green flowers and seeds. It's great for vermouths, shrubs, and cocktail bitters and is often pickled.

OTHER SEA VEGETABLES

Sea purslane
Grows in similar areas to sea beans and is rich in vitamins A and D. It is abundant around tidal pools and rocky cliffs and has yellow flowers and green leaves that look similar to sage.

Sea rosemary
A delicious wild herb that develops a natural saltiness and is great for seasoning roasted vegetables. The dark leaves grow up from a small upright shrub.

Salty fingers
Plump, edible leaves with a lovely crunch that burst in the mouth. These have a unique appearance and a marine bitterness that is lovely with pomegranate seeds.

Sea aster
A biennial with large, tender, semisucculent, straplike leaves and a sweet flavor.

Figure b.

Figure a.

CONT.

Figure c.

COOKING TIPS

Sea beans have a distinctive flavor, which means they don't require many added extras. They can be used raw in salads, steamed, or pickled. They tend to be very salty, so are often cooked with a little butter or oil or blanched briefly, and can also be used as seasoning. Don't add salt to any dish containing sea beans until you've tasted it!

For a traditional Norfolk serving suggestion, steam sea beans for 2 minutes, then dress with malt vinegar and black pepper. Or for a rustic Turkish recipe, steam the sea beans and serve with garlic and olive oil. I also regularly use sea beans for a salty zing in a brunch dish. I find it wonderful sautéed in olive oil with garlic and red chili for 3 minutes, then drizzled with lemon juice and sprinkled with fresh cilantro. (Lemon is the sea bean's best friend, as citrus balances the salty profile perfectly.) Serve a generous bunch on toasted sourdough with a poached egg and cracked black pepper.

ZERO WASTE

Sea beans don't last long once harvested, so forage them little and often. You only need a small portion to add a salty zing to a recipe. Keep it refrigerated, covered with a damp towel, for freshness. If you need to avoid waste, lightly pickled marsh sea beans can be delicious. Heat a white wine vinegar, water, and sugar solution at a ratio of 2:2:1, but allow it to cool for 5 minutes before adding the sea beans; otherwise, it will scald and become unpalatably limp too quickly. Try adding fennel seeds and coriander, which don't mask the delicate flavor. Store in the fridge and use within a week. Rock sea bean seed pods can also be pickled as above to reduce their bitterness; they can then be substituted for capers in pasta dishes, while pickled leaves are lovely with eggs, sushi, and salads. Sea beans also make an unusual garnish in a G&T with a slice of lemon. The bitterness lends itself to cocktail bitters and shrubs or infusing in gin for a complex Salty Dog—one of my favorite gin cocktails—with grapefruit juice and ice (**fig. c**).

MAIN MEAL

Sea Bean and Baby Zucchini Pasta

SERVES 2

For me, there's nothing better than being true to your roots and challenging yourself to reinterpret a classic with local ingredients. Try to find sweet yellow zucchini at a farmers' market or grow your own to sauté with the sea bean for this Italian pasta dish. The result is rustic and real, coastal and fresh.

INGREDIENTS

9 oz (250 g) trofie pasta

2 tbsp olive oil

2 garlic cloves, finely chopped

1 tbsp capers

2–4 baby zucchini, sliced

1 tbsp basil pesto

Large handful of marsh sea beans

1 tsp cracked black pepper

Handful of basil leaves

Zest and juice of 1 lemon

Grated Parmesan cheese, to garnish

Method

01 Bring a pan of water to a boil, add the pasta, and cook for 10–15 minutes.

02 Once the pasta is nearly ready, heat the olive oil in a large frying pan and gently fry the garlic and capers for 2–3 minutes.

03 Next, add the sliced zucchini. Cook for 4–5 minutes until they have caramelized slightly, then add in the pesto and sea beans. Stir and remove from heat—the residual heat in the pan will cook the sea beans effectively.

04 When the pasta is cooked, use a slotted spoon to transfer it right into the frying pan with the sea beans. Return the pan to the heat for a minute to emulsify the oils and moisture and toss gently to coat the pasta in the pesto and oil.

05 Season with the black pepper, then tear in the basil leaves as a garnish. Last, add the lemon zest and juice (if you add the lemon juice too early, it can brown the sea beans) and serve sprinkled with grated Parmesan.

MAIN MEAL

Katsu Curried Sea Vegetables and Tofu

SERVES 2

Sea beans, like many sea vegetables, have a complex umami flavor that provides tang and depth alongside their briny brightness. The unique salty bitterness is robust and works paired with a creamy curry. My twist on a katsu makes an exotic green bowl blown in from the shore. Try it with pickled rhubarb and ginger, jasmine rice, or rice noodles for a larger meal.

INGREDIENTS

1 tbsp sesame oil

9 oz (250 g) smoked tofu, diced

Large bunch of rock or marsh sea beans and other sea vegetables

1 lime

1 tsp sesame seeds

For the katsu curry sauce

2 tbsp sesame oil

2 carrots, chopped

1 onion, finely chopped

2 garlic cloves, chopped

1 tbsp grated fresh ginger root

1 tbsp mild curry powder

½ tsp turmeric

1 tbsp all-purpose flour

½ cup (100 ml) vegetable stock

1 cup (200 ml) coconut milk

2 tsp honey

2 tsp soy sauce

Method

01 First, make the katsu curry sauce. Heat the sesame oil in a saucepan; add the carrots, onion, garlic, and ginger; and fry until softened. Mix in the curry powder and turmeric, then allow the vegetables to caramelize for 10–15 minutes.

02 Sprinkle in the flour and cook out for 1 minute. Next, add the stock gradually, stirring continuously, and follow by pouring in the coconut milk and honey. Season with the soy sauce.

03 Simmer for 15 minutes until the carrots are fully soft, then use a hand-held mixer to blend until smooth.

04 Finally, heat the sesame oil in a wok and add the smoked tofu. Fry for 3–4 minutes until golden brown, then add in the sea beans and sea vegetables. Squeeze in the juice of a lime and sprinkle over the sesame seeds, then coat the tofu and sea beans in the katsu sauce and serve.

Sea Bean Pakora

MAKES 6–8

When you want an energy-packed snack, consider trying these sea bean pakora inspired by Nepalese small plates. I have wonderful memories of eating a wide selection of different vegetable pakora next to a lake under the Annapurna mountain range. They are rich, warming, and easy to make. The sea beans season the whole-wheat batter wonderfully, and the sweet potato provides golden color, allowing the green marsh grass to shine.

INGREDIENTS

1⅔ cups (150 g) whole-wheat flour

1 tsp baking soda

½ cup (100 ml) water

1 tsp garam masala

½ tsp ground cumin

½ tsp turmeric

½ tsp ground coriander

½ green chili, finely diced

7 oz (200 g) marsh sea beans

½ sweet potato, peeled and grated

Vegetable oil, for deep-frying

Sea salt

Method

01 Make a spiced whole-wheat batter by whisking the whole-wheat flour, baking soda, and water until smooth, then add in the ground spices and green chili. Next, mix in the sea beans and grated sweet potato.

02 Form the mixture into 6–8 loose patties, then heat the vegetable oil in a large saucepan or wok—the oil should be hot, at around 375°F (190°C). Carefully deep-fry the pakora in small batches for no more than 4–5 minutes, until golden brown. Remove from the oil with a slotted spoon, then allow to drain on paper towel before serving with a pinch of sea salt.

Fennel

YOU HAVE MY HEART, MANDOLINE SHARP

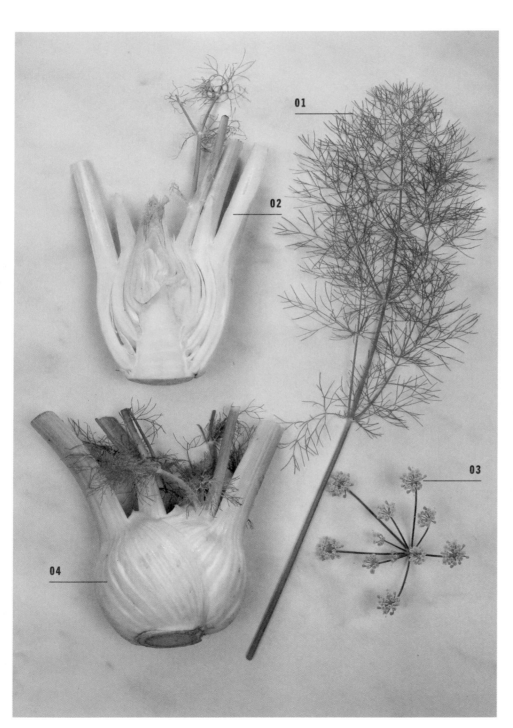

EDIBLE PARTS

01 FRONDS

The feathery fronds make the perfect garnish to delicately finish off a dish.

02 STEMS

The stems are edible and can be used as a crunchy replacement for celery or onion.

03 FLOWERS AND SEEDS

The flowers can be used as a beautiful garnish and provide perfumed fennel seeds that can be used in baking or curries.

04 BULB

Also known as the crown, what we know as the fennel "bulb" is actually a modified bulbous stem that grows in chunky, leaflike sections around the central core.

TAPROOTS

The taproots are also edible after you remove the soil and give them a clean.

In my garden, fennel wears the crown. It is the ultimate vegetable for cooking, from the root up to the feathery shoot. Fennel can be enjoyed cooked or raw and is unashamedly bold in taste, weaving anise flavor into a recipe's fabric.

PLANT

Fennel is a hardy perennial that grows well on dry soils and near the coast or riverbanks. Part of the carrot family, it grows to 3–10 ft (1–3 m) tall and is very aromatic due to a high potency of volatile compounds often prominent in herbs, including anethole and estragole. Anethole is a compound also found in star anise, and it is this that gives fennel its distinctive flavor. Fennel is good for you, too. It contains a combination of phytonutrients and boasts strong antioxidant properties as well. It's also known to aid digestion and reduce inflammation.

PREPARATION

I recommend using a pair of fine kitchen scissors to trim fennel fronds, a Japanese mandoline to shave the bulb (**fig. a**), a chef's knife to slice and dice, and a grater for making remoulade and slaw. The core of the bulb may need slicing more thinly to cook at the same rate as the rest of the bulb, and some sections of stalk are surprisingly tough and may need cooking. My advice is to taste as you go along and adjust your chopping size to suit the particular fennel part. When preparing dishes, a bowl of lemon ice water keeps fennel fresh and avoids browning until it's time to cook or serve (**fig. b**).

TYPES

COMMON

An aromatic herb with feather foliage and umbels of yellow flowers dusted in a bright pollen.

FLORENCE

This variety is of the same species as the herb but has a swollen, bulblike stem at its base that is eaten as a vegetable.

BRONZE

Because of its attractive purple-toned foliage, with a blend of blue-green and bronze hues, this variety is often grown for its ornamental qualities, but it is still very edible. It has a good, strong anise flavor, and as it is less bulbous than Florence fennel, I often use it as an herb.

BABY

Immature fennel bulbs and leaves are edible and tender. Grow as a succession crop— sown closer together—for young, bright-flavored plants with longer, thinner bulbs.

WILD

This is an invasive herbaceous perennial, because, like all fennel, it reproduces from both the crown and the seed. It has naturalized along roadsides and pasture land and has strong anise properties.

Figure a.

Figure b.

CONT.

Figure c.

COOKING TIPS

Fennel has a potent flavor—less is more, so don't feel obligated to use it all up in one recipe. That said, the bulb is excellent cooked whole, low, and slow on the grill or finely sliced and eaten raw. Mature bulbs require cooking and braising for longer to keep them tender, while smaller bulbs are better eaten raw. Diced, the bulb can also be used as a substitute for onion. The addition of acid can help balance any fennel dish—calm the wave of aniseed with some lemon juice or yogurt and cream. Fennel also works wonderfully well with desserts if handled carefully so as not to overpower the dish. Try mixing thin slices of bulb with apples in a twist on traditional apple crumble or apple pie. Or use the fresh fronds or crushed seeds to infuse a panna cotta or ice cream.

ZERO WASTE

Raw or cooked, fennel is entirely edible—it is the hero vegetable of zero-waste cooking—although the stalks, tops, fronds, taproots, and bulb all benefit from slightly different approaches. A bulb will keep in the fridge for a week, and if you have a surplus or leftovers, you can pickle (**fig. c**) or ferment it. I've enjoyed using fennel with radish, lemon, and white miso for pickles to serve with ramen or adding grated turmeric root and fermenting it as a golden kraut with a lovely anise note. Finely diced fennel makes a fantastic addition to chutney or piccalilli, and the flowers make a stunning garnish to cocktails and salads—for a delicate finish, shake off the pollen for a gorse-yellow dust. You can also try freezing chopped fennel fronds and storing them in a zipper-lock bag to add a quick herby hit to risottos, soups, and roasted vegetables. If you have fennel with the roots still attached, clean them, then dip in seasoned flour and fry as root chips or add to stir-fries. They possess the same sweet aniseed flavor and have a woody texture.

LIGHT LUNCH

Fennel and Cashew Salad
SERVES 2

My daughter Arrietty can be found hugging a fennel bulb at the kitchen table, exclaiming, "I love fennel!" It must run in the family. This salad combines thin slivers of the bulb with the feathery fronds for an anise explosion. The dish is balanced with sweet orange and honey-roasted cashews.

INGREDIENTS

1 tbsp coconut oil

2⅔oz (75g) cashew nuts

1 tbsp honey

1 tsp sea salt

1 tsp coconut flakes, plus extra for sprinkling

1 fennel bulb

1 orange, zested, peeled, and sliced

6 fennel fronds

Fennel flowers and/or calendula flowers, to garnish

Method

01 Preheat the oven to 400°F (200°C). Melt the coconut oil in an oven-safe pan.

02 Add the cashews and toss them in the oil until they are evenly coated. Then pour over the honey and roast in the oven for 10–15 minutes.

03 Remove the cashews from the oven to cool and sprinkle with the salt and coconut flakes while still warm.

04 Thinly slice the fennel vertically along the heart of the bulb, then build the salad with orange slices, orange zest, and fronds. Sprinkle with the honey-roasted cashews and finish with more coconut flakes and edible flowers.

SIDE OR MAIN MEAL

Fennel Gratin

SERVES 2 OR 4 AS A SIDE

This is my warm hug of a dish, designed to make you feel good. Summer fennel slowly cooked with a cheese sauce and crunchy gratin from yesterday's bread doesn't immediately shout "wow," but trust me. Whether served as a meal on its own or as a side, this dish is fennel's way of saying, "Come and join me for a rustic meal of pure comfort."

INGREDIENTS

3½ tbsp (50 g) salted butter
½ cup (50 g) all-purpose flour
1 tsp Dijon mustard
½ tsp grated nutmeg
½ tsp white pepper
¼ cup (50 ml) apple cider
½ cup (100 ml) heavy cream
3½ oz (100 g) grated
   Cheddar cheese
1 egg yolk
2 tbsp olive oil
2 fennel bulbs, roughly
   chopped
⅔ cup (75 g) breadcrumbs
Fennel fronds, to garnish
Sea salt

Method

01 Preheat the oven to 400°F (200°C). Make a roux sauce by melting the butter and adding flour. Stir until the flour cooks out, then add in the mustard, nutmeg, white pepper, and cider. Stir into a paste, then add in the cream.

02 Cook for 5–10 minutes on low heat until silky and smooth, then melt in the cheese. Remove from heat and stir in the egg yolk.

03 Heat 1 tablespoon of the oil in a pan and add in the chopped fennel. Cook on high heat for 5–10 minutes to bring some umami depth to the dish, then transfer to an oven-safe pan. Pour over the sauce, coating the fennel. Toss the breadcrumbs in the remaining olive oil and sprinkle over the top.

04 Bake for 25–30 minutes until the breadcrumbs are golden brown and the fennel is soft to the touch. Garnish with fennel fronds and season with sea salt.

MAIN MEAL

Fennel and Halloumi
SERVES 4

The combination of roasted fennel bulb and raw salad provides two different textures and flavors here. The raw citrus–dressed fennel salad has a bright anise tang. The roasted slices from the heart of the bulb, on the other hand, are full of umami depth, sweet caramelization, and a mellowed bitterness that works wonderfully with a nutty olive oil. The za'atar-coated halloumi and brined olives are the perfect accompaniment to the fennel. Serve with couscous, and, as this is a sharing dish, you could also provide some flatbreads to go with it.

INGREDIENTS

2 fennel bulbs

2 bell peppers (orange or yellow), sliced

3 tbsp olive oil

Sea salt and cracked black pepper

2 tbsp black olives

1 tsp sumac

1 preserved lemon, finely sliced

Zest and juice of 1 lemon

5½oz (150g) halloumi, sliced

1 tsp za'atar

7oz (200g) couscous

1 tbsp chopped parsley

Fennel fronds, to garnish

Method

01 Preheat the oven to 400°F (200°C). Prepare 1 fennel bulb by slicing it vertically, then add to a roasting pan with the peppers and toss in 2 tablespoons of the olive oil. Season with a pinch of sea salt and black pepper and roast for 25–30 minutes.

02 Meanwhile, slice the second fennel bulb crosswise and toss in a bowl with the olives, remaining olive oil, sumac, preserved lemon, and lemon juice and zest. The olives and preserved lemon should be salty enough to season the salad for you.

03 Fry the halloumi in a dry pan and coat it in the za'atar. Finally, make some couscous according to the package instructions and mix in the chopped parsley. Serve the roasted fennel, fennel salad, and halloumi on a bed of couscous and garnish with fennel fronds.

Tomato

MONEY CAN'T BUY HOMEGROWN TOMATOES

Classic vine tomato

Beefsteak

Gardener's Delight

Heirloom

Cherry

Grape

Plum

EDIBLE PARTS

01 SKIN

The skin provides up to 98 percent of the flavonols that are part of the phytochemicals in a tomato and are very good for your health. Peel if you want a more refined texture for a sauce, but I tend to keep the skin on.

02 FLESH

This is the juicy part of the tomato that holds most of the water. The fruit wall can be eaten raw and softens into a pulp when cooked. The flesh dissolves with heat and, as tomatoes are over 95 percent water, it can make a sauce wet if overcooked.

03 SEEDS

Each fruit contains at least two cells of small seeds, which are surrounded by a jellylike pulp. The seeds are a bit of a superfood: they are rich in dietary fiber, vitamin C, and vitamin A, and the clear gel that surrounds them helps improve bloodflow. I never remove the seeds for a salsa or sauce, because I like rustic texture and want all the goodness from my vegetables.

The arrival of tomato season remains every gardener's delight. A sun-ripened fruit plucked from the vine and eaten raw, cooked, or preserved always surpasses any store-bought variety for flavor and instills a great sense of pride.

PLANT

Tomatoes are part of the nightshade family and, although regarded as a vegetable, they are in fact a fruit. There are thousands of varieties, in all colors and sizes, which are easy to grow at home. The plant requires warm weather and plenty of sunlight, so in cooler climates, it grows best on sunny windowsills, in greenhouses, or under cover. In areas with higher rainfall, there is a greater risk of blight if grown outdoors. They typically grow to 3¼–9¾ ft (1–3 m) in height and can be cordoned or grown as bushes. The season will go from early summer until fall. Water regularly to avoid the fruit cracking and harvest with a pair of scissors, cutting just above the fruit so the stem isn't damaged and open to disease.

PREPARATION

A ripe tomato should be uniformly colored true to its variety, plump and glossy, and not too hard to the touch. If it's oversoft, you should consider using it for sauces rather than salads. For tomato prep, use either a serrated tomato knife or a paring knife. Smaller blades allow you to seed the tomato if you want a firmer salsa, segment it into a salad, or easily halve larger fruits for roasting. Also consider working on a board with a groove to channel the juices. You can remove tomato skins by scoring the bottom of the fruit with a cross, dropping into boiling water to blanch for 30 seconds, then immersing in ice water—the skin will slip off.

TYPES

CHERRY

These enticingly firm fruits are barely larger than candy and grow in red, orange, yellow, and purple. A sweet, crisp bite.

BEEFSTEAK

A large variety perfect for stuffing, with a firm skin, juicy, meaty flesh and mild flavor.

HEIRLOOM

Also known as heritage, heirlooms have deep, rich colors and a variety of textures are sweet to tangy and often very juicy. Perfect eaten raw.

PLUM

A cooking fruit with fewer seeds and a tougher, denser skin than other varieties. Its well-balanced flavor means it's the go-to choice for stews, pastes, or sauces.

GRAPE

This variety has an oval "grape" shape and is crisp and crunchy, with a sweet-to-tangy flavor.

GREEN

Underripe tomatoes are tart, tangy, and bright green, with a firm, meaty texture. There are also some heirloom varieties that remain green when they are ripe.

GARDENER'S DELIGHT

A small, sweet, flavorful tomato, great for snacking. It's heavy cropping and grows well in pots and grow bags.

CONT.

Figure a.

Figure b.

COOKING TIPS

Tomatoes have a very high water content, so you can either cook them down into a sweet sauce or sear to keep them juicy inside while holding their form. You can also use a tomato like a lemon to add acidity to a dish with a fresh squeeze of juice. Wrap half a tomato in muslin to catch the seeds and squeeze over salads, then use the flesh in a cooked recipe. Another favorite for me is roasting halved tomatoes for 20 minutes at 425°F (220°C) with a drizzle of olive oil, a pinch of salt and pepper, and some dried oregano. Cherry tomatoes also work well slowly and gently cooked under oil in a confit with garlic.

Of course, the ultimate companion for tomato is basil, and how better to enjoy the two than on a mozzarella pizza? Tomato sauce provides the base layer of acidity, while extra slices on top caramelize, bringing out the sweetness and umami flavors. Also try serving raw slices with burrata (**fig. a**) or on toasted sourdough for a bruschetta with olive tapenade.

ZERO WASTE

The tomato season is relatively short, but fortunately there are many ways to preserve the fruit. Ketchups, sauces, or pastes are a great way to use a bumper crop, and adding salt, sugar, or vinegar and cooking out the moisture will preserve yours for longer. Tomato juice is another great use for a surplus and makes for an excellent Bloody Mary: mix ¼ cup (50 ml) vodka, 1 cup (250 ml) tomato juice, 1 tablespoon of lemon juice, 3 drops of hot chili sauce, and a pinch of celery salt and cracked black pepper, then garnish with celery, lemon, and fennel flowers (**fig. b**). Also try making your own sun-dried tomatoes by drying sliced tomatoes on lined trays in a dehydrator at 120°F (50°C) or in the oven at 200°F (100°C) for 6–12 hours. Then store in an airtight jar or submerged in olive oil with some dried herbs (**fig. c**).

Near the end of the season, you may be left with a surplus of green tomatoes. Rather than discard them, try making green tomato chutney with vinegar, spices, and sugar.

Figure c.

MAIN MEAL

Tomato Stew

SERVES 4

Many countries have a twist on this rustic mix of summer vegetables: France has ratatouille; Italy has minestrone. This is my homage. It has tomato at its heart, binding everything with a sweet sauce and a perfect balance of acidity. Simplicity is what makes this dish rich, taking it from humble beginnings to vegetable royalty.

INGREDIENTS

2 tbsp olive oil

8 large tomatoes, roughly chopped

6 green beans, roughly chopped

6 radishes, quartered

4 spring onions, roughly chopped

3 carrots, sliced

2 zucchini, roughly chopped

2 red bell peppers, roughly chopped

1 leek, roughly chopped

1 white onion, roughly chopped

3½ pints (2 liters) vegetable stock

5½ oz (150 g) chickpeas or beans, drained

Handful of snow peas or sugar snap peas

Bunch of basil and chopped fennel fronds, to garnish

Sea salt and cracked black pepper

Method

01 Warm the oil in a large saucepan or casserole dish over medium-high heat. Add all the chopped vegetables and soften for 15 minutes, stirring continuously.

02 Next, add the stock and bring to a rolling boil.

03 Reduce the heat and simmer for 45 minutes, stirring occasionally until the vegetables are soft and tender and the tomatoes have broken down into a rich sauce. For the last 5 minutes of cooking, add the chickpeas or beans and the snow peas or sugar snaps.

04 Serve and finish with the basil and fennel fronds and season to taste with salt and black pepper.

MAIN MEAL

Stuffed Tomato
SERVES 2

I love a classic stuffed vegetable recipe, but I often find that, despite looking impressive, a stuffed pepper can taste bitter or a marrow too soft. But I've found the perfect showstopper. Robust enough to withstand the heat from the oven, a beefsteak tomato has an earthy sweetness and takes the umami flavor to the next level. The aromatic stuffing stays moist, protected by a crunchy crumble topping of pistachios and pine nuts.

INGREDIENTS

*1 large beefsteak tomato,
    about 4–6 in (10–15 cm)
    in diameter*

*5½ oz (150 g) cooked
    couscous*

2 tbsp finely diced zucchini

*1 preserved lemon,
    finely sliced*

*6 sun-dried tomatoes,
    chopped*

1 tsp capers

½ tsp fennel seeds

1 tsp sumac

2 sprigs of mint, to garnish

For the crumble topping

2 tbsp pine nuts

*2 tbsp pistachios, roughly
    chopped*

1 tbsp finely chopped mint

Pinch of dried rose petals

Sea salt

Method

01 Preheat the oven to 400°F (200°C). Start by slicing the top off the tomato and setting to one side—this will be the lid for roasting. Then scoop out half of the flesh and seeds; to avoid waste, use these in a salsa or ketchup. If required, use a sharp knife to turn the tomato and carve through the cell walls and make scooping easier.

02 In a bowl, mix together the couscous, zucchini, lemon, sun-dried tomatoes, capers, fennel seeds, and sumac, then fill the tomato to the top with the mixture.

03 To make the crumble topping, pulse all the ingredients except the salt in a blender to a coarse texture, then season with a pinch of salt. Sprinkle the crumble over the stuffing, then replace the lid and put the stuffed tomato on a lined baking sheet and roast for 20–30 minutes.

04 Serve warm with a sprig of mint to garnish.

SIDE

Roasted Tomatoes and Mozzarella

SERVES 4

Although it may appear simple, this is probably one of my most extraordinary recipes. Heirloom tomatoes are full of variety; the golden cherries roasted alongside deep reds is sensational with the basil and balsamic, and the mozzarella provides creamy notes. This dish is the ultimate celebration of tomatoes and one to revisit time and time again.

INGREDIENTS

2¼ lb (1 kg) heirloom tomatoes

2 tbsp olive oil, plus extra for drizzling

1 tsp balsamic vinegar, plus extra for drizzling

1 tsp sea salt

9 oz (250 g) mozzarella cheese

8 basil leaves

Method

01 Preheat the oven to 425°F (220°C). Cut larger tomatoes in half and keep the smaller ones whole, then place them in a large roasting pan.

02 Dress the tomatoes with the olive oil and balsamic vinegar and season with the salt.

03 Roast for 20–25 minutes until the tomatoes soften and the skin starts to blister and caramelize in places.

04 Tear the mozzarella and basil leaves and scatter them over the tomatoes. Drizzle with a little more olive oil and vinegar and serve warm.

Beans

CLIMB THE BEANSTALK

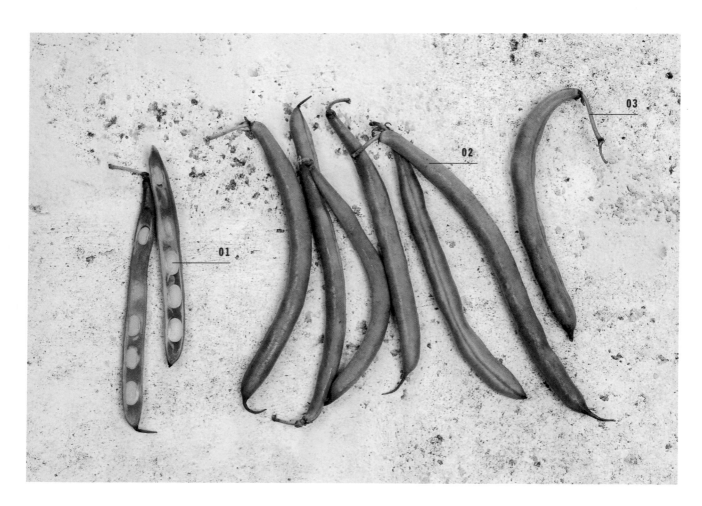

EDIBLE PARTS

01 BEANS

Immature beans or peas are small and usually lime green in color; they are protein-packed with a creamy texture when cooked. They can mature into larger beans that are more robust to cook with and ideal to preserve.

02 POD

The pod is edible in most varieties of bean. They have a sweet, grassy flavor that becomes slightly bitter as they mature.

03 STEM

The stems are inedible when mature but, when very young, they can be cooked and eaten.

Beans epitomize the potential in life. Harvested fresh, they are a bright emerald green; dried, they store for months like depositing savings for the future; cooked, they are rich and restorative. Beans are magical—worth swapping for a cow any day.

PLANT

Like the naturalist Henry David Thoreau, I've always been "determined to know beans." There are many different types, but in most cases, the whole pod and the peas inside can be cooked. In the garden, they grow upward in uniform rows, signifying good things to come. They are an excellent source of fiber, iron, potassium, and phosphorous and are particularly high in vitamins K and C. From young pods to mature beans, they provide nutrient-packed bulk to stews and soups; crisp texture in salads; or creamy, slow-cooked comfort. They are generally at their most tender when picked smaller and more frequently.

PREPARATION

For younger beans, I either cook them whole or slice diagonally to provide individual sections that contain the immature peas inside the shell. For larger bean pods, blanch before cooking to soften them and reduce bitterness. They are wonderful sweated in a lump of butter or a little oil. Beans are also widely available already processed, canned or cooked, but they are far cheaper to buy in bulk dried. When dealing with dried beans, my advice is to place them in a pan of water and bring to a boil. Leave to cool and soak for several hours, then replace the water before boiling until soft. The soaking shortens the cooking time and results in a more even texture.

TYPES

GREEN

The three main types of common bean are string or runner, stringless or French, and flat-podded snap beans. They are primarily grown for their edible pods instead of their immature peas, though both are edible. Bright-red flowers produce thin pods. The peas within are semistarchy with a sweet, grassy flavor. There are dwarf, climbing, and self-supporting varieties, and they have superb nitrogen-fixing qualities for the soil in the garden.

KIDNEY

Also known as the red bean, this variety has a dark-colored skin and is named for its shape. A versatile bean with a sweet, nutty flavor and soft, creamy texture when cooked, it is often served with rice for a classic Creole dish or in chili con carne.

BLACK

Sometimes called turtle beans or black Mexican beans, these have an oval, jet-black pea with an earthy, sweet taste and soft texture. The small, shiny bean has a delicate mushroom flavor and goes extremely well with corn or in a burrito.

EDAMAME

Edamame are actually a preparation of immature soybeans rather than a different type. They are a rich source of protein and therefore used widely in vegan diets and for meat-replacement products.

PINTO

A rust-colored bean popular in South American and Mexican cuisine. It has a speckled appearance and, once cooked, can be eaten whole or mashed. Pinto beans are great for spiced, refried beans or a cooking pot of cowboy beans when camping.

MUNG

This bean is green in color and grows in more tropical climates. I buy them dried, but you don't need to soak them before cooking. They are also dried as a split bean for dal and are lighter yellow when their skins are removed. The sprouted beans are a popular source of beansprouts.

NAVY

Small, oval, creamy-white beans that are widely used in baked beans and soups for their buttery, smooth texture. They are very mildly flavored, so they absorb sauces and spices easily. Other popular varieties include cannellini or lima beans. These are sweet and creamy with high starch levels that provide bulk.

BORLOTTI

Originally bred in Colombia, these have distinctive plump red pods speckled with creamy yellow that contain dappled ivory- and hazelnut-colored beans splashed with magenta. Popular in Northern Italy, they have a sweet, chestnutlike flavor and creamy texture.

CONT.

Figure a.

Figure b.

COOKING TIPS

Beans can be eaten raw or cooked. Whole or sliced pods are great sautéed in oil or blanched in boiling water for 2–3 minutes. Young beans are also fantastic cooked on the grill for a tasty contrast of sweet and smoky flavors. Cooked lima beans make a fantastic substitute for chickpeas in hummus if blended with olive oil, garlic, and lemon. The result is a soft, creamy, and utterly delicious white bean dip. A mix of navy and pinto beans is ideal for baked beans. Soften some diced red onion in oil with chopped garlic and plenty of paprika, then add the cooked beans and some chopped tomatoes and cook slowly. Finish with fresh cilantro and plenty of black pepper, and try adding a splash of bourbon for a drunken version (**fig. a**). But one of my favorite recipes for beans, which I had a few years ago at a local restaurant, is to fry sliced garlic and red chili in coconut oil, then add green beans and garnish with coconut flakes (**fig. b**). The combination is simple but tastes sublime.

ZERO WASTE

Bean pods are a good source of fiber, so try cooking with all parts of your bean to avoid waste. If shelling the beans, the larger pods can be used for stocks and to add a legume flavor to sauces.

Also try chopping whole green beans into a summer chutney recipe or freezing in batches once blanched. For larger bean pods with mature peas, try drying them and storing in an airtight container for up to 12 months.

You can oven-dry beans by first podding them into cold water and blanching for 2 minutes. Then spread them out in a single layer on a baking sheet and dry in an oven at 200°F (100°C) for 4–5 hours or in a dehydrator for 5–6 hours at 120°F (50°C) before packing in sealed containers. They will then require soaking before use, so try to get into the habit of soaking them the night before you want to use them.

MAIN MEAL

Bean Burger with Sorrel and Wasabi Mayo

SERVES 2

Bean burgers come in all shapes and sizes, and every chef has their own favorite recipe. I always used to love a good black bean burger, but recently I've been searching for something a bit brighter and less heavy. This recipe celebrates beans and has a slight Japanese twist with kimchi and a zingy sorrel mayo. Try serving with sweet potato fries.

INGREDIENTS

For the burgers

5½oz (150g) edamame beans

2½oz (75g) chickpeas

3½oz (100g) cooked quinoa

2 garlic cloves, finely diced

2 tbsp whole-wheat flour

2 spring onions, finely sliced

1 tbsp nori flakes

1 tbsp chopped fresh cilantro

1 tbsp grated fresh ginger root

½ tsp sea salt

2 tbsp sesame seeds or raw quinoa

2 tbsp sesame oil

For the sorrel mayo

12 sorrel leaves or spinach leaf or watercress

2 tbsp mayonnaise

Juice of 1 lime

½ tsp wasabi paste

To serve

2 burger buns

A few bok choy leaves

Salad leaves, such as mizuna, fennel fronds, and baby leaves

Kimchi

Method

01 Mix all the burger ingredients together except the sesame seeds and oil. Mix thoroughly, then, using a hand-held mixer, pulse the mixture to make it soft enough to form into patties. Try to retain some texture; you want a coarse bean burger that can be formed by hand.

02 Mold the mixture into 2 large patties, then roll them in the sesame seeds or raw quinoa and refrigerate for 30 minutes.

03 Meanwhile, make the sorrel mayo by blending all the ingredients in a food processor, then cut the burger buns in half and toast them.

04 Char a couple of bok choy leaves on a dry griddle, then mix a simple bitter salad with some mizuna, fennel fronds, and baby leaves.

05 Fry the seeded burger patties in hot sesame oil for 4–5 minutes on each side. Finally, build the burgers with the crunchy salad as the base, followed by the bean burger, drizzled in spicy sorrel mayo and topped with kimchi.

SIDE OR MAIN MEAL

Torched Green Bean and Radish Salad

SERVES 2 AS A SIDE OR 1 AS A MAIN

The beans are the star in this summer salad. The whole dish is dramatically charred to melt the cheese and provide some theater at the table. Caramelized shallots; sour, crunchy pickled radishes; salty blue cheese; and tender, bittersweet green beans complete the flavor show. A salad of multiple parts that play as one, this is a marvelous magic-bean performance.

INGREDIENTS

Large handful of young green beans

2 shallots

1 tbsp olive oil

1 tbsp grated orange zest

½ tsp sea salt

½ tsp cracked black pepper

3½ oz (100 g) blue cheese, crumbled

Parsley sprigs, to garnish

For the pickled radishes

2 tbsp granulated sugar

¼ cup (50 ml) cider vinegar

12 radishes, trimmed

Method

01 First, make the pickling solution by dissolving the sugar in the vinegar and ¼ cup (50 ml) boiling water. Bring to a boil, then remove from heat and submerge the trimmed radishes. Leave to cool for about 30 minutes, then drain. The radishes should still be crunchy and taste lovely and tart.

02 Meanwhile, blanch the green beans whole in boiling water for 3 minutes, then plunge into ice water to refresh.

03 In a ridged skillet, char the shallots whole until sweet and tender. They should only need 5–10 minutes.

04 Next, toss the blanched beans in a bowl with the olive oil and orange zest, then season well with the salt and pepper.

05 Serve the beans on a plate with the shallots and pickled radishes and sprinkle over the crumbled blue cheese. Use a blow torch or grill for 4–5 minutes to melt the cheese and char the beans and radishes, then garnish with parsley.

Huevos Rancheros

SERVES 2

This all-day bean breakfast is comforting and full of flavor. The beans provide creamy substance and soak up the spices like a sponge. By caramelizing the base of onion and garlic first, you can build a real depth of flavor, which then works wonderfully with the lighter profiles of grilled peppers, zingy lime, and fried eggs. Add a selection of salsa, guacamole, pickles, and flatbread for a real feast.

INGREDIENTS

1 tbsp olive oil

4–6 eggs

For the beans

2 garlic cloves, chopped

½ red onion, diced

2 tbsp olive oil

1 tbsp chopped jalapeño

1 tsp smoked paprika

1 tsp oregano

½ tsp ground cumin

½ tsp ground coriander

7 oz (200 g) navy beans

1¾ oz (50 g) chopped tomatoes

1 tsp sea salt

1 tsp cracked black pepper

For the rajas

1 tbsp olive oil

½ red bell pepper, finely sliced

½ yellow bell pepper, finely sliced

1 onion, finely sliced

1 tsp dried oregano

Juice of 1 lime, plus extra to serve

Method

01 Start with the beans, as the longer you cook them, the more fully the warming flavors will develop. Sauté the garlic and onion in the olive oil with all the spices for 4–5 minutes until soft and caramelized.

02 Add in the beans and tomatoes. Reduce the heat and cover the pan with a sheet of parchment paper to act as a cartouche. Simmer for 20–25 minutes until creamy and soft. Avoid stirring so the beans retain their texture.

03 In another pan, make the rajas. Warm the oil in a pan over high heat and fry the peppers and onion with the oregano for 5–6 minutes. Once caramelized, remove the vegetables and set aside, then deglaze the pan with lime juice. Use the same pan to heat a little more oil over medium heat and fry the eggs the way you like them.

04 Now return to the beans. Use a wooden spoon to mash some of them into a refried-bean-style paste, then season to taste with the salt and pepper. Serve with the rajas and eggs and an extra squeeze of lime.

Sweet Corn

MYTHICAL MAIZE

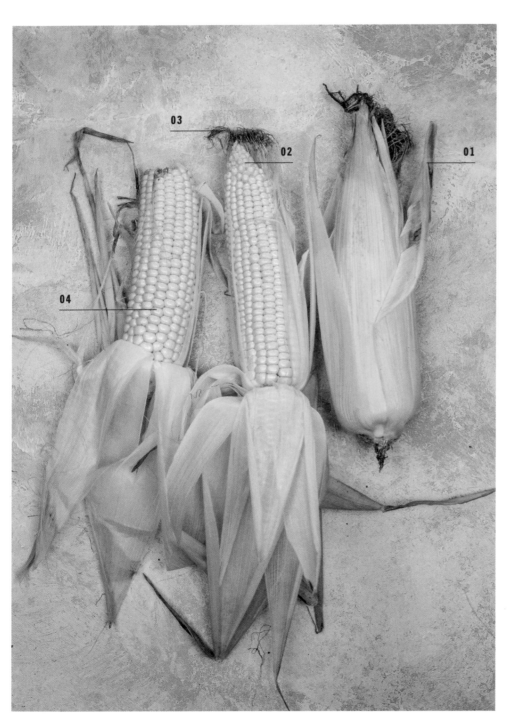

INEDIBLE PARTS

01 HUSKS

These are useful for protecting the corn when baking or steaming. They impart a subtle corn flavor but are inedible.

02 CORN COB

The central cob of mature corn is inedible, but it can be consumed raw on baby corn. The corn cob becomes tough as the plant matures. They make great grill fuel when dried.

EDIBLE PARTS

03 CORN SILK

These threads or tassels protrude from the tip of the ear of corn and are used in some natural remedies as a diuretic, but I strip them off before cooking.

04 KERNELS

Sweet corn kernels are all edible and can be dried to preserve them. Once harvested, the sugars start converting to starch.

Sweet corn inspires a humble feeling of awe. Within the lime-green husk is a hidden core of gold that shines when freshly shucked. Heavy and firm, juicy and sweet—it's no surprise to me that in Mayan culture, this vegetable was worshipped.

PLANT

There are thousands of ancient types of corn grown in Mexico and South America. All the varieties are types of maize that have high sugar levels and are therefore suited to harvesting as vegetables rather than grain crops. Sweet corn is harvested when young and immature rather than being left on the plant for the kernels to mature and dry out like the types of maize used for polenta. And for a good crop, long, hot summers are best.

I have thoroughly enjoyed replicating the American Indian "Three Sisters" method of growing it, where you plant your sweet corn blocks with climbing beans and squashes. The corn acts as a natural trellis for the beans, while the squashes cover the ground, preventing weeds and retaining moisture. It's a great symbiotic way of companion planting. Corn is a highly nutritious vegetable full of vital minerals like calcium, niacin, and riboflavin. It's also a superb source of fiber and beta-carotene, which produces vitamin A to promote healthy vision and support your immune system.

PREPARATION

A good rule is to harvest corn once the tassels turn dark brown. Test it first by peeling back a little of the husk and piercing a kernel with a skewer or knife tip: if watery liquid squirts out, it is unripe; if it's creamy, then the cob is ready. Twist and pull off the stem sharply. When buying corn, choose ones with a firm feel that are in their bright-green husks. The husk should be tucked tightly around the corn. The sugars in the corn turn to starch once picked, so always look for produce that is as fresh as possible. To shuck, peel the green leaves away (**fig. a**), remove the silk strands from the top of the ear, then either cook the cob whole or carve off the kernels. A well-sharpened knife and a tender steamed core make it easier to slice vertically down and keep the kernels attached to each other.

Figure a.

TYPES

YELLOW SWEET CORN

Sweet cobs with sugar that quickly turns to starch. The yellow kernels are packed in bountiful, uniform rows with up to 400 in one cob. Peak ripeness is when they have just been harvested and the kernels are succulent and sweet.

SUPERSWEET CORN

Usually found in supermarkets, these have 30 percent more sugar than standard corn. The kernels can be slightly chewy. There are hybrids that contain large amounts of beta-carotene.

BABY CORN

Very small, with a mild flavor, because it is picked early when less sugar has developed. Mostly sold shucked, it is often used whole or chopped into stir-fries.

BLACK CORN

An heirloom variety with purple, blackish kernels. The plant pigment contains anthocyanins, which are known to be rich in antioxidants and have anti-inflammatory properties, but also stain your fingers.

RED CORN

An increasingly popular variety for its striking color, red corn is actually a grain maize crop that can be harvested young as a vegetable. Tends to be higher in protein than yellow corn.

PERUVIAN CORN

Rich in fiber, with larger kernels and less sugar than standard corn. Available in many colors, it has a starchy, nutty flavor.

CONT.

Figure b.

Figure c.

COOKING TIPS

Cooking corn is great fun—you can try almost anything. When cooked on the grill, soak the corn for 1 hour first in water to then steam them in their husks on the grill for 20 minutes. You can then strip back the husks and baste with lashings of herby butter to char directly on the grill. For an Asian twist, grill the cobs, then glaze with soy sauce, or try glazing with a sticky Korean barbecue sauce and serving with kimchi. You can add the shaved-off kernels to chowder (see *opposite*) for creamy texture and sweetness or make zingy salsas with tomato and chili or South American–style bean salads.

Another fun recipe is to make a large sweet corn fritter (**fig. b**). Combine the sweet corn with some grated zucchini or blanched green beans and season with paprika and coriander. Fry for 4 minutes on either side like a pancake and top with a dollop of labneh, salad, and pickles. This makes a lovely lunchtime meal, and the corn adds a sweet, crunchy texture to the fritter.

ZERO WASTE

Making popcorn is a great way to avoid waste. This involves drying the husked corn for 3–4 weeks by hanging the cobs in a warm, well-ventilated space or using a dehydrator for 4–8 hours at 125°F (52°C). Once dry, the kernels can be stripped from the cob and stored in an airtight container. To pop them, heat 1 tablespoon of oil in a saucepan and add a handful of kernels. Cover with a lid and, after 2–3 minutes, they will start to pop. Try a savory seasoning of dried cheese, chives, and black pepper. To rehydrate the corn for cooking, soak in a bowl of water for 4–6 hours.

Freezing is also a good way to preserve corn. Blanch for 3–4 minutes and refresh in ice water first, then spread the kernels on a lined baking sheet and freeze. I also make sweet corn relish with sliced red onion, cider vinegar, and chopped garlic—a must-have for any summer barbecue. Add fresh cilantro, lime, and red chili for a spicy hit that works well with the sweet relish—it will inject a refreshing zing into a veggie burger (**fig. c**).

Corn Chowder

SERVES 4

This chowder has a feel-good factor that will help you bounce back from any bad day. My version captures the feeling of a fresh coastal breeze with sea beans and sea vegetables. It's a well-seasoned recipe that I've cooked on beaches and quays to warm up after a wild swim or a long sail. The water crackers and steamed corn croutons provide real crunch to contrast with the creamy chowder beneath.

INGREDIENTS

2 ears of sweet corn, husked

3½ tbsp (50 g) butter

½ leek, finely sliced

4 potatoes, peeled and diced

1 shallot, diced

1¾ oz (50 g) peas

2 cups (500 ml) vegetable stock

1 tsp ground white pepper

½ tsp cracked black pepper

½ tsp grated nutmeg

1 bay leaf

2 cups (500 ml) whole milk

1 tsp sea salt

Handful of sea vegetables (sea beans, sea purslane, or sea beet—see page 118)

Flat-leaf parsley, to garnish

4 water crackers, to garnish

Method

01 First, boil the corn in a large saucepan of salted water for 5–10 minutes until the kernels are soft.

02 Melt the butter in a saucepan and add in the leek, potatoes, and shallot. Sweat for 10–15 minutes on a low heat and avoid caramelizing.

03 Strip the kernels from one of the boiled cobs and add them to the pan along with the peas. Cover with the stock, then add the white and black pepper, nutmeg, and bay leaf. Bring to a boil and simmer for 10 minutes or until the potatoes are completely soft.

04 Remove the pan from heat, then add the milk and blend with a hand-held mixer into a coarse chowder. Return to just below boiling point and season to taste with the salt.

05 Finish by adding the sea vegetables just before serving, then garnish with more sweet corn stripped off the second boiled cob and some flat-leaf parsley. As a final touch, break up the water crackers and scatter on top.

SIDE OR SNACK

Grilled Corn on the Cob with Chili Cheese

SERVES 6

This is a throwback to the days when I cooked my way through university as a chef at a Mexican restaurant. The chili, lime, and cilantro-infused butter bastes the cobs to keep them sweet and moist and the chili cheese is a fiesta in the mouth. You can keep the husks attached for this one, but strip them back so they don't catch on the grill—it adds a rustic look and makes them easier to turn without tongs.

INGREDIENTS

10½ tbsp (150 g) salted butter

Zest and juice of 1 lime, plus extra to garnish

2 tbsp roughly chopped cilantro, plus extra to garnish

1¾ oz (50 g) jalapeño, chopped

6 ears of sweet corn, with husks

3½ oz (100 g) chili cheese, grated

Method

01 Preheat the grill until you have a good bed of glowing embers, or preheat a griddle pan in a hot oven at 425°F (220°C).

02 Melt the butter in a saucepan, then remove from heat and infuse it with the lime zest and juice, cilantro, and jalapeño for 10–15 minutes.

03 Pull back the husks of the sweet corn and lay the cobs directly on the grill or griddle pan.

04 Brush the corn with the flavored butter and grill for 15 minutes, turning regularly and basting every few minutes until juicy and chargrilled on all sides.

05 Serve with the grated cheese sprinkled on top while still warm, plus some extra cilantro and lime juice.

Burnt Corn Hummus
SERVES 2

I love hummus, but too often it can look a bit beige and uninspired. This dip, however, is the dream child of trips to the sunny coast of Mexico, inspired by memories of sipping golden beers and being dazzled by spicy bright color in every dish. In recent years, I've been searching for something smoky and sweet to relive those warm nights and serve to friends as a party starter, so coming up with this dip was like discovering Montezuma's treasure.

INGREDIENTS

2 ears of sweet corn, husked

3½ oz (100 g) cooked chickpeas, drained

4 garlic cloves, grated

1 tbsp tahini

2 tbsp lime juice

1 tbsp sweet paprika

Smoked sea salt

2 tbsp olive oil

Tortilla chips, to serve

Method

01 Either roast the corn in the oven at 425°F (220°C) or grill for 15 minutes or until they caramelize. Then, while still tender and juicy, strip the kernels off the cobs and place in a food processor, reserving one handful as a garnish.

02 Add the chickpeas, garlic, tahini, lime juice, and paprika to the food processor and blend until smooth, then season to taste with the smoked sea salt.

03 Transfer the hummus to a serving bowl, stir in the olive oil, and garnish with the handful of the reserved corn kernels. Serve with tortilla chips warmed for 5 minutes in the oven.

Chard

RAINBOW LEAVES

EDIBLE PARTS

01 LEAVES

Chard leaves grow in an impressive bouquet and should be harvested from the outside inward. When young, the small baby leaves are very tender and mild in flavor. As they mature, they grow from delicate oval shapes with thin veins into large, wrinkled, deep-green leaves with a waxy, firm texture. As with the stems, cook them when mature.

02 STEM

When young, the tender stems are delicious eaten raw as baby leaf salad. As the plant matures and the stems thicken, they become stringy and require cooking. Large stems should be separated from the greens and sautéed or braised before adding the rest of the leaves to soften.

Cooking with chard is like painting. The sap-green leaves and the cadmium-red and chrome-yellow stems are ornamental and richly layered. Grow it for edible color and form and enjoy mixing the simple, rustic colors on your palette.

PLANT

Chard is also known as leaf beet; it is from the same subspecies as beets but is selected for its leaves, as it doesn't have a bulbous root. It's an extremely hardy plant—tolerant of cold, shady conditions—and is a prolific cropper over a long period, providing multiple harvests. This makes it ideal for small spaces and urban kitchen gardens. Harvest regularly to ensure regrowth, removing the outer leaves so the center can grow out. As it's a prolific cut-and-come-again crop, you can harvest manageable amounts to avoid waste. Nutritionally, it is also rich in minerals and vitamins C, K, and E; beta-carotene; calcium; and zinc.

COOKING TIPS

As you can eat chard raw or cooked, it's another highly versatile vegetable, although typically mature chard leaves are best cooked for a more refined flavor. Start by sautéing and wilting the leaves if you are unfamiliar with chard. Then, as you grow in confidence, try using it more creatively. The stalks work well in stir-fries or when roasted or braised. The leaves can be used in smoothies or green soups and can often be substituted in recipes that require spinach or kale, such as saag aloo. A Spanish omelet or tortilla is also yummy with chard stalks softened in butter, then folded in with the fluffy eggs and boiled potatoes.

PREPARATION

You can harvest young, fresh green leaves or wait for them to mature for tougher, more bitter stems. Wash the leaves under cold water and shake dry before preparing. Separate the stems and the leaves and treat them differently for best results. Slice off larger stems where they join the leaf and slice diagonally so they have a large surface area that will help them cook more quickly. As they become older, they may become a bit stringy and more fibrous, so they will need to be cooked for longer. The leaves can be shredded finely like a napa cabbage or roughly chopped so as to be quickly braised or wilted.

ZERO WASTE

If you harvest chard leaves little and often, it's easy to avoid waste. But if you do need to use up a surplus, separate the stalks and leaves, blanch both, and freeze them separately, ready for cooking later. Alternatively, try fermenting. Rainbow chard kimchi is a recipe I love—the sour fermentation adds a lacto-tang to the earthy leaves. Finely chop the chard and combine with chopped chili, ginger, and garlic. Then add 4 percent total weight in sea salt. Massage, cover, and leave overnight, then press into a sterilized jar and top up with a 4 percent brine. Leave to ferment for 7–10 days, then store for 3–4 months.

TYPES

RAINBOW SWISS CHARD

My favorite chard due to its colorful pageant of stems forming a dense rosette. It has a subtle earthy flavor with a slight metallic tang. The succulent young leaves become bitter as they mature.

RED CHARD

The baby leaves of red chard resemble beet greens or red spinach. They have a delicate flavor, less earthy than Swiss chard, and are far less bitter when harvested as a baby leaf compared to mature chard. The oval leaves have thin red veins and a mild, spinachlike flavor with nutty notes. There is a woody, wet-earth aroma due to a volatile compound called geosmin, which provides its distinctive taste.

SWISS CHARD

Grows very tall when mature and can also be harvested as a baby leaf for salads. It has less wrinkled leaves than other chards and white/silver ribbed stems. More succulent and buttery in texture than most chards, it has a mild, sweet flavor and a slightly salty profile. Very good braised and finished in the pan with lemon juice and sea salt.

SEA BEET

An ancestor of chard that can be readily found near the coast. Its thick, diamond-shaped leaves are succulent and dark waxy green, with wrinkled edges. Rich in vitamin C and available all year round, it tastes great cooked, like a robust, salty spinach.

MAIN MEAL

Chard and Triple-cheese Cannelloni

SERVES 2

In my reimagining of this family favorite, I've used chard instead of spinach—a fresh take to reinvigorate what can be a nostalgic pasta dish with earthy depth, more texture, and a bitterness under the rich melted cheese. Casting chard in the lead role of a much-loved meal is a risk, but I think it has paid off and could even be an improvement—only time will tell.

INGREDIENTS

8–12 cannelloni tubes
Cracked black pepper
Small bunch of chives, chopped, to garnish

For the tomato sauce
1 tbsp olive oil
1 garlic clove, finely chopped
5½oz (150g) tomato purée
1 tsp dried oregano
1 tsp balsamic vinegar
Sea salt and cracked black pepper

For the cheese sauce
3½ tbsp (50g) butter
2 tbsp all-purpose flour
½ cup (100ml) milk
½ tsp grated nutmeg

1¾oz (50g) Parmesan cheese
1¾oz (50g) mozzarella cheese
1¾oz (50g) Cheddar cheese
1 egg yolk

For the filling
1 tbsp olive oil
1lb 2oz (500g) chard, roughly chopped
1 tbsp pine nuts
1 tsp grated lemon zest
½ tsp grated nutmeg
9oz (250g) ricotta cheese
Sea salt and cracked black pepper

Method

01 First, make the tomato sauce by heating the olive oil in a saucepan, then adding the garlic to soften. Next, add the purée, oregano, and balsamic vinegar. Season to taste with salt and pepper and simmer for 10 minutes, then remove from heat, set aside, and allow to cool.

02 For the cheese sauce, melt the butter in a saucepan and stir in the flour to form a roux. Once you have a smooth paste, add in the milk a little at a time and cook until smooth and silky, stirring continuously. Then add the nutmeg and the three cheeses. Melt the cheese over low heat, then remove from heat and finish by stirring in the egg yolk while the cheese sauce cools.

03 For the filling, heat the olive oil in a frying pan, then add the chopped chard with the pine nuts, lemon zest, and nutmeg. Allow the chard to wilt for 4–5 minutes, then stir in the ricotta and season to taste with salt and pepper. Remove from heat and allow to cool, then stuff the mixture into each pasta tube.

04 Preheat the oven to 400°F (200°C). In a casserole dish, pour the tomato sauce into the base and line up the stuffed cannelloni tubes on top, then pour over the cheese sauce. Roast for 20–25 minutes in the oven until the cheese is golden and the pasta is perfectly cooked. Season to taste with cracked black pepper and garnish with some fresh chives.

MAIN MEAL

Rainbow Pie with Fenugreek and Lentils

SERVES 6

I bake this pie for a late-summer lunch. The earthy chard balances beautifully with the diced sweet potato, nutty lentils, and fenugreek seeds. And like a pot of gold at the end of a rainbow, it's all wrapped in a rich, buttery pastry. You can add diced cheese for an even richer version, but there is plenty to be said for keeping this all about the vegetables.

INGREDIENTS

3½ tbsp (50 g) ghee

2 sweet potatoes, peeled and diced

1 tbsp fenugreek seeds

2¼ lb (1 kg) rainbow chard, roughly chopped

1 cup (250 ml) coconut milk

9 oz (250 g) French green lentils, cooked

1 tsp sea salt

1 tbsp all-purpose flour, for dusting

1 lb 2 oz (500 g) puff pastry

1 egg, beaten, for glazing

Method

01   Melt the ghee in an oven-safe frying pan or cast-iron skillet and add the diced sweet potato and fenugreek seeds. Sauté for 5–10 minutes, then add the chard.

02   Braise the mixture until the chard wilts and the stems soften, then add in the coconut milk, cooked lentils, and salt. Stir well and simmer for 5–10 minutes, then remove from heat and leave to cool.

03   Preheat the oven to 400°F (200°C). Dust your work surface with the all-purpose flour and roll out the puff pastry, then cut it into a large circle to fit your pan. Place the pastry circle over the pie filling and crimp the edges, then carefully cut a hole in the center to allow steam to escape. Brush with the beaten egg.

04   Bake the pie for 35 minutes or until the pastry is golden brown and the filling is piping hot.

BREAKFAST OR BRUNCH

Chard-stalk Shakshuka

SERVES 2

A good brunch on a Saturday morning is the best start to some much-needed time off on the weekend—it wakes up your appetite. This baked-egg dish treats the chard stems like tender asparagus for a scattering of color and the leaves as an earthy pesto wilted beneath.

INGREDIENTS

1 tbsp olive oil

9 oz (250 g) chard stalks, chopped

8 cherry vine tomatoes, halved

9 oz (250 g) chard leaves, finely sliced

2 tbsp chopped cilantro

1 tbsp lemon juice

4 free-range eggs

1 tbsp za'atar

2 tbsp plain yogurt

1 tsp harissa sauce

Method

01 Preheat the oven to 400°F (200°C). In an oven-safe frying pan or skillet, heat the olive oil and add in the chard stalks and cherry tomatoes. Sauté for 3–4 minutes, then remove from the pan with some tongs and set aside.

02 Next, add the finely sliced chard leaves to the pan. Wilt these until they soften, then add 1 tablespoon of the cilantro and the lemon juice. Once you have a good base of wilted greens to line the bottom of the pan, start building your shakshuka.

03 Return the chard stems and tomatoes to the pan. Make a shallow indent in the chard leaves with each egg before cracking them carefully into the holes. Next, place the whole pan in the oven to bake for 5 minutes.

04 Remove from the oven and garnish with the za'atar and the remaining freshly chopped cilantro. Finish by mixing the yogurt and harissa in a small bowl to drizzle over the aromatic baked eggs and wilted chard.

Garlic

AMPLIFYING FLAVOR

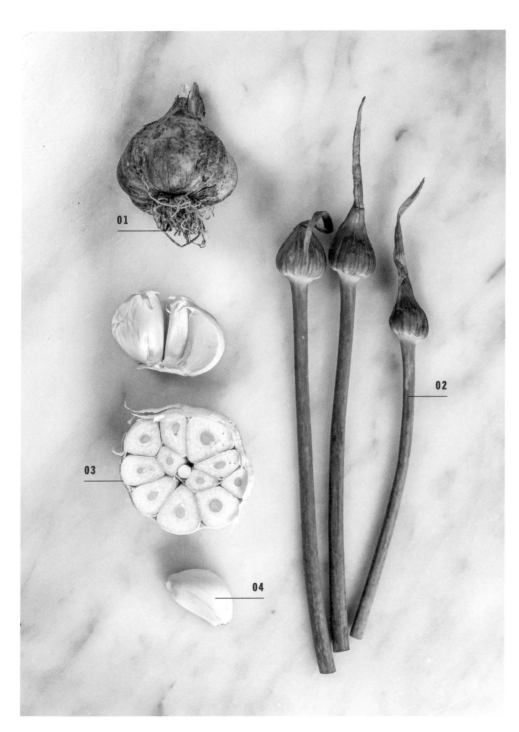

EDIBLE PARTS

01 ROOTS

The small roots are edible and make a great crispy garnish when washed and fried in oil.

02 SCAPES

The scapes are green shoots or stems that hold the garlic flower; their season is therefore short and sweet. When the hard-neck garlic plant throws out scapes with a teardrop-shaped bulb near its end, it diverts energy away from the bulb. Growers will therefore snip off the scapes to increase the size of the bulb. They are fresh, vegetal, and delicious cooked like tender asparagus spears or fried in oil and used as a garnish.

03 BULB

The garlic skin is technically edible and full of flavor if cooked for longer, but I tend to squeeze garlic from it after roasting. Generally, it is papery, tough, and fibrous, so it is usually discarded, but it works well for infusing in soups and stocks if strained before blending.

04 CLOVES

There are normally 10–12 cloves in each bulb, and they are the prime part of the garlic plant. When crushed or cut, the flavor compounds in the cloves release a sulfur-based molecule called allicin, which provides their pungent flavor. This is why whole cooked cloves taste sweet rather than pungent.

As far as I'm concerned, there is no such thing as "a little garlic." It provides something deep and sweet, pungent and strong. I've been known to add whole bulbs to my dishes, so turn your recipes up to 11 and try adding an extra clove.

PLANT

Garlic should be planted in fall and harvested in summer from sets sown directly in the ground. It has great immunity-boosting properties, as it is rich in vitamins C and B6 and phosphorus. Hard-neck varieties have a stem that sprouts from the center of the bulb and are ready to lift once the leaves turn yellow and start to dry out, while soft-neck varieties are comprised of leaves and don't produce a central flowering stem. They are ready to harvest when the leaves start to yellow and fold down to the ground. Once lifted, garlic is usually left to dry and can then be braided or bunched. Alternatively, you can forage for wild garlic.

COOKING TIPS

Garlic bulbs are a cooking essential, providing allium flavor, heat, sweetness, and a pungent aroma to almost any dish, while the green leaves can be used as a garnish or sautéed with oil and herbs.

Try using garlic cloves with all sorts of fresh herbs, from sage to sorrel, in a pesto—blend with olive oil, pine nuts or pumpkin seeds, lemon juice, and sea salt. Also try making your own garlic oil by heating several chopped cloves in 1¾ pints (1 liter) olive oil. Bring to a boil, then remove from heat and allow to infuse. Once cool, strain the oil and use the oil-coated garlic to start a risotto or curry sauce.

PREPARATION

To prepare, try peeling the cloves and then slicing, grating, or simply crushing them in a pestle and mortar to release the volatile flavor compounds. A useful way to process larger quantities of garlic all at once is to place two dozen peeled cloves with a pinch of sea salt in a food processor and pulse until they have a coarse diced texture. Then submerge in olive oil and keep in a sealed container in the fridge. Whenever you need some garlic for a recipe, you can simply dip a clean teaspoon in and start cooking—it's a kitchen hack that saves lots of time and effort, and you'll be hard-pressed to taste the difference.

ZERO WASTE

Store garlic in a warm, dry place—not in the fridge, as it may begin to shoot in the cold and damp conditions. (The exception is wild garlic and green garlic.) If you are wasting garlic, you are probably not using enough in your recipes. If in doubt, add another clove, but if you do still end up with a surplus, slice them and make fermented garlic in a 3 percent brine solution for a sweet-sour super ingredient perfect for curries, stir-fries, or ramen dishes. Soft-neck garlic can be dried in a dehydrator at 120°F (50°C) for 6–8 hours to make garlic salt or powder, while wild garlic can be easily preserved—blanch and freeze or make plenty of pesto.

TYPES

COMMON

Common garlic has a mild allium aroma and delicate taste. These bulbs range in size and contain several cloves in a protective layer of pale thin skin. Hard-neck garlic has more flavor than soft-neck varieties.

BLACK

Not its own variety, but garlic that has been cured with heat in a fermentation chamber for about a month. The Maillard reaction transforms the cloves into sweet, balsamic-tasting black garlic with a jellylike texture and plummy tones like a dried fruit. It has a less pungent smell than fresh garlic.

ELEPHANT

Can grow up to 4 in (10 cm) in diameter and produces far fewer cloves. Milder and sweeter than common garlic, closer to leek or onion, often with a yellow hue.

GREEN/SPRING

Thin, green stalks harvested in early spring before the bulbs mature. Sharp and tangy, with a firm texture and strong flavor. It can be used raw or cooked. It is great added to mashed potatoes.

WILD/RAMPS/RAMSONS

The long green leaves, white flowers, scapes, and rhizome roots are all edible. It grows as a leafy perennial most commonly in damp woodlands. It looks similar to the toxic lily of the valley, but when in doubt, the smell is unmistakable.

LIGHT LUNCH

White Garlic Soup

SERVES 4

I first tasted this when I ran a Chateau Takeover at my dad's place in France with some chefs and foodie friends. It seems like an appropriate dish to celebrate again, as it uses the entire garlic bulb and can be served hot or cold, making it a really versatile zero-waste recipe. My version is a combination of what I like best from both the French and Spanish traditions.

INGREDIENTS

½ cup (100 ml) whole milk

1 bouquet garni (bundle of thyme, bay, and parsley)

3½ oz (100 g) yesterday's baguette, plus extra for croutons (if using)

5 tbsp (75 g) butter

6 heads of garlic

½ cup (100 ml) white wine

3½ oz (100 g) blanched almonds

1 tbsp Spanish sherry vinegar

1¾ pints (1 liter) vegetable stock

2 egg yolks

Sea salt and cracked black pepper

Green grapes or croutons with black garlic and Gruyère cheese, to serve (optional)

Method

01 Warm the milk in a small saucepan with the bouquet garni, tearing in chunks of the stale bread. Heat gently for 5 minutes to allow the herbs to infuse and the bread to soften, then remove from heat and set aside.

02 In a large stock pot, melt the butter and add the whole garlic heads. Cook on high heat for 5–10 minutes, stirring regularly so they don't burn but are allowed to caramelize and start browning to create lots of flavor.

03 Pour in the white wine and deglaze the pan, then add in the blanched almonds and sherry vinegar. Follow with the vegetable stock and reduce the heat. Simmer for 45 minutes.

04 Once the garlic has all softened, blend the mixture with a hand-held mixer—the entire garlic bulbs and cloves should turn into a coarse purée.

05 Pass the garlic purée through a sieve, then remove the bouquet garni from the infused milk and mix in the garlic purée. Blend again and, while still warm, pour some into a small bowl with the egg yolks and stir. Once incorporated, add the egg yolk mixture back in with the main soup and stir until smooth and glossy.

06 Season to taste with salt and pepper and garnish with grapes if you plan to serve it cold like a gazpacho or, if serving hot, with croutons made from toasted slices of day-old bread rubbed with black garlic, topped with grated Gruyère, and drizzled with oil.

Smoked Garlic Butter

MAKES ABOUT 14 OZ (400 G)

Homemade butter is a blank canvas for bold flavors, and oak-smoked garlic is my favorite. It's pungent and sweet, rich and creamy, with woody caramel notes peppered with crunchy sea salt flakes. You could also try adding fresh chopped herbs for a splash of color. It's delicious with freshly baked bread, in scrambled eggs, or for sautéing summer greens.

INGREDIENTS

4 tbsp oak wood chips

12 garlic bulbs (you only need 2–3 cloves for this recipe, but it's worth smoking as many as you can manage—they keep for 4–6 weeks)

1¾ pints (1 liter) heavy cream

1 tsp sea salt

Method

01 Start by cold smoking the garlic the day before. You'll need a kettle grill or cold smoker. I light my wood chips in the base of my smoker with the garlic bulbs on a grill above them. I then close the lid and leave for 4–6 hours to smoke—make sure the temperature is 50–85°F (10–30°C). Alternatively, you can leave them overnight for a heavier smoke.

02 To make the butter, remove the cream from the fridge an hour before you start so it's room temperature.

03 Beat the cream in a large bowl with an electric whisk for 4–5 minutes until the cream thickens and forms stiff peaks. Continue whisking past this point until it resembles scrambled eggs. The cream will then separate, leaving pools of buttermilk. Squeeze the buttermilk from

the yellow butter fats and reserve to use later in a smoothie or pancakes.

04 Next, wash the butter by dabbing it repeatedly with clean cheesecloth. Squeeze out as much of the moisture as you can from the cloth each time and rinse it under cold running water.

05 Once you have removed all the water from the butter, mix it with 2–3 cloves of peeled and chopped smoked garlic and season with a generous pinch of salt.

06 Form into a traditional butter-pat shape with some ice-cold wooden pats or a couple of wooden spatulas. Wrap in parchment paper and store in the fridge for up to 1 week. Alternatively, the butter will keep in the freezer for up to 3 months.

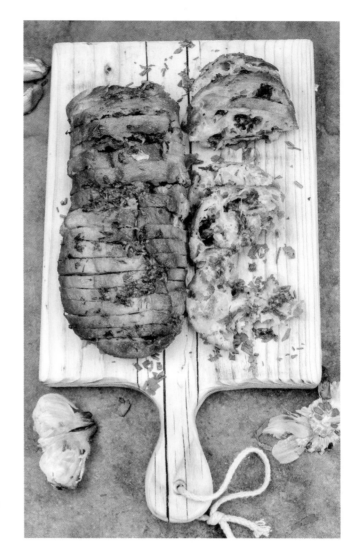

SNACK OR SIDE

Hasselback Smoked Garlic Bread

SERVES 4

Conventional garlic bread is almost always the supporting act in a meal. It's beige and shy and modest and a bit tired of performing the same old songs. But we all know deep down that a good garlic bread can steal the show, and I reckon my version is a cult classic waiting to explode. I love the wave of buttery smoked garlic and herbs between each golden crust. If you want to supercharge this recipe even more, try sprinkling with grated cheese before baking.

INGREDIENTS

2 loaves of ciabatta sourdough

6 smoked garlic cloves, crushed (see opposite)

7 tbsp (100 g) butter, softened

4 tbsp flat-leaf parsley, chopped, plus extra to garnish

2 tbsp olive oil, plus extra for drizzling

Sea salt

Method

01 Preheat a barbecue oven or hot smoker to 350°F (180°C) or a conventional oven to 400°F (200°C).

02 Slice the bread like a Hasselback potato into slices less than ½ in (1 cm) thick.

03 In a bowl, combine the garlic, butter, parsley, and oil, then season with a pinch of salt.

04 Next, carefully spread a generous amount of the herby garlic butter evenly onto each slice of bread.

05 Place the stuffed loaves on a baking sheet lined with foil and drizzle the tops with a little more oil, then bake in the barbecue oven, hot smoker, or conventional oven for 10–15 minutes until the bread is crisp with a golden garlic liquid filling the dough.

06 Sprinkle with some extra parsley and serve hot.

"

There's nothing quite like a bowl of warming pumpkin soup or sweet potato pie on a crisp day as the leaves start to fall outside.

"

FALL

Squash

STOREROOM HERO

Jack O'Lantern

Red Kuri

01

03

02

04

Thelma Sanders

Butternut

05

Becky

INEDIBLE PART

01 STEM

The woody stem is usually brown or dark green and is inedibly fibrous.

EDIBLE PARTS

02 FLESH

This is the prime cut of the squash and is normally orange or pale yellow in color. It can have a spongy-to-firm texture and is often sweet tasting, with a wholesome flavor that develops depth when roasted.

03 PULP

The pulp is often removed and composted, as it is slightly more bitter than the sweet flesh. It also has a stringy texture that makes it unsuitable for many recipes, but it is edible and, once roasted, can be puréed into a soup.

04 SEEDS

Usually cream or light brown, the seeds can be saved for planting and also taste good roasted or fried. They are nutty and a good source of fiber.

05 SKIN

The skin of all squashes and pumpkins is edible, but some types have a thicker skin that resists cooking and is unpleasant to eat. For others, it softens to a sticky, caramelized texture that is delicious when roasted.

Each squash variety has its own unique character and nuanced flavor—and I love each of them equally, with all their quirks and flaws. A jamboree of winter squashes is like a good family get-together—fun, loud, and full of love.

PLANT

Summer squashes, such as pattypan, are the more perishable type, with a thin skin and tender flesh—they are mostly treated like zucchini. Winter squashes mature at the end of summer and have thick skins, hard seeds, and firmer flesh. Most are vine-type plants that are harvested when fully mature. After harvesting, squashes are cured to further harden the skin. This involves air-drying in a warm, well-ventilated place for 7–10 days. They can almost all be stored for months in a cool room. Squash and pumpkin seeds are very high in zinc, and the flesh is rich in vitamins C, A, E, and B, as well as magnesium.

PREPARATION

When choosing squash, always opt for those with smooth, unblemished skin; a firm texture; and a hard stem. I regard them as something of a danger vegetable when chopping or peeling, as the skin can be very strong, as well as being smooth. Use a large, sharp chef's knife for slicing to avoid slipping and hurting yourself, and try using an ordinary vegetable peeler for removing the skins. A robust spoon is also useful when scooping out the pulp and seeds from the internal cavity. I've bent many a spoon scooping out squashes before I settled on a strong favorite for this task. I usually separate the seeds while prepping and clean them up for roasting or drying (see overleaf). Wash off the pulp, dab with paper towel, then dry or cook for a zero-waste snack.

Figure a.

TYPES

BUTTERNUT

A large, bell-shaped squash with light tan skin. It has dense orange flesh with a buttery flavor, a small seed cavity, and tender skin once cooked.

RED KURI

A gorgeous teardrop shape with a smooth skin in vibrant red or orange, with pale-yellow ridging. It has firm, dry skin; a smooth texture; and strong flavor.

PUMPKIN

A long vining plant that has a mild flavor. Inside is a large cavity, making it good for stuffing. Stores very well.

ACORN

A fast-growing ovoid squash in deep orange, pale yellow, and dark green. The skin is ridged and firm, while the flesh is moist, spongy, tender, and sweet.

SPAGHETTI

An oblong squash with pale-yellow skin similar to a melon. The mild flesh is dense but pulls apart into long, translucent strings when cooked.

SWEET DUMPLING

Small, decorative squashes that can be striped with mottled green, yellow, or orange. They have scalloped lobes and a light gold flesh (fig. a). Tender and sweet, they are lovely roasted.

BLUE HUBBARD

A squash with pale-pewter skin and bright, golden flesh. The thin but hard skin covers starchy, semisweet flesh.

CONT.
___

Figure b.

Figure c.

COOKING TIPS

Squash will roast well whole, sliced, or diced. I always try to roast it with the skin on for added flavor. Whole roasted Hasselback squash is certainly worth trying for something a little different (**fig. b**). Preheat the oven to 400°F (200°C) and slice the whole squash in half, then lay it flat and carefully slice down through the skin and flesh, though not all the way through. Stuff a sage leaf in each section, drizzle with olive oil, season with sea salt, and bake for 40–45 minutes. This is a delicious way to cook squash and can be easily served by slicing a few sections onto each plate. Alternatively, if you want to boil or steam your squash, remove the skin first and use it to start off a stock or gravy (see *Zero Waste*). To make a purée suitable for pumpkin pie (see page 167), slice the squash into large segments, remove the seeds, then roast in a preheated oven at 400°F (200°C) for 45 minutes. Peel off the skin, then either mash or blend the flesh into a smooth purée.

ZERO WASTE

Squash opens up huge potential to avoid food waste if you try to cook creatively. All parts except the stem are edible and can release tons of flavor into your recipes. Try roasting, toasting, or frying the seeds rather than throwing them away, and season with chili salt for a snack or crunchy crouton in soups. The skin is tasty when roasted but also makes a rich base for gravy or stock. Fry the skin in a little oil in a saucepan, then enrich with a tablespoon of miso paste before adding in the water. The depth of flavor from the caramelized skin will add a real umami profile to a gravy or rich sauce.

I also strongly recommend trying out fermented squash (**fig. c**). A few years back, I had a try and ended up putting it on a zero-waste menu at a fall pop-up with chestnut-stuffed cabbage (see page 203). After fermenting slices in a 3 percent brine with the skin on, the squash developed a fabulous sweetness, a complex sea-mineral profile, and a sour tang. You can mash it, roast it, or serve it raw in salads.

MAIN MEAL

Squash Gnocchi
SERVES 4

I used to hate making gnocchi with squash, because it is so much wetter than when made with a potato base. That was until I realized that you can simply add a little more flour until you can roll it out easily, and it still ends up tasting fantastic without the same mess. The less flour you add, the lighter the gnocchi, but once cooked, the orange dumplings indented with fork marks take on lots of extra flavor from the rich sage oil and fermented chili.

INGREDIENTS

1 small butternut squash, peeled and roughly diced, seeds removed

1¼–1½ cups (150–200g) all-purpose flour

1 egg, beaten

½ cup (50g) grated Parmesan cheese

½ tsp sea salt, plus extra for seasoning

2 tbsp olive oil

4 pickled garlic cloves, finely sliced

2 tsp fermented chili (see pages 282–285)

8–12 sage leaves

3½oz (100g) kale, roughly chopped

Cracked black pepper

Method

01 Steam the squash for 20–30 minutes until tender, then cool for 10 minutes.

02 Mash the squash or blend in a food processor to a purée, then lay on paper towel to absorb the extra moisture.

03 In a bowl, combine the squash purée with the flour, egg, Parmesan, and salt until you have a doughlike consistency.

04 On a floured surface, roll into 1 in (2.5 cm) cylindrical lengths, then, if time allows, chill in the fridge for 30 minutes. Cut the lengths into 1 in (2.5 cm) sections with a floured knife and mark each gnocchi with the back of a fork.

05 Heat the oil in a frying pan, then add the garlic, chili, sage, and kale.

06 Boil the gnocchi in salted water for 2 minutes until they float, then remove with a slotted spoon, add to the frying pan, and cook for 2–3 minutes. Season with salt and black pepper, then serve.

MAIN MEAL

Pumpkin Soup and Squash Bread
SERVES 4

The bar for this recipe was set pretty high, as my children love eating pumpkin soup and adding their own pinch of salt. I decided to go all out and make a spiced bread with maple-roasted squash and pumpkin seeds, too, in an attempt to win their approval. Luckily, they loved it.

INGREDIENTS

For the bread
1 lb 2 oz (500 g) white
  bread flour
2 tbsp olive oil
2 tsp dried yeast
1 tsp ground cinnamon
1 tsp ground ginger
½ tsp ground nutmeg
½ tsp sea salt
12 oz (350 g) squash, peeled
  and diced
2 tbsp maple syrup
4 tbsp pumpkin seeds

For the soup
1 lb 2 oz (500 g) pumpkin,
  diced and seeds removed
2 onions, chopped
1 red bell pepper, chopped
1 carrot, roughly chopped
4 garlic cloves, chopped
1 tbsp paprika
2 sprigs of thyme
2 tbsp olive oil
1¾ pints (1 liter) vegetable
  stock
1 tsp sea salt
½ tsp black pepper

Method

01 Preheat the oven to 425°F (220°C). To make the bread dough, mix the flour with ¾ cup (200 ml) warm water, 1 tablespoon of the olive oil, the yeast, spices, and salt. Knead for 10 minutes on a floured surface, cover, then proof for 45 minutes to 1 hour.

02 In a roasting pan, drizzle the diced squash for the bread with the remaining olive oil and the maple syrup, then roast in the oven for 20–25 minutes.

03 For the soup, add the pumpkin or butternut squash, vegetables, and garlic to a second roasting pan. Sprinkle with the paprika, thyme, and oil, then roast in the oven for 35–40 minutes.

04 Once the squash for the bread is ready, remove from the oven and allow to cool slightly. Then fold and knead it into the dough with the pumpkin seeds as you punch down the dough. Next, shape and gently lay the dough in a greased loaf pan and allow to proof for 45 minutes more.

05 When the roasted vegetables for the soup are ready, blend in a food processor with the stock and season.

06 Once doubled in size, bake the bread for 35–40 minutes until golden. Serve warm with butter and a bowl of the soup.

DESSERT

Salted Pumpkin and Pecan Pie

SERVES 6

My dad cooked pumpkin pie versus me in a competition years ago on TV, against the dramatic backdrop of the Minack Theatre in Cornwall. I think I lost that battle, but now I've taken my recipe to the next level with a pinch of sea salt in the caramel and a toasted-pecan topping.

INGREDIENTS

1 lb (450 g) shortcrust pastry

For the filling

1 lb (450 g) pumpkin purée (see page 164)

1⅓ cups (200 g) dark brown sugar

1 tsp ground cinnamon

½ tsp ground nutmeg

½ tsp ground ginger

Pinch of ground cloves

3 eggs, beaten

1 tsp cornstarch

¾ cup (200 ml) heavy cream

For the crumble topping

3½ tbsp (50 g) butter

5½ oz (150 g) pecans, crushed

½ cup (100 g) golden sugar

⅓ cup (75 ml) heavy cream

1 tsp sea salt

Method

01 Preheat the oven to 400°F (200°C). Roll the pastry into a circle about 14 in (35 cm) in diameter. Line a 9 in (23 cm) pie pan with the pastry and trim off any excess. Cover with parchment paper, fill with baking beans, then blind bake for 15 minutes. Remove from the oven, remove the beans, and let the case cool in the pan.

02 To make the filling, whisk the pumpkin purée, sugar, spices, eggs, cornstarch, and cream in a large bowl. Pour the mixture into the baked pastry crust, leaving space for it to rise. Bake in the oven for 50 minutes until nearly set.

03 Next, make the crumble topping. Melt the butter in a saucepan and add the crushed pecans and sugar. Cook for 3–4 minutes until the butter browns and the sugar caramelizes. Then add in the cream and season with the salt. Remove from heat and spread over the top of your pumpkin pie for an even layer of salted caramel and pecan crumble.

04 Bake the pie for a final 5–10 minutes, then allow to cool on a wire rack. Serve sprinkled with a pinch of sea salt.

Beet

HUMBLE AND SWEET

'Burpees Golden'

'Chioggia'

'Detroit'

EDIBLE PARTS

01 LEAVES

The iron-rich, heart-shaped leaves grow 2–8in (5–20cm) long. They are edible when young and have a semibitter taste similar to chard. Baby leaves can be eaten raw as the tastiest of salad greens, but larger leaves should be cooked.

02 STEMS

These brightly colored, tender stems are wonderful cooked and can be sautéed, steamed, or added to stir-fries.

03 SKIN

The skin is often tougher than the flesh but is edible and has a robust, earthy flavor. Cooking the bulb with the skin on helps retain nutrients and keeps the flesh moist. If peeling, try frying the skin for beet-peel chips.

04 FLESH

The vibrant, firm flesh of a beet has a sweet and earthy flavor. The texture is crunchy but softens when cooked. Younger bulbs can be eaten raw, but larger, mature globes benefit from roasting or pickling.

05 TAPROOT

Remove and clean the taproot before cooking. They are very good added to stir-fries or pickled. I find they taste similar to young bulbs but can be less sweet and a little more woody.

Beets may appear humble on the outside, but the jewel-like bulb brings a very earthy flavor and a star quality all its own. The beet is the proverbial peasant poet—deep rooted and with much to say—worthy of all our praise.

PLANT

Beets are a hardy crop that yield both bulbs and leaves. They can be sown densely in rows to then harvest the delicate baby leaves. Once thinned out, the bulbs grow quite large depending on the variety. The larger the bulb, the tougher and woodier the core; young, smaller beets tend to be sweeter. All of the plant is edible, and there are some wonderful heritage varieties. Beets are very high in vitamins A and C, beta-carotene, and potassium and boast numerous health benefits, including lowering cholesterol and supporting liver function. When selecting beets, look for firm, smooth bulbs with undamaged skins.

COOKING TIPS

Beets are best pickled, roasted, or raw as a dramatic garnish. You can also steam them if you want to retain a clean flavor. They're cooked when you can slide a knife into the center without much resistance.

Beets pair perfectly with any lactic or acidic tang. One of my favorite combinations is to pickle fine slices in raspberry vinegar for an enriched acidic note—try serving with horseradish crème fraîche and toasted walnuts. Alternatively, a goat cheese salad with fig and balsamic never fails.

Beets are also ideal for sweet dishes. Try salted chocolate brownies enriched with grated beets. I also use beet juice for a refreshing sorbet or winter berry smoothie.

PREPARATION

Butchering a beet can feel like dealing with a bleeding vegetable. It requires a range of knife skills—trimming the leaves, peeling with a paring knife, chopping julienne—or you can simply grate, dice, or finely slice. Pick similar-sized beets when preparing to roast so that they cook at the same rate, and before cooking, trim off the leaves and stems and remove the taproot. These are all edible, but they will overcook if dealt with in the same fashion as the bulb. Always try to keep the skin on when cooking to retain nutrients and color. And if roasting or steaming whole, leave on ½–¾ in (1–2 cm) of the stems so the color doesn't leak out.

ZERO WASTE

Beets seem to multiply in the fridge in fall, but there are lots of ways to avoid wasting them. Try shredding the stems into a coleslaw or gently sautéing them with lemon and olive oil. The leaves can be cooked in a similar way to spinach or chard, and, once blanched, they also freeze well. The taproots are excellent cooked in a pan with a little oil or butter. They can also be fried whole and added to vegetable-peel chips.

My go-to zero-waste recipe is beet hummus. Roast the beets first, then blend with garlic, tahini, lemon juice, dried apricots, and cumin seeds for a delicious mauve dip. Beets are also fantastic preserved in vinegar with red onion.

TYPES

GOLDEN

A heritage beet; when harvested young, the roots, sweet bulb, and delicate stems are particularly tasty. It has long, crisp leaves, and the bulb tapers slightly at the end. Beneath the orange skin is yellow flesh ringed in white gold. It is crunchy and tender, mild, sweet, and earthy. A striking addition to salads and slaw.

LARGE RED

The most popular type of beet. It varies in size but is generally a larger bulb. Under the firm red skin is a deep-crimson flesh that is dense and crunchy. When cooked, it develops a sweet flavor and soft texture. The leaves are edible but tend to be more bitter than those of smaller beets, similar to mature rainbow chard.

STRIPED

These are predominantly Italian heirloom varieties that come with pink and white stripes or colorful rings in the flesh. They taste as delicious as they look.

WHITE

Easily mistaken for a radish or baby turnip, these white bulbs are moist and crisp with a gentle, sweet, earthy flavor.

CYLINDRA

An elongated beet with dark-maroon skin and a sweet flavor, also called half-long or stump-rooted. Their long, cylindrical roots can grow up to 8 in (20 cm). The greens are sweeter than other varieties and taste particularly "beety." Best sliced on a Japanese mandoline.

MAIN MEAL

Beet Wellington
SERVES 4

A Wellington takes time, but it's worth it when you have such a celebration of beets to enjoy. The chard leaves replace a classic pancake for wrapping, and my duxelles is a blend of herby mushrooms and walnuts, providing more earthy support for the sweet beets. Serve this as a lovely sharing dish with salad or roasted vegetables and horseradish mustard.

INGREDIENTS

4 large beets, leaves removed

2 tbsp olive oil

1 lb 2 oz (500 g) puff pastry

9 oz (250 g) large chard leaves

1 egg, beaten

1 tsp cracked black pepper

For the duxelles

2¼ lb (1 kg) mushrooms, finely diced

2 shallots, finely diced

2 tbsp olive oil

4 garlic cloves, chopped

2 tsp chopped rosemary

3½ oz (100 g) walnuts, chopped

⅓ cup (75 ml) sweet sherry

½ cup (50 g) breadcrumbs

Sea salt and cracked black pepper

Method

01 Preheat the oven to 400°F (200°C). Roast the beets for 1 hour coated in the olive oil.

02 Once cooked, peel the beets and trim off their bases, then slice into rounds ½ in (1 cm) thick.

03 Make the duxelles by softening the diced mushrooms and shallots in the olive oil. Add in the garlic, rosemary, and walnuts. Cook for 4–5 minutes, then add in the sherry. Sauté for 3–4 minutes until the sherry reduces, then combine with breadcrumbs in a mixing bowl. Season to taste with salt and black pepper.

04 Remove any large stems from the chard leaves and blanch in salted boiling water for 2–3 minutes, then drain and allow to cool on a kitchen towel.

05 Roll out the puff pastry into 2 large rectangular sheets of about 8 × 12 in (20 × 30 cm). Arrange a sheet of puff pastry on a lined baking sheet. Top with the chard leaves, then spread out one-third of the duxelles mixture along the center.

06 Place the slices of cooked beets on top of the duxelles mixture to form a long cylinder. Cover with the remaining duxelles and wrap with the chard into a tidy log shape.

07 Cover with the second pastry sheet, use a fork to crimp the pastry edges together, then score the top to allow steam to escape while baking. Wash with the beaten egg and sprinkle with black pepper. Bake for 25–30 minutes until the pastry is golden and flaky. Serve warm.

Beet Dough Balls and Dill Butter

MAKES 12–15

I first tried beet bread when a good friend of mine set up his artisan bakery over a decade ago. It quickly became his signature bread, and he still bakes it today. The delicate beet sweetness in the dough provides a wonderful flavor and fun pink color. For my version, I've served the warm dough balls with dill butter and some pickled beets on the side.

INGREDIENTS

For the dough balls
2½ tsp (7g) dried yeast
3½ tbsp (50g) butter, melted
⅓ cup (75ml) beet juice
1 tsp granulated sugar
1¾oz (50g) grated beets
Sea salt
1 tbsp olive oil
2½ cups (300g) all-purpose flour

For the pickles
1 tbsp granulated sugar
⅓ cup (75ml) cider vinegar
½ tsp mustard seeds
1 tsp chopped dill stalks
1 beet, leaves removed and sliced
½ small cucumber, sliced
½ red onion, sliced

For the dill butter
5¼ tbsp (75g) butter, softened
1 tbsp chopped dill

Method

01 For the dough, whisk together the yeast, ½ cup (100ml) warm water, melted butter, beet juice, and sugar in a bowl and leave to ferment for 15 minutes.

02 In a separate bowl, combine the grated beet, a pinch of salt, the oil, and flour and gradually stir in the beet water. Knead on a floured surface for 10 minutes, then leave covered in a bowl to proof for 1 hour.

03 Meanwhile, make the pickles. Heat the sugar, vinegar, mustard seeds, dill stalks, and ¼ cup (50ml) boiling water in a small pan and bring to a boil. In a container, submerge the sliced vegetables in the hot liquid. Seal and allow to cool for 20–25 minutes, then drain.

04 Whip together the softened butter and chopped dill.

05 Once proofed, punch down the dough, divide into 12–15 lumps, and form into small balls. Place on a lined baking sheet to rise for 30 minutes more and preheat the oven to 425°F (220°C).

06 Bake for 20–25 minutes until just starting to brown, then serve with the pickles and dill butter.

SIDE OR STARTER

Dirty Beets and Labneh with Black Dukkah

SERVES 2

This recipe shows how candy-sweet beets can be. The super-fresh sweetness, earthiness, and delicate nuttiness are sealed in by harsh, dirty cooking on a bed of glowing coals. I've paired them with acidic strained yogurt, peppery nasturtium oil, and a charcoal-black dukkah. Wilt the beet tops over the grill until they soften for a mild bitterness that completes the dish.

INGREDIENTS

8–12 small beets, bulb and leaves separated
12 nasturtium leaves
⅓ cup (75 ml) olive oil
5½ oz (150 g) labneh

For the dukkah
1 tbsp charcoal salt
1 tsp nori flakes
Pinch of dried rose petals
1 tsp black sesame seeds
½ tsp thyme
½ tsp smoked chili flakes
1 tbsp roasted walnuts

Method

01 In a grill or pit, build a fire with charcoal or wood. Allow to burn for 45 minutes, then spread out the coals.

02 Cook the beets directly on the hot coals for 30–45 minutes depending on their size. Turn with tongs every 15 minutes. Once the skin has blackened and the flesh inside has softened, remove from the fire and allow to cool slightly.

03 Wilt the beet tops for 2–3 minutes over the coals in a wire basket or on a grill.

04 Blend the nasturtium leaves with the oil, then warm the mixture over the coals in a pan. Once it reaches boiling point, cool and strain through a fine sieve.

05 Next, make the dukkah by blending all the ingredients in a spice blender.

06 Halve or slice the beets and serve with the labneh. Dress with the nasturtium oil, a sprinkling of black dukkah, and the wilted greens. (Don't eat the charred skin; the flesh easily comes away from it.)

Broccoli

FLOWER POWER

Purple sprouting

Calabrese

01

02

03

04

Tenderstem

Broccolini

EDIBLE PARTS

01 FLORETS

The tight clusters of unopened flowers form either around a central head or on elongated stems. These florets can be eaten raw or cooked for a couple of minutes to enhance the color and soften the stems.

02 LEAVES

All broccoli leaves are edible and can be cooked along with the florets or sautéed in a little oil with lemon juice. Larger, darker-green leaves will taste more bitter than younger ones.

03 STEM

The stem of all broccoli is edible and doesn't need to be discarded. Some varieties have a thicker stem with a slightly woody texture, so may require longer cooking than slender stems.

04 FLOWERS

Once the broccoli plant is fully mature or has bolted, it produces edible flowers that are a bright canary yellow. They have a subtle peppery flavor and look fantastic on salads.

You must eat your broccoli—it's a vegetable commandment.
It may have arrived late to the superfood game, but broccoli is
one of the healthiest—and tastiest—plants to cook at home.
It is bright, snappy, and flowery, like a '60s rock song.

PLANT

One of the reasons I love broccoli so much is that it has a wide range of tastes and textures, from soft and flowery to fibrous and crunchy. It's a nutrient-packed green vegetable from the cabbage family that is high in fiber, phosphorous, potassium, iron, and zinc, with an edible treelike trunk that sprouts branches or forms clusters of small flower heads that turn bright green when cooked. The plant provides many edible parts over a long growing season. When harvesting, use a sharp garden knife to remove the stems without bruising them.

COOKING TIPS

The most important thing to remember when cooking broccoli is that it only requires steaming or boiling for a few minutes, while roasting releases unforetold umami profiles, as does slow-roasting the stems. Alternatively, the stems and florets can both be eaten raw—try grated stems in a slaw or grated florets as a crunchy topping for salads. For me, the flavors go particularly well with rich, savory ingredients such as Parmesan, black garlic, blue cheese, hazelnuts, and fermented chili. Italian herbs and Indian spices also bring out the delicate natural sweetness.

PREPARATION

Choose firm stems and dark-green heads for freshness. If it looks yellow, the broccoli is probably past its freshest, though it will still be good for soups or roasting (see *Zero Waste*). My knife of choice for breaking down broccoli is a boning knife with a sharp point and flexible profile that enables you to easily turn around the plant. I break it down into florets on small bunches, which take far less time to cook than the stems. You should be left with the heart if working on a central head. This and the thicker stems can be chopped into smaller pieces and cooked at the same rate as the finer tender branches.

ZERO WASTE

Unwashed broccoli keeps for 7–10 days in the fridge. When florets develop a yellow tinge, try making broccoli soup: blanch in boiling water, then blend with leek and potato or blue cheese and celery root. Broccoli rice is another favorite for avoiding waste. I often combine grated broccoli 50:50 with grated cauliflower, then roast them with coconut oil. Blanched and frozen, broccoli can be stored for up to a year—I sometimes use it in a smoothie instead of frozen spinach or avocado; the grassy flavor is delicious with oat milk, ginger, and lime.

The tougher stems are often the part left over, so try shaving them into ribbons to add to stir-fries or slicing them thinly and pickling in a sweet vinegar solution.

TYPES

CALABRESE

Often sold just as "broccoli," this is a bright-green variety that does have a central head but, once cut, grows many. It's an older variety with thick stems and petite frilly leaves. The small florets are fast to bolt, thus providing flowers.

HEADING BROCCOLI

Also known as cauliflower broccoli, this is a large, tightly formed variety with dense curds that form off a central branch. It's easy to break down into smaller sections for cooking.

BABY

Also known as sprouting broccoli, this variety has far smaller heads with long, thin stalks that emerge from a central branch. The popular Tenderstem is a relatively new hybrid of Chinese kale and broccoli. It arrives in summer and produces vigorous side shoots that have a tender, mild flavor. Can be eaten raw and is great in stir-fries.

PURPLE SPROUTING

A late-cropping variety with elegant silvery-green leaves; long, stiff stems; and tiny deep-purple flowers. The flavor is somewhat peppery. They lose their vibrant purple color when cooked for longer. It's also possible to get white sprouting broccoli.

ROMANESCO

Ornate clusters of yellow-green flowers are packed around a tight fractal spiral that radiates upward. Intense in flavor, it is nutty and slightly sweet, crunchy and tender, with a crisp bite.

MAIN MEAL

Miso-roasted Broccoli Stems and Floret Rice

SERVES 2

I've made this dish a few times using different techniques and, after some practice, I've found the winning recipe. This is the easiest and tastiest version. It's not slowly poaching, confit, or roasting—it's a combination of all these. The broccoli stems are cooked in a pan with stock and sesame oil, regularly tilting the pan to baste them with the hot miso glaze as it reduces and becomes thick and glossy. The stems are then roasted in the oven for a final umami char.

INGREDIENTS

2 tbsp sesame oil

2 calabrese broccoli stems, trimmed

2 sheets of nori, to serve

For the miso glaze

2 tbsp red miso paste

2 tbsp agave nectar

2 tbsp soy sauce

1 tbsp kombu flakes

1 tbsp mirin

2 cups (500 ml) dashi stock

For the floret rice

2 heads of calabrese broccoli

3½ oz (100 g) cashew nuts

1 tbsp coconut oil

1 tbsp soy sauce

Method

01 Preheat the oven to 400°F (200°C), then prepare the floret rice. Blend the broccoli heads and cashew nuts coarsely in a food processor until you have a chunky consistency. Spread out on a baking sheet, then drizzle with the coconut oil and soy sauce and set aside.

02 In an oven-safe frying pan, heat the sesame oil and sear the broccoli stalks on all sides for 2–3 minutes.

03 Mix all the glaze ingredients except the dashi stock together in a small bowl and add to the pan to start glazing the broccoli. Once the miso glaze has begun to reduce and bubble, start spooning it over the stalks to baste them. Add the dashi stock gradually to keep the glaze slack enough to spoon over the stalks while maintaining a high rolling boil. After 10 minutes, the glaze should have reduced and the stalks should be well coated and sticky.

04 Place both the baking sheet of floret rice and the oven-safe pan containing the glazed stalks into the oven and roast for 15 minutes.

05 Serve the floret rice and stalks on an edible sheet of nori.

SIDE

Tandoori Purple Broccoli with Masala Sauce

SERVES 2

Cook this dish either in a hot oven or over glowing embers. The blackened purple broccoli tips take on a deep, earthy flavor that sings alongside the sweet stems and delicate flower shoots. It's colorful and bold and unleashes another side to this tender vegetable. You could also try a whole tandoori-roasted broccoli served in a rich curry sauce.

INGREDIENTS

12 purple-sprouting
  broccoli stems
Sea salt
Pink pickled onions,
  to garnish
Charcoal salt

For the tandoori rub
1 tsp paprika
1 tsp turmeric
1 tsp coriander seeds
1 tsp fennel seeds
1 tsp sea salt
½ tsp Kashmiri chili
  powder
2 tbsp canola oil

For the masala sauce
3½ tbsp (50 g) ghee
1 tsp grated garlic
1 tsp grated fresh ginger root
½ onion, finely diced
1 tsp garam masala
1 tsp ground coriander
½ tsp red chili powder
½ tsp turmeric
1 tsp ground cardamom
1 tbsp tomato paste
Sea salt

Method

01 Preheat the oven to 425°F (220°C) or light a fire under a grill. First, mix the tandoori spices with the canola oil, then rub this over the broccoli.

02 For the masala sauce, start by melting the ghee in a saucepan. Blend the garlic, ginger, onion, and spices in a food processor, then mix into the ghee to form a smooth paste. Add the tomato paste and a splash of water to slacken the mixture and simmer for 5–10 minutes. Season to taste with the salt.

03 Either roast or grill the spiced broccoli stems for 8–10 minutes until charred and crispy in places, turning if necessary. Season with the sea salt.

04 Serve the charred broccoli with the masala sauce spooned over the top. Garnish with pink pickled onions to cut through the rich spice and season to taste with the charcoal salt.

SIDE OR LIGHT LUNCH

Tempura Broccoli with Soy Sauce
SERVES 2

Tempura vegetables go through phases of popularity a bit like music, but like any good song, they come back around for a retro revival. This recipe was cool to me back in the '90s with my baggy jeans and bowl haircut, and I'm digging it again now that I've given it a fresh seaweed twist. Biting through the light, crisp, golden batter into tender, sweet-stemmed broccoli beneath, you find a gently spiced but umami-packed treat that rocks loudly.

INGREDIENTS

Vegetable oil, for deep-frying

10–12 Tenderstem broccoli stems

2 tbsp all-purpose flour

For the dipping sauce

2 spring onions, finely sliced

½ red chili, seeded and finely diced

⅓ cup (75 ml) soy sauce

1 tbsp mirin or rice vinegar

1 tsp sesame oil

1 tsp honey

1 tsp sesame seeds

1 tsp grated fresh ginger root

For the tempura batter

½ cup (50 g) all-purpose flour

⅓ cup (50 g) cornstarch

1 tsp baking powder

½ cup (100 ml) sparkling water, chilled

1 tbsp nori flakes

1 tsp shichimi

Method

01 First, make the dipping sauce by whisking all the ingredients together in a bowl, then leave to marinate while you make the tempura.

02 Preheat the vegetable oil in a large wok or fryer to 350°F (180°C).

03 Blanch the broccoli spears for 1 minute in boiling water, then drain and dredge in the all-purpose flour.

04 Make the tempura batter by whisking the ingredients together in a bowl until smooth and bubbly. Evenly coat the dredged broccoli spears in the batter before frying them in small batches so you don't lower the temperature of the hot oil. Cook for 3–4 minutes until the batter is golden and crisp. Remove from the oil with a slotted spoon and place on a sheet of paper towel to drain off any excess oil. Serve with the soy dipping sauce.

Mushrooms

MYSTERY MADE MANIFEST

Portobello

Baby portobella

01

02

Shiitake

Cremini

White cap

Button

Oyster

Large flat

03

EDIBLE PARTS

01 STEM

The stem tends to be the most robust part of a mushroom and can withstand the most cooking. Trim larger stems and try frying or sautéing in butter to release the woody aroma.

02 GILLS

Delicate gills form the underside of most mushrooms and can be easily damaged when cleaning or cutting. Avoid overstirring in the pan, as they can disintegrate quickly and leave your mushrooms bruised and dirty.

03 CAP

The top of a mushroom is the prime cut and may sometimes need peeling or gently brushing with a mushroom or vegetable brush to remove any soil or growing medium. Smaller caps can be cooked whole or halved and larger mushrooms can be cleanly sliced to pickle, fry, or add to stews.

Like alien eruptions, the mushrooms we cook with are the fruiting bodies of a vast, unseen underground network, and their bursting forth is one of the great wonders of the plant world. It's a mesmerizing process that fills me with awe.

PLANT

It takes years to fully understand how mushrooms grow—I can recognize some types of fungi, but there are several hundred that I just don't know. And as the old saying goes, all mushrooms are edible, but some only once in a lifetime, so treat them with care and never pick and eat them if you are not 100 percent certain what they are and how to cook them safely. I won't offer a wild guide to these tasty plants in this book, as advice is like the mushrooms themselves: the wrong kind can be dangerous. Instead, I want to focus on cultivated mushrooms that you can commonly buy from grocers, artisan growers, and markets (**fig. a**).

Figure a.

PREPARATION

When selecting mushrooms from stores, choose firm, undamaged ones that have a taut skin on the cap and clean gills. The stems should have been cut cleanly and they should smell sweet and earthy, not musty and damp. Gently brush off any soil, straw, or growing compost. Wash under a cold tap if required, but dry well before storing in the fridge.

For most mushrooms, I treat the stem and cap as the two major parts to be cooked together; for large mushrooms, I often remove the stem, as it's more fibrous, but I like to cook it by slicing into similar-sized pieces to the cap. Small mushrooms, such as the button mushroom and enoki, can be cooked or pickled whole.

Use a paring knife when working with delicate mushrooms. You may want to use a teaspoon to remove the dark gills, as they can darken a dish and leach a mushy texture into the recipe when cooked. But don't discard these parts; use them in a mushroom ketchup or dry them on a baking sheet for an intense seasoning to add to a barbecue sauce, nut roast, or stew.

TYPES

CHANTERELLE

Yellow to orange mushrooms with a frilly trumpet shape, firm flesh, and slightly rubbery texture. They have a fruity, earthy taste.

BABY PORTOBELLA

A closed-cup mushroom with a strong flavor and meaty texture. Similar to button and cremini in appearance but darker in color.

OYSTER

A delicate shell shape that grows in overlapping tiers in gray, pink, or yellow. They can lose their color when cooked but keep their chewy texture and robust flavor.

SHIITAKE

Has a firm cap, light-brown flesh, chewy stem, garlic-pine aroma, and smoky flavor.

CEPS

Also known as porcini and often sold dried or as a powder, these have a rich flavor; red-brown top; and meaty, velvety texture.

ENOKI

A favorite in Japan, these long white mushrooms are good in soups, with noodles, or pickled.

PORTOBELLO

A large brown mushroom with a meaty texture that can be stuffed or baked whole. A good veggie alternative to a burger.

CREMINI

Light tan to rich brown and stronger than their button cousins, with an earthier taste and firmer texture.

CONT.

Figure b.

Figure c.

COOKING TIPS

Don't overcrowd the pan when you cook mushrooms. They leach out lots of stored water, and if you try to cook too many in one pan, they'll sweat and remain limp and soggy. Whereas if you cook them in a large pan with room for the water to evaporate and with oil or butter working the edges, they will brown with an umami charm while the flavor intensifies.

Deviled mushrooms on sourdough toast has to be my favorite brunch dish. The mushrooms are sautéed in butter with a pinch of paprika. Once browned, add sherry and reduce, then add cream and fresh thyme. I love the rich paprika, velvety cream, and butter-fried mushrooms. Adding a splash of sherry, white wine, or vermouth elevates the dish, and the cooked mushrooms soak up the flavor as you deglaze the pan.

A fun idea I picked up from an American chef is to use large mushroom stems like scallops in a risotto: pan seared in a beurre noisette and flambéed for dramatic effect in Marsala wine. You then use the diced caps sautéed for a rich mushroom and saffron risotto with a dusting of porcini powder to finish (**fig. b**).

ZERO WASTE

Mushrooms have a notoriously short shelf life. I store them in a paper bag in the fridge but always try to use them within a few days of buying. One go-to recipe for using them up is to soften them with shallots, rosemary, garlic, and thyme, then blend until smooth. Add milk, cream, and stock for a smooth autumnal soup that freezes well.

The best preserving method is to dehydrate them. Thinly slice larger mushrooms and wash and dry smaller ones, then dry in an oven or dehydrator at 130°F (55°C) for 8–14 hours. Store in an airtight container or blend into a dried mushroom powder for an umami seasoning.

Smaller mushrooms were made to be pickled. Allow the solution of 2:2:1 vinegar, water, and sugar to cool for 15 minutes before pouring over the mushrooms so it doesn't scald and soften them. Add other bold flavors such as Sichuan pepper, star anise, mustard, radish, red onion, and chili (**fig. c**). Use within 10–14 days once opened, and serve with ramen or stir-fries.

MAIN MEAL

Mushroom Hand Pie
MAKES 4

Every country has their version of a pie to eat on the move. Where I live in Cornwall, we call it a pasty; in Mexico, an empanada; in Poland, a pierogi, and in New Zealand and Australia, it's a hand pie. For this version, I've paired earthy baby portobella mushrooms, a leek for allium warmth, and tarragon for sophisticated anise notes. It's a pocket full of comfort-food joy.

INGREDIENTS

1 lb 2 oz (500 g) puff pastry
3½ tbsp (50 g) butter
9 oz (250 g) baby portobella mushrooms, diced
1 small leek, finely sliced
⅓ cup (75 ml) white wine
1 tbsp chopped tarragon
1 tsp lemon zest
½ tsp sea salt
Ground white pepper
1 tsp cornstarch
1 egg, beaten

Method

01 Preheat the oven to 400°F (200°C). Roll the pastry into 2 sheets about 8 × 12 in (20 × 30 cm) and select 2 large pastry cutters—one about ¾ in (2 cm) larger than the other. Cut out 4 pastry disks with the larger cutter and 4 with the smaller one.

02 Add the butter to a pan and sauté the mushrooms and leek for 4–5 minutes. Add the white wine, tarragon, and zest, and season with salt and white pepper.

03 Cook for 3–4 minutes until the wine has reduced, then add the cornstarch. Stir, then remove from heat and allow to cool.

04 Put a small handful of the filling in the center of each smaller pastry disk. Then wet the edge, lay the larger disk on top, and gently press with a fork to seal. Score and make a small hole in the top for steam to escape.

05 Lay on a lined baking sheet. Brush with egg, bake for 20–25 minutes, and enjoy.

MAIN MEAL

Chicken Fried Mushroom Burger

SERVES 2

I confess I have a soft spot for takeout and fast-food burgers. But I try to avoid eating processed ingredients, so I've often found myself in a quandary. My answer is to create delicious, seasonal alternatives at home. I think this whole trend is now called "fakeouts," but I call it eating with a conscience. Every so often, one of my fast-food substitutes becomes more than just an imitation, and this recipe is a case in point. I'm glad to share my secret 11-spice mix in the hope that you enjoy it as much as I do.

INGREDIENTS

12 oyster mushrooms
2 tbsp all-purpose flour
2 eggs, beaten
Vegetable oil, for deep-frying
2 brioche buns, halved and toasted
Barbecue sauce, pickled onions, sea beans, and truffle, to serve
2 rosemary skewers

For the spiced crumb
2 tbsp paprika
1 tbsp ground white pepper
1 tsp ground ginger
1 tsp ground black pepper
1 tsp dried mustard
1 tsp garlic powder
1 tsp smoked salt
½ tsp dried thyme
½ tsp oregano
½ tsp celery salt
½ tsp grated nutmeg
½ cup (50 g) panko breadcrumbs

Method

01 Start by combining the 11 spices with the panko breadcrumbs in a large bowl. I use breadcrumbs to coat rather than all-purpose flour because I like the crunchy contrast with soft, meaty mushroom.

02 Pane the mushrooms by dipping them in the all-purpose flour, then the beaten eggs, and finally the spiced crumb. Repeat if you want a thicker layer of crispy coating on the mushrooms.

03 Deep-fry a few coated mushrooms at a time in hot oil at 375°F (190°C) for 4–5 minutes until golden and crispy. Don't crowd the pan to maintain a high temperature. Remove from the oil with a slotted spoon and drain on paper towel, then keep warm in the oven at 250°F (130°C) while you fry the next batch.

04 Serve on toasted brioche buns with barbecue sauce, pickled onions, sea beans, and slices of truffle. Skewer each burger together with a woody sprig of rosemary.

MAIN MEAL

Fire-roasted Mushrooms and Cured Egg Yolk

SERVES 2

This dish tastes best with the smell of leaf mold at your feet and sweet woodsmoke rising from the grill. The fierce heat and wood compounds infuse the mushrooms with fire flavor, while the lacinato kale shields them as you cook. The semicured egg yolk caps it all off for an umami, salty finish.

INGREDIENTS

2 egg yolks

4 tbsp seaweed salt

1 tsp cracked black pepper

2¼ lb (1 kg) mixed mushrooms

4 lacinato kale leaves, roughly chopped

1 tbsp truffle oil

1 tbsp chopped rosemary

Black truffle, to garnish (optional)

Method

01 Lay the egg yolks on a bed of seaweed salt and black pepper and cure in the fridge for 1 hour on each side.

02 Build a fire and let it die down to hot, glowing embers.

03 In a bowl, dress the mushrooms and lacinato kale in the truffle oil and rosemary. Then lower them over the fire in a wire basket to within an inch of the hot coals. Cook for 2–3 minutes and toss to char on all sides.

04 Brush off some of the salt and pepper from the egg and serve with the mushrooms and lacinato kale. To elevate the dish further, grate over some fresh black truffle.

Carrots

SWEET, CRISP, AND FULL OF PROMISE

EDIBLE PARTS

01 LEAVES

The feathery leaves are highly perishable, lasting only 1–2 days in the fridge. They have a delicate parsley flavor and can be eaten raw or wilted or puréed into pesto. They also crisp up very nicely in hot oil and can make a lovely fried snack. Larger leaves are more bitter.

02 STEMS

The thin green stems are fibrous and often discarded but can be sautéed in oil and cooked like pea pods or asparagus spears. They have a peppery flavor similar to dill and fennel, which both happen to be relatives, and a subtle bitterness that responds well when citrus is added. The carrot stems can also be blanched and incorporated into pesto or soups.

03 SKIN

Like other vegetables, the majority of the nutrients in carrots are just under the skin, so they are best scrubbed or scraped rather than peeled.

04 ROOT

The entire carrot root, including the thin root hairs, is edible. The flesh itself is crisp and crunchy when raw, with a slightly tougher core. Carrot roots are usually conical and tapered but grow gnarly and forked depending on the cultivar and soil conditions.

Bright, plump, and crisp, plumed with feathery green tops, carrots boost broths and stews and make meals instantly more nutritious, but we've only recently started to discover the full culinary potential of this sweet, earthy root.

PLANT

The carrot is a root vegetable with a piney, fruity, woody flavor. Second only to beets in sugar levels, they are highly suitable for both savory and sweet recipes. They vary in length—typically 4–10 in (10–25 cm)—and grow in a range of colors, from orange to purple, red to yellow. The darker the color, generally the sweeter the flavor. Carrots are low in calories, high in flavor, and brimming with beta-carotene—the main dietary source of vitamin A, which supports normal growth and benefits our immune system, skin, and vision. They're also an excellent source of vitamins B1, B2, B6, C, and K; potassium; and magnesium.

Figure a.

PREPARATION

Choose stiff, firm carrots with bright, feathery tops. If they bend or have cracking on the skin, they are probably old and starting to wilt. Always remove the greens as soon as you have them in the kitchen and store them separately wrapped in a sheet of damp paper towel. The carrot root will dry out otherwise, as the tops suck out the moisture. Use the tops within 1–2 days. Clean the root with a stiff kitchen brush to remove any soil. Peel if desired, but I tend to keep the skin on, as it is rich in nutrients. You can grate them, spiralize them, or cook them whole. They can also be diced, sliced, or prepared julienne, so get ready to test out your vegetable knife skills.

TYPES

PURPLE

*Many are purple on the outside but remain pale orange or white at the core (**fig. a**). They are intensely sweet and slightly peppery. The color fades when cooked, so they are best pickled or raw.*

RED

These taste similar to orange carrots. The color comes from the antioxidant lycopene, which has been linked to better heart health and protection against sunburn and some cancers.

GOLDEN

Also known as white carrots, with a subtle cream or yellow color and mild, sweet flavor. They work well roasted with maple syrup, honey, or thyme.

CHANTENAY

An heirloom variety that's shorter in length but greater in girth than standard carrots. Available in many colors, they have a smooth skin and a snappy texture when raw and develop earthy notes when cooked.

NANTES

Neatly cylindrical with a rounded tip, it has firm orange skin and long, leafy greens. The fine-grained flesh is crisp with little to no core in the center. It has a tender and sweeter flavor profile than most carrots.

BABY

Refers to any variety that is harvested early for a smaller root. Crunchier and sweeter than mature carrots, they are therefore favored in salads.

CONT.

Figure b.

Figure c.

COOKING TIPS

Carrots are notoriously sweet, and even more so when lightly cooked. They lose very few nutrients in the process; it can even make some nutrients more digestible. They can be roasted, boiled, steamed, stir-fried, or grilled and can also be used in desserts. My favorite flavor combinations for carrots are caraway and cumin seeds, dill, thyme, or ginger. If you are looking for a stock-pot essential, carrot will be first in line. The trio of carrot, onion, and celery fried in oil forms the flavor base of many dishes—a classic mirepoix in French cuisine and soffritto in Spanish. Soffritto is fried slowly and cooked with generous amounts of olive oil. You can also add garlic, parsley, rosemary, and bay leaf for a more aromatic version.

For something a little more unusual, carrot jerky is my hybrid idea to cure baby carrots in a sweet, dry cure with sugar, sea salt, spices, and vinegar. After a few days, you wash off the cure, pat dry, then cold smoke the carrots for 12 hours. You can then dehydrate them further for a chewy snack similar to biltong (**fig. b**). It's a fun thing to try, and I believe we will see plenty more creative vegetable charcuterie concepts over the coming years.

ZERO WASTE

Carrots are best kept in a fridge with good air circulation around them and can store for up to a month. To reduce waste, consider juicing them as the base for smoothies with ginger root and turmeric. Carrot juice can also be fermented by adding 3 percent sea salt—it adds a tangy, sweet flavor to meals—or combined with oil and vinegar for a sour-tang vinaigrette.

A go-to recipe for carrot tops has to be pesto (**fig. c**); it preserves them for 2–3 weeks in oil. Try it with cumin, cardamom, and orange for an Indian slant or pumpkin seeds, garlic, and parsley for a more classic version. Carrot tops can also be used to infuse oils, or fry them in hot oil with a pinch of coconut sugar, coconut flakes, and sea salt for a snack like crispy seaweed.

If you'd rather preserve the roots, blanch in salted water, dunk in an ice bath, then dry and freeze them. Grated carrot also makes a delicious golden kraut fermented in a 3 percent brine. It's sweet, sour, and earthy—perfect for salads and veggie burgers.

SNACK

Carrot Bhaji

SERVES 2–4

Spices seem to go off with a bang when paired with carrots. I adore a bhaji, and this recipe includes some real aromatic flavor bombs. The whole-wheat flour boosts the nuttiness of the mix and the grated carrots are blended with fenugreek, black onion, and coriander—plus a few other friends from my spice rack. The result can be served with a colorful selection of pickles, mango chutney, coriander achaar, and raita.

INGREDIENTS

1 tsp fenugreek seeds
1 tsp black onion seeds
1 tsp coriander seeds
1 tsp turmeric
½ tsp ground cumin
½ tsp chili powder
½ tsp ground ginger
14 oz (400 g) carrots, grated
½ red onion, finely sliced
½ green chili, seeded and finely diced
2 tbsp slivered almonds
1 tsp sea salt
2 eggs, beaten
⅔ cup (75 g) whole-wheat flour
Vegetable oil, for frying

Method

01 Carefully toast the spices for 2–3 minutes in a dry frying pan on medium-low heat, stirring so they don't burn, then allow to cool.

02 Combine the grated carrot, onion, chili, and almonds with all the toasted spices and the salt and mix thoroughly. Then fold in the beaten eggs. Sift in the flour a little at a time until you can form the spiced carrot mixture into a loose patty.

03 Heat some oil, about ½–¾ in (1–2 cm) in depth, in a frying pan and fry the bhajis for 4–5 minutes on each side until golden. Finish in a preheated oven at 400°F (200°C) for a few minutes if you've made big, chunky bhajis like me, then serve with your pickles and chutneys of choice.

Miso-roasted Carrots with Pink Dukkah

SERVES 2

A chef should probably never have one favorite dish, but this is very close to being mine. Creating it was a real high point in the book, as I loved the taste; the vibrant colors; and, most of all, the simple act of rolling a sweet roasted carrot in a crunchy dukkah to coat it. That moment was eminently satisfying but also, for me, happened to create the perfect mouthful. The carrot-top chermoula with cumin and chili has since been made several times and served with all sorts of other meals.

INGREDIENTS

2 tbsp olive oil
12 purple carrots
1 cup (250 ml) miso stock
2 tbsp honey
1 tsp sea salt

For the dukkah
1 tbsp sunflower seeds
1 tsp pink Himalayan salt
1 tsp paprika
1 tsp coriander seeds
1 tsp pink peppercorns
Pinch of dried rose petals

For the chermoula
1¾ oz (50 g) carrot tops, plus extra sprigs to garnish
2 garlic cloves
1 tbsp pine nuts
1 tsp cumin seeds
½ green chili, seeded
½ tsp sea salt
2 tbsp lemon juice
2–4 tbsp olive oil

Method

01 Blend together the pink dukkah ingredients in a spice blender and set aside. (You can add all sorts of other ingredients to this blend if you want to—try sesame seeds, hemp seeds, and herbs for extra depth of flavor.)

02 To make the chermoula, first blanch the carrot tops in boiling water for 2 minutes, then drain and pat dry. Blend in a food processor with the garlic, pine nuts, cumin seeds, green chili, and salt. Drizzle in the lemon juice and olive oil until you reach the desired consistency; I like a slack chermoula, so I tend to add lots of oil.

03 For the carrots, heat the olive oil in a pan and add the carrots whole. Sauté for 4–5 minutes, then add in the miso stock. Keep the stock simmering until it reduces, and after 15–20 minutes, add in the honey and sea salt. Reduce further until the carrots are soft and sticky.

04 Last, roll the carrots in the dukkah mix. Slice some of the carrots, then serve with the carrot-top chermoula and a few sprigs of raw carrot leaf.

DESSERT

Carrot and Cardamom Ice Cream
MAKES 4

Several years ago, I branched out from my baking business to start an artisan ice cream company. We only made three flavors: spiced toffee apple pie, lemon curd, and the one shown here—carrot and cardamom. The project was short-lived, but the ice cream was good, so I thought I'd bring out this old favorite of mine one last time to share with the world.

INGREDIENTS

4 carrots, chopped, plus extra to garnish

4 green cardamom pods, lightly crushed

¾ cup (200 ml) heavy cream

¼ cup (50 ml) whole milk

2 egg yolks

½ cup (100 g) granulated sugar

¼ cup (50 ml) apple juice

Edible flowers, to garnish

Method

01 Start by simmering the carrots in a small amount of boiling water with the crushed cardamom pods. Simmer for 20–25 minutes until the carrots are very soft and infused with a sweet, spiced flavor. Then drain, remove the cardamom pods, and allow to cool.

02 In another pan, warm the cream and milk. Combine the egg yolks and sugar in a bowl, then slowly pour in a little of the warm cream mixture and whisk continuously until smooth. Gradually add more until you have one mixture. Return to low heat and stir all the time until the cream thickens into a custard— do not boil or it will curdle. Leave to cool, then seal in an airtight container.

03 Blend the carrots with the apple juice into a smooth purée and combine with the cooled custard. Then place the mixture into an ice cream machine to churn and freeze for 1 hour, processing according to the ice cream maker's instructions.

04 When ready, serve your soft-scoop ice cream garnished with edible flowers and freshly grated carrot.

Sweet Potato

HEART OF GOLD

EDIBLE PARTS

01 FLESH

Sweet potato flesh can vary in color and firmness, but it's all edible. Some types might better suit baking or mashing, depending on their moisture levels. You can cook the flesh in many ways or eat it raw; unlike potatoes, sweet potato flesh doesn't contain the poisonous enzyme solanine. Neither does it contain toxins like many yams, which require cooking first.

02 SKIN

The skin is edible and full of nutrients—antioxidants are three times more concentrated in the skin than in the flesh, so use it whenever you can.

SHOOTS AND LEAVES

These are both edible and taste delicious, though they are rarely sold in the UK. I ate the tuber leaves in Fiji when I worked out there, and they are great as an edible parcel to wrap food in before baking or chopped and wilted like spinach.

One of my proudest moments as a grandson was harvesting a sweet potato that my grandpa had grown in his vegetable patch. I remember rubbing off the jet-black soil to reveal an earthy copper skin glinting beneath—I've been mining for gold ever since.

PLANT

The sweet potato is an herbaceous perennial vine from the same family as tomatoes and peppers, which produces impressive morning-glory heart-shaped flowers. The edible tuberous roots vary in size but can grow up to 12 in (30 cm) long. Hundreds, if not thousands, of varieties are grown around the world. The skin color varies; paler flesh tends to be firmer, while the deep-orange hues are softer and moist. Generally, they all have a sugary flavor with buttery, earthy undertones. It's regarded as a super-healthy vegetable—it is particularly high in vitamins A and C, iron, potassium, and fiber—and a good source of complex carbohydrates.

COOKING TIPS

Sweet potatoes can be boiled, roasted, mashed, puréed, or grilled, to name a few options. Partner with pungent flavors and strong spices such as cumin, chipotle, paprika, cinnamon, and nutmeg. Iron-rich spinach and kale also pair well to cut through the natural sweetness. They are superb baked with cinnamon butter and smoked sea salt. For a real rustic cooking method, try baking them dirty, right on the coals, until the skin blackens and the flesh is soft and fluffy. Also try roasting or frying your own sweet potato fries—season with paprika and sea salt and serve with a mango salsa or herby chimichurri salt—or skin-on wedges for a thicker slice of sweetness.

PREPARATION

Choose unbruised sweet potatoes that feel heavy to hold and firm rather than soft. Don't store them in the fridge, as it will give this tropical vegetable a hard core and degrade the flavor. Most of the time, I cook sweet potato with the skin on, as it's nutritious and stops the flesh from collapsing under intense heat; I gently scrub the skin and then use a chef's knife or vegetable cleaver to slice or dice the tuber. If you are peeling, try to only trim off thin layers of skin to avoid waste, and always store the flesh in cold water or in a sealed container in the fridge afterward to prevent it from drying out and discoloring.

ZERO WASTE

Some of my favorite ways to use up sweet potato are diced with black beans for a spicy vegetarian chili, fried with kale and lima beans as a hash for brunch, or grated in a quesadilla with grilled cheese and cilantro. You can dice, blanch, and freeze it to easily add a portion to stews, chili, or soups. It can also be used in desserts. Try replacing pumpkin with sweet potato purée for a sweet pie (see page 167) or swapping out the carrot in a carrot cake. Sweet potato-peel chips are also the tastiest you can make. Try roasting with a drizzle of oil or deep-frying for real crunch. Then, while still hot, sprinkle with smoked sea salt, smoked chili flakes, and coconut flakes.

TYPES

BEAUREGARD

The most common variety found in stores, with a fairly uniform elliptical shape and only slightly tapered points, making them easy to prepare. Has a semismooth skin; fine-grained, dark-orange flesh; and a sweet, slightly nutty flavor. Lends itself to baking, boiling, or mashing.

PURPLE

Has a firm magenta flesh with a low moisture content and a sweet flavor with a slight tartness. Works well when seasoned heavily for roasted dishes. It is also suited to desserts. Like many purple foods, it is high in antioxidants.

HANNAH

A medium-to-large sweet potato with a bulbous oblong shape and russet- or tan-colored skin. The off-white interior transforms to pale yellow when cooked. It is dense but mild, with a less sweet flavor and a dryer texture than Beauregard, with a consistency similar to a white potato, making it good for mashing.

JEWEL

Another highly popular variety, especially across the US, with copper skin and a deep-orange flesh that is moist and tender.

GARNET

Has a red or purple skin with heavy orange flesh and a good, full-bodied flavor when baked. It makes great gnocchi.

LIGHT LUNCH

Sweet Potato and Red Lentil Soup
SERVES 4

There are few ingredients that can be so casually added to a soup, stew, or dhal and make such an impact as sweet potato. It lifts a basic recipe with a sweet, punchy tang and a down-to-earth profile. It also erupts in the bowl with a deep-orange color that makes it one of my favorite ingredients to cook with in the darker months. My mom's sweet potato soup is a family favorite and uses red lentils to add earthy body. It is clean and bright on the palate and goes wonderfully with some crusty bread. Thanks, Mom!

INGREDIENTS

2 tbsp olive oil

1 onion, chopped

2 garlic cloves, grated

1 tbsp grated fresh ginger root

1 carrot, diced

3 sweet potatoes, diced

1 red bell pepper, chopped

1 celery stalk, chopped

7 oz (200 g) red lentils, washed and drained

14 oz (400 g) can chopped tomatoes

2¾ pints (1.5 liters) vegetable stock

1 tbsp lemon juice

1 tsp paprika

1 tsp sea salt

½ tsp cracked black pepper

Chopped parsley, to garnish

Method

01 Heat the olive oil in a large pan and sauté the onion gently for 5 minutes, with the lid on, until soft.

02 Add the garlic, ginger, carrot, sweet potatoes, bell pepper, and celery to the pan. Sweat for another 3–5 minutes with the lid on.

03 Add the washed lentils, stir for a minute to coat them with oil, then add the tomatoes and stock.

04 Add the lemon juice, paprika, and salt and pepper to taste. Bring to a boil, then reduce heat and simmer for 20 minutes (or until the vegetables are soft) with the lid on, stirring occasionally and adding a little boiling water if necessary to prevent sticking.

05 Blend in a food processor or with a hand-held mixer to your preferred texture, adding more boiling water if necessary to achieve the consistency you want. Sprinkle with chopped parsley and serve.

MAIN MEAL

Sweet Potato Falafel with Quinoa Tabbouleh and Turmeric Flatbreads

SERVES 4

Roasted sweet potato adds deep caramelized notes to my falafel recipe, and the apricots accentuate its natural sweetness. I've added spice to the flatbread, chili to the tangy yogurt, and aromatic herbs to the tabbouleh to boost the earthy flavors. The starchy textures hold the dish together, soaking up all the noisy chatter like a convivial host.

Method

01 Preheat the oven to 400°F (200°C). To start the falafel, drizzle the sweet potatoes with olive oil and roast for 30–35 minutes.

02 Combine the flatbread ingredients with 3½ cups (100 ml) water in a bowl and knead into a firm dough. Leave to rest, covered, for 30 minutes, then divide into 4 portions and roll out on a floured surface into large rounds. Cook on a hot griddle pan for 2–3 minutes on each side, then keep warm under a kitchen towel.

03 Blend the sweet potatoes in a food processor with the chickpeas, garlic, apricots, whole-wheat flour, baking powder, and harissa. Season with salt and roll the mixture into balls. Add more whole-wheat flour if they feel too wet. Roll in sesame seeds and bake on a lined baking sheet for 45 minutes to 1 hour.

04 For the tabbouleh, stir the herbs into the quinoa and mix with the tomatoes, capers, and oil. Serve with the falafel, flatbreads, yogurt or labneh, and zhoug.

INGREDIENTS

For the falafel

2 sweet potatoes, peeled and diced

1 tbsp olive oil

7 oz (200 g) chickpeas, cooked and drained

2 garlic cloves, finely sliced

1¾ oz (50 g) dried apricots, diced

2 tbsp whole-wheat flour

1 tsp baking powder

1 tsp harissa

½ tsp sea salt

2 tbsp sesame seeds

For the flatbread

2 cups (250 g) all-purpose flour

2 tbsp plain yogurt

1 tbsp olive oil

2 tsp ground turmeric

½ tsp salt

For the tabbouleh

4 tbsp chopped mint

4 tbsp chopped parsley

1 lb 2 oz (500 g) cooked quinoa

1¾ oz (50 g) sun-dried tomatoes, diced

1 tbsp capers

1 tbsp olive oil

To serve

4 tbsp strained yogurt or labneh

1 tbsp zhoug

Sweet Potato Toast with Miso Butter

SERVES 2

Sweet potato toast was a huge trend a few years ago and would be right at home in the cafés of Byron Bay—this is my twist. The miso butter provides a very malted depth and a silky umami spread melting over the charred toast. A pinch of cinnamon is my secret ingredient.

INGREDIENTS

1 sweet potato, sliced into lengths ½in (1cm) thick

3½ tbsp (50g) vegan butter spread

1 tsp miso paste

Pinch of ground cinnamon

1 avocado, peeled, stoned, and sliced

2 tbsp sauerkraut

Handful of salad leaves

1 tbsp toasted seeds (sunflower, pumpkin, and hemp seeds)

1 tbsp olive oil

½ tsp sea salt

Method

01 Toast the sweet potato slices in a toaster. Repeat 3–4 times until they soften slightly and start to blister and char in places.

02 In a small bowl, mix the vegan butter spread and miso paste and add a pinch of cinnamon. Spread on the sweet potato toast while still hot.

03 Plate up with the sliced avocado, sauerkraut, salad leaves, and toasted seeds. Dress with a drizzle of olive oil and a pinch of sea salt.

> *Hardy, humble winter veggies like brassicas and root veggies, simply cooked in the colder months, provide comfort food that nourishes body and soul.*

WINTER

Winter Cabbage

GOOD TO THE CORE

Red

Savoy

01

02

White

EDIBLE PARTS

01 LEAVES

All cabbage leaves are edible. They often have a waxy coating, and you may want to remove the veins from larger leaves, as they take longer to cook. Outer leaves tend to be darker in color and are rich in vitamin C.

02 CORE

Also known as the heart, the core of many cabbages is more fibrous than the rest and may need to be grated into a coleslaw or finely diced. It also tastes more bitter and requires longer cooking than the leaves.

STALK

Cabbage stalks are edible but are notoriously woody and can taste unpleasant. I avoid cooking them and start my vegetable butchery from the point where the leaves join the stalk.

Childhood memories of overcooked cabbage haunt many people, but sauerkraut has led the charge back into the trendy mainstream. This revival is great news—if cooked right, cabbage adds refined flavor and sartorial elegance to a dish.

PLANT

Cool-weather cabbages form a tight head of leaves around a distinct core or heart. They have a unique peppery, grassy, sweet flavor and are part of the brassica or *Cruciferae* family; "cruciferous" refers to the slightly bitter flavor that cabbage, sprouts, and cauliflower give off due to the sulfurous compounds, or glucosinolates, in the leaves. It grows with a short stem and is also called head cabbage due to its characteristic shape. It is an excellent source of vitamins C, K, and B6, as well as potassium, riboflavin, and iron. The outer leaves are higher in vitamin E and may taste more cabbagey than the inner leaves.

COOKING TIPS

Cabbage can be steamed, blanched, braised, roasted, or stir-fried. Generally, it's key not to overcook it; it will smell unpleasant and lose all its nutrients. When blanching, never boil for longer than 3–5 minutes, then refresh in cold water if you are planning to sauté or fry it later. Try serving it raw in slaw or marinated with oil and lemon. Stir-frying is also pretty foolproof. That said, red cabbage responds well to slower cooking if pickling or using a strong braising liquid. Alternatively, it can be braised in stock or red wine for just 5–10 minutes to retain its bite and natural sweetness. The mildly bitter flavors go well with soy sauce, aromatic herbs, dried fruit, toasted nuts, and spices.

PREPARATION

Try to select a cabbage that looks bright, with crisp, firm, tightly packed leaves. They should feel heavy. Avoid any with holes where insects could have burrowed inside, remove any damaged outer leaves, and cut out central stalks that feel too tough to eat. Rinse if necessary. Cabbage benefits from simple cooking methods, so prepare the leaves simply, too: shredded, chopped, or whole. Slicing thinly increases the surface area so that you reduce the risk of overcooking.

ZERO WASTE

Store cabbages in a cool, dark place for up to 7 days. In the fridge, they may even last longer. Try finely chopping any leftovers and frying in a British bubble and squeak with roast potatoes. Serve with a poached egg and cranberry sauce for a zero-waste brunch. Leftover cabbage also makes a great addition to egg-fried rice with soy sauce, toasted sunflower seeds, and diced pepper. It's a well-known secret that crispy seaweed is often made with finely shredded cabbage— fry in hot oil and season with soft light brown sugar, sesame seeds, five-spice, and sea salt. Cabbage is also famously used in krauts and kimchi (see pages 284–285), and this is the best way to preserve it in my eyes.

TYPES

GREEN

A common type with broad, waxy green leaves that form a dense overlapping ball around the heart. The texture is firm when raw but softens when cooked. It has a sweet, grassy flavor with a mustardy finish.

SAVOY

A loose-headed variety with green crinkled leaves that cluster into a dense heart. The large surface area makes them superb grilled, braised, or fried with butter and sage. They have a crunchy bite when shredded and eaten raw and a sweet, earthy flavor when cooked, with a slightly bitter aftertaste.

RED

Has burgundy-colored, thick, waxy leaves. The anthocyanin pigments produce pink, red, and magenta colors, making it even healthier than green varieties. The bold, peppery flavor and crunchy texture can be paired with rich spices, fruit, and nuts, with strong festive connotations.

WHITE

White cabbage has a sweet, mild flavor and is excellent raw. If overcooked, it can become mushy and sulfurous. It contains as much vitamin C as lemon juice.

BOK CHOY

Also known as pak choi or Chinese celery cabbage, this has thick, crunchy white stems, with pliable oval green leaves. The flavor is mild and has an earthy sweetness when cooked. Can also be eaten raw.

MAIN MEAL

Stuffed Savoy Cabbage with Fermented Squash and Madeira-soaked Prunes

SERVES 2

My wife Holly is my severest critic, and she loves this dish—
a compliment that makes me feel proud to share it with you.
The stuffed cabbage leaves are filled with chestnuts and
herby mushrooms, the fermented squash works really well
with the earthy roasted cabbage leaves, and the rich prunes
provide an umami-sweet sauce.

INGREDIENTS

6–8 large Savoy cabbage
leaves, thickest parts of
the veins removed

1 tbsp walnut oil

1 lb 2 oz (500 g) fermented
squash, sliced (see pages
282–285)

Sea salt

Calendula petals, to garnish
(optional)

For the stuffing

3½ tbsp (50 g) butter

3½ oz (100 g) mushrooms,
finely diced

1 shallot, finely diced

1 garlic clove, finely diced

1 tsp chopped thyme

1 tsp chopped rosemary

½ cup (50 g) panko
breadcrumbs

½ tsp sea salt

½ tsp cracked black pepper

3½ oz (100 g) chestnuts,
cooked, plus extra to
garnish

1 tbsp grated orange zest

For the purée

9 oz (250 g) fermented
squash

½ tsp xanthan gum

½ tsp sea salt

For the prunes

12 prunes

⅔ cup (150 ml) Madeira
wine

¾ cup (200 ml) vegetable
stock

1 sprig of thyme

scant 2 tbsp (25 g) butter

Sea salt

Method

01 Blanch the Savoy leaves in boiling water for 2–3 minutes until pliable. Remove and refresh in ice water. Then preheat the oven to 400°F (200°C).

02 To make the stuffing, melt the butter in a frying pan; add the mushrooms, shallot, garlic, thyme, and rosemary; and soften. Remove from heat and allow to cool.

03 Season the breadcrumbs with the salt and pepper, then pulse the mushroom mixture in a food processor with the seasoned breadcrumbs, chestnuts, and orange zest until you have a very coarse mixture.

04 Place a handful of the stuffing onto each Savoy leaf and fold into a parcel. Place on a baking sheet and brush with the walnut oil. Add the sliced fermented squash to the sheet and bake with the parcels for 20 minutes.

05 Meanwhile, in a saucepan, soak the prunes in the Madeira over medium heat for about 20 minutes. Add the stock and thyme, then reduce. Simmer gently for 10–12 minutes, then reduce the liquid further for about 10 minutes until sweet and sticky. Add in the butter and a pinch of salt and mix for a rich, glossy sauce.

06 To make the purée, blend the fermented squash in a food processor with the xanthan gum and salt until smooth, then warm through in a pan.

07 Plate up the parcels, roasted squash, purée, and soaked prunes, then finish with a grating of cooked chestnut, a pinch of sea salt, and the calendula petals (if using).

SIDE

Braised Red Cabbage, Sloes, and Chestnuts

SERVES 4

There are many subtle nuances to observe in a seasonal kitchen. Over the year the produce changes, of course, but so do the smells from the stove. Every year when red cabbage starts being delivered to our door, I look forward to cooking this dish and trying out a new version. This recipe fills the house with winter warmth and marks a new season beginning. It is simple, rustic food brightening up the darkest months.

INGREDIENTS

3½ tbsp (50 g) butter

1 red cabbage, cored and finely sliced

2 red onions, sliced

4 cloves

3 star anise

1 cinnamon stick

9 oz (250 g) apples, peeled, cored, and diced

5½ oz (150 g) cooked chestnuts, roughly chopped

⅔ cup (150 ml) sloe gin (with berries, optional)

3 tbsp cider vinegar

½ cup (75 g) soft light brown sugar

¾ cup (200 ml) water

½ tsp sea salt

½ tsp cracked black pepper

3–4 sprigs of thyme, to garnish

Method

01 Preheat the oven to 300°F (150°C). Melt the butter in a lidded casserole dish over medium heat and fry the cabbage and onions with the cloves, star anise, and cinnamon stick for 10 minutes with the lid on.

02 Add in the diced apple, chestnuts, sloe gin (with the soaked berries if you have them), vinegar, sugar, and water. Cook for 5 minutes, stirring well.

03 Transfer to the oven with the lid on and braise the cabbage for 1–2 hours. Stir every half an hour or so and cook until the water has evaporated and the cabbage is tender and sweet.

04 Season with the salt and pepper, remove the cinnamon stick, then garnish with the thyme leaves and serve.

SIDE

Winter Slaw

SERVES 4

Slaw is probably the greatest zero-waste recipe ever invented, and this one is a proper celebration of cabbage—an inviting, colorful winter slaw with a tart mustard dressing mixed with orange and fennel tops. It makes for a versatile side dish that can be served with baked potatoes, burgers, salads, or sandwiches.

INGREDIENTS

¼ red cabbage, finely sliced

¼ white cabbage, finely sliced

2 spring onions, sliced diagonally

1 large red carrot, grated

1 apple

1 tbsp fennel tops

For the dressing

1 tbsp orange juice

1 tsp cider vinegar

1 tsp whole-grain honey mustard

1 tsp olive oil

Sea salt

Method

01 In a small bowl, whisk together all the dressing ingredients except the salt, then season to taste.

02 Mix the cabbage, spring onions, and carrot together in a large bowl. Core and grate the apple, then add last of all to avoid discoloration. Add the fennel tops and coat evenly with the orange and mustard dressing.

03 Serve fresh for a light, crunchy side or keep in the fridge for 2–3 days. It's best made regularly in small batches, as the vegetables can lose their vibrancy when stored.

Cauliflower

FLAVORFUL FLORETS

Purple

01

White

02

03

EDIBLE PARTS

01 STALK

The central stalk is thick and tougher than the florets but still edible. It is good added to stocks, roasted whole, or grated into salads. I like to avoid discarding the stalk and enjoy finding creative ways to cook it.

02 LEAVES

The leaves can be steamed, sautéed, or roasted. Larger ridged leaves with prominent veins running down to the base of the stalk are better removed and added to stock or roasted. Tender young leaves can be treated like cabbage or spring greens. Avoid overcooking.

03 HEAD

The head, or curd, is comprised of what are technically called aborted floral meristems but are generally referred to as florets. These small edible flower buds can be crumbly and soft or firm, depending on the variety. The head can be broken down into clusters or roasted whole.

Cauliflower is a bombshell of a vegetable with the power to either blend in or astonish. It is low in fat and high in fiber and nutrients. But it's not just healthy; it has a cruciferous complexity, meaty texture, and bouquet bursting with flavor.

PLANT

Cauliflower is a brassica that normally produces a large central head with the leaves folded over it to protect the flowers from sunlight, which would cause them to brown and develop a bitter flavor. It is a superfood high in vitamin C, fiber, and selenium. The flavor is mild but with sweet and bitter notes. Avoid overcooking it, as, like all cruciferous vegetables, it can smell sulfurous and become unpleasant to eat. Choose cauliflowers that have a uniform shape, a dense head, and no discoloration. Look for deeply ribbed, crisp green leaves rather than wilted or yellow. The color at the base indicates how recently it's been picked—the whiter it is, the fresher it is.

COOKING TIPS

Cauliflower is an ideal replacement for rice, potatoes, and other foods that are high in carbohydrates and calories. The robust structure of a cauliflower head makes it ideal to marinate and baste when roasting to enhance the flavor. The cruciferous flavor also works extremely well with a rich cheese sauce. Chicken fried cauliflower is a super-tasty dish to cook with a spicy hot sauce. Try roasting the cauliflower florets for 20 minutes coated in a dry Cajun spice rub, then roll in spiced cornflakes and breadcrumbs. Fry in hot oil for 6–8 minutes, then toss in Nashville hot sauce. It's finger-licking good!

PREPARATION

When preparing cauliflower, first remove the surrounding leaves and slice out the thicker veins if using them as spring greens. Keep the thicker stalks for stock. After removing the leaves, I use a boning knife to trim the branches from the base upward, cutting the florets from the central stalk. At this point, I switch to a paring knife and trim down the florets into equal-sized portions so they cook evenly. For steaks, adopt a different approach and slice through the entire head, using the stalk to guide you. Normally, you can slice 2–3 steaks from the center. Then you are left with the florets, which are easy to pickle, steam, or blend into cauliflower rice (see page 211).

ZERO WASTE

You can store cauliflower in the fridge for 7–10 days, but if you need to use it up, lactofermentation is really worth trying (see pages 282–285). Ferment trimmed florets in a 3 percent brine with chili, grated root turmeric, ginger, and dried mango. Add some coriander seeds, mustard, and peppercorns and leave for 7–10 days for some wonderfully sweet, tangy sour pickles. You can also preserve cauliflower by blanching and then freezing. Boil for under 5 minutes so the florets retain some crunch when you defrost and cook them later. Refresh in cold water after boiling, then freeze and store for up to 12 months.

TYPES

WHITE

The classic cauliflower has a dense head and a singular trunk with clusters of firm, dense florets forming around it. They have a soft, crumbly texture and a mild nutty flavor, which is amplified when roasted. All of the plant is edible.

GREEN

This colorful variety is a hybrid of cauliflower and broccoli. It is sweet, mild, and not bitter. The texture is less crumbly than white cauliflower, and it has a firm bite when cooked.

PURPLE

Vibrant violet hues make this an impressive vegetable, though the stem and core remain a subdued cream color. It has a milder flavor free of bitterness and soft, crumbly florets, and it is a visually strong counterpart to green vegetables on the plate.

SPROUTING

Sometimes called flowering cauliflower, this is longer than other varieties—the result of overgrown heads or secondary growth from the base of older leaves. It has thin, edible stems that shoot off with small clusters of florets on the tops. The stems vary in length but commonly grow up to 4in (10cm) long. It has a milder flavor than a full-grown cauliflower.

MAIN MEAL

Cauliflower Steak
SERVES 2

I first started serving cauliflower steaks on restaurant menus a few years back, and they quickly became a personal favorite. This recipe is an homage to pub grub—a classic indulgent date-night steak, cooked in a skillet to bring out the inherent meaty texture and nutty flavors, with roasted vegetables and a boozy peppercorn sauce.

INGREDIENTS

2 cauliflower steaks (see Preparation, page 207)

1 tsp sea salt

1 tsp cracked black pepper

2 tbsp olive oil, plus extra for drizzling

3½ tbsp (50g) butter, diced

2 sprigs of thyme

2 garlic cloves, crushed

1 beefsteak tomato, halved

2 portobello mushrooms

Small bunch of chard or kale

1 tbsp lemon juice

Onion rings, to garnish (optional)

For the peppercorn sauce

3½ tbsp (50g) butter

1 shallot, finely diced

2 garlic cloves, diced

½ tsp green peppercorns, crushed

½ tsp black peppercorns, crushed

½ tsp dried thyme

¼ cup (50ml) brandy

⅔ cup (150ml) heavy cream

Method

01 Preheat the oven to 400°F (200°C).

02 Season the 2 large cauliflower steaks with salt and pepper. Drizzle with the olive oil and start heating a heavy cast-iron skillet or oven-safe frying pan.

03 Add the steaks to the pan when hot and sear for 3–4 minutes on each side, then add the butter, thyme leaves, and crushed garlic. Cook for another 4–5 minutes, spooning the hot butter over the steaks, then transfer the pan to the oven and roast for 15–20 minutes.

04 Place the tomato and mushrooms on a baking sheet, drizzle with a little oil, and roast in the oven at the same time as the cauliflower, also for 15–20 minutes.

05 In a pan, wilt the chopped chard or kale in a little oil and drizzle with the lemon juice.

06 Finally, make the peppercorn sauce. Melt the butter in a pan, then add the shallot, garlic, crushed peppercorns, and thyme, then soften for 5 minutes. Add in the brandy and reduce for 2–3 minutes. Then follow with the cream. Stir to combine, then remove from heat.

07 Serve the cauliflower steaks with the roasted vegetables and wilted chard, drizzled with the warm peppercorn sauce. Garnish with battered onion rings for an extra treat.

SIDE OR MAIN MEAL

Roasted Cauliflower with Tahini and Turmeric

SERVES 4

I don't think I'll ever get tired of roasting whole cauliflowers. My version is tender in the middle, with charred yellow, chewy florets on the outside. As a centerpiece or part of a mezze, it is rich in umami flavor and heavy with spice but light and clean-tasting at the same time.

INGREDIENTS

1 whole cauliflower

For the shawarma spice marinade
2 tsp turmeric
1 tsp ground cardamom
½ tsp ground cinnamon
½ tsp ground coriander
½ tsp ground cumin
1 tsp sea salt
1 tbsp tahini
2 tbsp canola oil
1 tbsp plain yogurt

To serve
4 tbsp chopped parsley
4 tbsp chopped mint
1 tsp za'atar
1 tbsp pomegranate seeds
½ tsp pink salt
1 tbsp lemon juice
1 tbsp plain yogurt

Method

01 Preheat the oven to 425°F (220°C) or light a grill. In a small bowl, combine the shawarma spices with the tahini, oil, and yogurt. Mix until smooth, then brush half the marinade onto the whole untrimmed cauliflower.

02 Place the cauliflower in the oven on a lined baking sheet on its stalk so that it sits upright to roast for a total of 40–45 minutes. Reduce the temperature to 400°F (200°C) after the first 10 minutes of cooking, and halfway through roasting, brush again with the remaining spice marinade.

03 Check with a toothpick that the cauliflower is soft in the center and, if so, serve whole or sliced in half on a bed of chopped parsley and mint, sprinkled with the za'atar, pomegranate seeds, and salt and dressed with the lemon juice and yogurt.

SIDE

Cauliflower Rice

SERVES 2

I don't regret a single meal where I've swapped basmati rice for cauliflower rice. This is my go-to version—it is earthy, sweet, and works perfectly with pickles and a good vegetable curry, but it's also flexible. You can roast it with different spices, fruit, nuts, and oils for nuanced little changes to the recipe, so experiment and add your own twists.

INGREDIENTS

3 cardamom pods, lightly crushed
1 tsp turmeric
1 tsp fennel seeds
½ tsp nigella seeds
½ tsp brown mustard seeds
2 tbsp coconut oil
1 whole cauliflower
2 tbsp slivered almonds
1¾ oz (50 g) raisins
½ tsp sea salt

Method

01 Preheat the oven to 400°F (200°C). In a dry frying pan, gently toast the spices over low heat for 1–2 minutes, then add the coconut oil. Mix into a paste, then remove from heat.

02 Pulse the cauliflower in a food processor into a coarse rice texture. Include the stalk and some smaller leaves.

03 Add the rice, almonds, and raisins to the spice paste and stir. Transfer to a baking sheet and roast for 15–20 minutes.

04 After the first 10 minutes, open the oven briefly to let steam escape and to stir the rice once. Remove the cardamom pods, season with the salt, and serve.

Leeks
LAYERS OF SWEETNESS

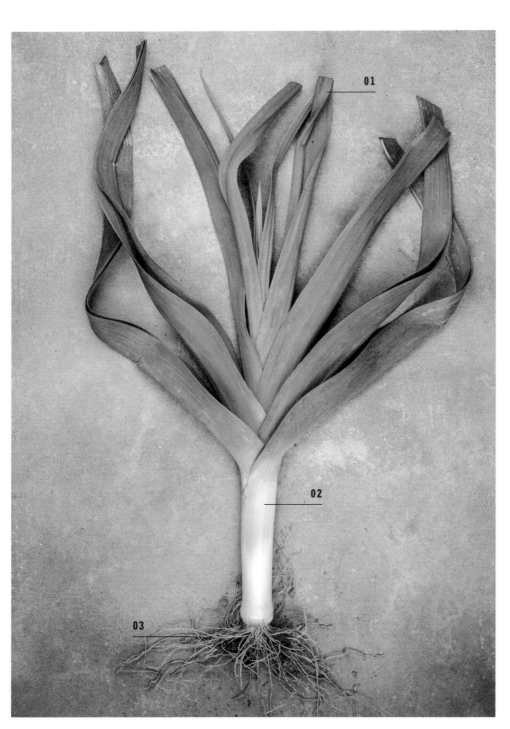

EDIBLE PARTS

01 LEAVES

Sometimes called flags, the flat leaves fan out at the top of the stalk. They are darker green and have a beautiful winter-blue tint. They can grow to nearly 3 ft (1 m) in height. All the leaves are edible, but the ends are often discarded, as they are fibrous and prone to rust.

02 STALK

The stalk is cylindrical with a rounded bulb at the base and grows straight up in a tightly overlapping pattern. Leeks are always white at the base and can be trenched up for a larger white section.

03 ROOTS

These are edible and, despite being a challenge to clean, they make a delicious fried garnish for soups and also work chopped right into a stir-fry like garlicky bean sprouts.

SCAPES

Leek scapes are the long, tender stalks and young flower buds that grow when the leek bolts in late spring. The edible tips have a mild allium flavor and subtle garlic aroma. They are soft like asparagus in texture.

Leeks have been a constant throughout my life. To me, their flavor has it all: from the sweet white bulb to the bitter, grassy green tips. Holding one of these sturdy stems, with their sweet allium profile, I know the meal to come will taste delicious.

PLANT

Leeks are an allium, related to garlic and onion, though they have a milder flavor and are sweet, grassy, and tender. Many growers will pile up soil at the base of the bulb to limit chlorophyll production and thereby lengthen the tastier white portion. This pushing up of soil around them is called blanching or trenching. Overwintering leeks have the strongest flavor, while smaller, younger ones raised in spring are sweeter, more delicate, and soft in texture. All of them are a rich source of vitamins B6 and K. Additionally, leeks contain prebiotics, insulin, and folates, which promote healthy digestion, blood-sugar levels, and cell growth.

Figure a.

PREPARATION

Try to go for leeks that are about 1 in (2.5 cm) in diameter, smooth, and perky looking, with a firm, unblemished lower white part and stiff, bright green leaves where possible. Rust does occur on the leaves at certain times of the year, so don't be alarmed by some yellow spots at the tips, but avoid eating these diseased parts. The texture should feel crisp and snappy.

To prepare a leek, trim off the leaves a few inches below the splayed V-shaped section above the stalk. As they grow, leeks can collect a lot of dirt between their leaves, so they almost always need cleaning. I split them lengthwise from halfway up the stem, up through the tips of the leaves, and repeat into quarter-sections (**fig. a**). I then spread the leek out slightly and rinse it under cold running water. I then shake off the excess water, and it's as simple as that.

Leeks are a chopping dream. The roots hold the stalk together while you cut and make them a pleasure to slice or thinly dice. I also recommend trying to split the stalk with a cut down the length of one side and then flattening out the layers into large rectangular sheets. These make a great substitute for pasta in a lasagna.

TYPES

EARLY LEEKS

These are varieties that are ready in fall. 'King Richard' can be harvested as early as August. 'Jaune de Poitou' is another productive, quick-growing variety that has yellow leaves in contrast to the bluish-green foliage of most types. They tend to be less winter hardy and are designed to be lifted early before it gets too cold. 'Carlton' is a quick-growing variety and can be lifted from September to December—it's a good, mild, midseason leek.

LATE LEEKS

'Musselburgh' is a popular variety bred in Scotland that does very well over winter. It's a hardy late-season variety with crisp, sweet white stems. Another reliable variety with sturdy stems is 'Bleu de Solaise', which has leaves that turn a dark blue-green color after the first frost and is very cold-resistant.

BABY

These slender cylindrical stems that look like spring onions are leeks that have not been allowed to plump up, so they lack the thicker fanned foliage of mature leeks. They have a lovely tender texture and are meltingly soft when cooked. Entirely edible, they are very good for grilling and are actually mild enough to eat raw.

CONT.

Figure b.

COOKING TIPS

Leeks are mucilaginous—they contain a substance called polysaccharide, which, when extracted during cooking, creates a uniquely slippery, unctuous feel and a natural thickener that makes leeks well suited as an ingredient in soups and stews. I like to pair leeks with lemon, tarragon, cider, mustard, smoked cheese, brown butter, and fennel. The delicate profile also suits chervil, pastis, coriander seeds, and celery salt.

Leek risotto with tarragon, preserved lemon, and mushroom is a classic for good reason. The combination is simple and delicate. After sautéing the leeks with garlic, mushrooms, capers, and tarragon, add in some white wine, stock, and preserved lemon. Finish with crispy leek tops fried in a little oil and drizzle with tarragon oil (fig. b).

Leeks can also make extremely good kebabs on skewers. Blanch the whole stem in a tall stock pot for 4–5 minutes, then cut into chunky 1–2 in (2.5–5 cm) rings. Skewer through the side and season with a Sichuan dressing or some sriracha sauce. Cook on a yakitori grill or a grill over charcoal and watch the outer layers char while the inner layers remain tender and sweet.

ZERO WASTE

To keep leeks fresh for longer, don't trim them before storing and don't freeze them, as this results in a more bitter flavor and a soft texture. Ideally, store them in the ground. They will happily keep over winter. For bought leeks, keep them in the fridge and use within 5–10 days. To preserve them, try making potted leeks. Sauté with tarragon and mustard, then pack tightly into a sterilized jar. Top with a ¾ in (2 cm) layer of clarified butter spiced with mace. Potted leeks are delicious on toasted sourdough.

Alternatively, try making leek ash—this sounds like a ridiculous thing to do, but it tastes surprisingly delicate and makes a dramatic seasoning. Preheat the oven to 475°F (240°C) and turn on the range hood or open a window. Place a leek on a baking sheet and roast until completely blackened, dry, and crisp; this can take 60–90 minutes. Allow to cool and use as broken shards or blend into a powder for seasoning. Store in an airtight container for up to 1 month.

Leek and Seaweed Croquettes

MAKES 12–16

The problem with these croquettes is knowing when to stop eating them. The bite-sized, richly savory nuggets are dangerously addictive and creamy—crunchy on the outside and soft and succulent inside. I have always loved croquettes, but for me, if they don't have leek in them, they're probably not worth making. The leek provides a valuable allium pungency without overpowering the other flavors, and this recipe is a great way to bring together those best of friends, leek and potato.

INGREDIENTS

3½ tbsp (50 g) butter

1 large leek or 2 small ones, finely sliced

1 tbsp dried tarragon

1 tbsp nori flakes

1 lb (450 g) mashed potatoes

5½ oz (150 g) grated Gruyère cheese

4 tbsp all-purpose flour

1 tsp sea salt

2 eggs, beaten

Vegetable oil, for frying

For the herby breadcrumbs

1 cup (100 g) panko breadcrumbs

1 tsp nori flakes

1 tsp lemon zest

½ tsp sea salt

½ cracked black pepper

For the mustard mayo

4 tbsp mayonnaise

2 tsp whole-grain mustard

Method

01 Melt the butter in a frying pan, add the leeks, and sauté over medium-to-low heat. After 5–6 minutes ,add the tarragon and nori flakes. Remove from heat and allow to cool.

02 Combine the mixture with the mashed potatoes, Gruyère cheese, and 2 tablespoons of the all-purpose flour. Season with the salt and form into 12–16 croquette-shaped balls. If time allows, chill in the fridge for 30–40 minutes, as it helps them keep their shape.

03 Mix together all the ingredients for the herby breadcrumbs in a bowl. Next, roll each of the leek croquettes in the remaining flour, then in the beaten egg, then coat them in the herby breadcrumbs.

04 Fry the croquettes in ½–¾ in (1–2 cm) of oil for 4–5 minutes until golden brown, while you mix the ingredients for the mustard mayo in a bowl. When ready, serve the croquettes warm with a dollop of the mayo.

MAIN MEAL

Leek and Cider Terrine
SERVES 4

Terrines are regarded as pretty old-fashioned, and I wanted to cook one that felt up-to-date. The gently cooked leeks provide bite and counter the cider jelly's soft texture. The result is a spreadable terrine with anise and apple notes, delicate allium pungency, and a citrus aroma—a perfect recipe for early-season leeks that are still sweet and tender. Try served on toasted sourdough with a bitter radicchio salad, lemon oil, sprouted seeds, and tarragon.

INGREDIENTS

7 tbsp (100 g) butter

2 leeks, sliced into ½ in (1 cm) coins

2½ cups (600 ml) cider

¾ cup (200 ml) vegetable stock

2 tbsp roughly chopped tarragon

1 tbsp whole-grain mustard

1 tbsp grated orange zest

1 tsp sea salt

4 g sachet of vegetarian gelatin

Method

01 Melt the butter in a saucepan over low heat and add all of the sliced leeks. Make sure they cover the entire bottom of the pan, then add ½ cup (100 ml) of the cider and the stock. Cover with a disk of parchment paper to act as a cartouche and reduce heat. Poach the leeks for 20–25 minutes until soft and tender—avoid caramelizing them.

02 Meanwhile, heat the remaining cider in a pan with the tarragon, mustard, orange zest, and salt until it boils, stirring occasionally. Then remove from heat and stir in the gelatin until it dissolves. Allow to cool for no longer than 5–10 minutes.

03 Next, neatly arrange the poached leeks in two layers in a lined terrine mold. Pour over the cider jelly liquid, leave for 1–2 hours at room temperature to set, then serve.

Leek Gratin on Sourdough Crumpets

SERVES 4

These are my mom's sourdough crumpets. The leek topping is the perfect twist on rustic Welsh rarebit, with grilled cheese and mustard back notes. They're easy to make, but I'd urge you to use crumpet rings—and to serve them with Worcestershire sauce and a watercress salad.

INGREDIENTS

For the crumpet batter

9 oz (250 g) sourdough starter

1 tbsp granulated sugar

½ tsp sea salt

½ tsp baking soda

Oil, for greasing 3½ in (9 cm) crumpet rings

For the leek gratin

3½ tbsp (50 g) butter

1 leek, finely sliced, roots retained

1 tbsp all-purpose flour

½ cup (125 ml) heavy cream

1 tbsp whole-grain mustard

3½ oz (100 g) grated mature Cheddar cheese

½ tsp nutmeg

Pinch of ground white pepper

1 tbsp olive oil, for frying

Method

01 For the batter, mix the starter with the sugar and salt, then stir in the baking soda. Grease a griddle pan and 2 crumpet rings with oil and, over medium heat, spoon the batter into the rings, leaving ½ in (1 cm) at the top for them to rise. Cook for 3–4 minutes until the batter comes away from the edges. Transfer to a cooling rack and repeat until the batter is used up.

02 For the leek gratin, melt the butter in a pan, add the leek, and soften. After 6–8 minutes, add in the flour and cook it out. Then stir in the cream and mustard.

03 Cook until the cream thickens, then add the cheese, nutmeg, and white pepper, stirring until all the cheese has melted. Remove from heat and allow to cool.

04 Place the crumpets on a baking sheet and spoon a generous dollop of the gratin on top of each one. Grill for 4–5 minutes until the cheese bubbles.

05 Fry the leftover leek roots in the olive oil and serve the crumpets garnished with a nest of the roots on top.

Kale

HEALTHY HIPSTER

Red Russian

01

Lacinato

Siberian

02

EDIBLE PARTS

01 LEAVES

The leaves have a deep, earthy flavor with a metallic tang and savory notes. Edible raw or cooked, they are highly versatile and retain their chewy texture when cooked. Occasionally, I will roast whole leaves of lacinato kale or steam Siberian kale to use as a wrap instead of tortilla for burritos or for nut roast sausage rolls.

02 STEM

All kale stems and thicker veins are edible, but some can be woody and are best removed if steaming or sautéing the leaves. On younger leaves, the stems are tender and can be cooked along with the leaves. For larger cuts, try to trim out the stem, then braise or stir-fry. The thickest stems are also a good addition to a green stock.

Many vegetables have tried to dethrone the head of the hipster tribe, but kale wins every time in both style and substance. It brings a pop of color and texture; tastes spicy, sweet, and bitter; and is a nutrient powerhouse. All hail the kale.

PLANT

Kale is a hardy winter vegetable that is easy to grow. It's a nonheading form of primitive cabbage descended from wild cabbages. The loose head provides a colorful rosette of leaves from the thin stems, which range in color, size, and shape and in structure from flat to frilly. Many gardeners grow kale in borders for ornamental value over winter, but it's also the poster child of healthy eating, with sky-high levels of nutrients. It has more iron than red meat and more vitamin C than other greens. It's even got more calcium, gram for gram, than milk. Harvest young leaves from the top of the plant first. This stimulates more tender leaves.

COOKING TIPS

Kale is versatile but should not be overcooked, as it will lose nutrients. A good introductory method is to sauté it with butter, garlic, and black pepper until wilted. Another is to steam it with a splash of water. It's delicious as chips (see page 223), roasted, stir-fried, boiled, or stewed. To braise, cook for 20–25 minutes in stock until tender and sweet.

Kale is a punchy way to elevate most dishes, but also a shortcut to adding extra nutrients at a late stage—a superfood hack. Add it to stews and pasta sauces for the last 10–20 minutes of cooking time for a chewy texture and burst of color. It pairs well with comforting winter flavors like rosemary, orange, apple, cinnamon, and hazelnut.

PREPARATION

Choose kale with the stems intact, not chopped, if possible. It lasts longer this way and allows you to decide how to prepare it yourself. Leaves should be a vibrant color and feel firm and crisp to the touch. Avoid any with a yellow tinge. The butchery is relatively basic. A rough chop through tender leaves before cooking means you can fit more in a pan (although bear in mind that as kale wilts, it reduces in volume). To remove thicker stems, use a paring knife to slice up to a natural snapping point. Make a V cut and remove the woody section if necessary. This can then be cut finely and cooked along with the rest or added to stock.

ZERO WASTE

Wet kale leaves wilt much faster when stored, so only wash them prior to cooking. Store in the fridge for 5–7 days. A smoothie is an excellent way to use up a handful of kale. You can blanch first or blend the chopped leaves raw. Add honey, berries, ginger, or banana to sweeten and work with kefir, oat milk, or yogurt. For something special, try with apple and cinnamon kombucha.

To preserve kale, blanch for 2–3 minutes, drain, then refresh in ice water. Squeeze out excess water and form into balls. Freeze on a tray, then store in the freezer for up to 4 months. Alternatively, dried kale makes a lovely furikake seasoning: mix with toasted sesame seeds, gochugaru, sugar, and salt.

TYPES

GREEN CURLY

Also called Scottish kale, this is the most common type, with frilly green leaves and thick stems. It is tender as a baby leaf, but as it matures, the stems become more fibrous. The tightly curled leaves retain a good tough bite once cooked, tasting sweet and slightly bitter.

RED CURLY

A red version of curly kale that looks extremely attractive in salads with other greens. It is visually stunning and has an earthy sweetness.

SIBERIAN

Also called Hungry Gap or rape kale lutes, this has plain leaves with shades of sea green; soft, wavy edges; and pale-green veins. The leaves are more tender than curly kale, similar to spring greens when cooked.

RED RUSSIAN

This purple heirloom variety has ruffled leaves and reddish stems and can be bicolored with green variegations. It tastes more like cabbage, with a robust flavor and a semicrisp texture.

LACINATO

Also called cavalo nero or Tuscan kale, this variety has distinctive scales and deeply veined leaves that are green-purple, bluish, or almost black. The leaves are narrow, with thin, ribbed stems. It provides a hearty, tangy bite and earthy sweetness and retains its firm texture when cooked. Perfect for pizza toppings, pasta recipes, braising in broth, or rustic stews.

BREAKFAST

Green Eggs and Kale
SERVES 2

What does a hipster have for breakfast? This. It's a kale-centric twist on shakshuka, with baked eggs and kale pesto on a bed of wilted greens. The flavors are clean and bright, and the dish goes perfectly with a cup of turmeric latte or chai. The roasted butternut squash could be substituted with other leftover roasted vegetables, peppers, or beets if you'd like.

INGREDIENTS

7 oz (200 g) squash, sliced
1 tbsp olive oil
9 oz (250 g) kale
3½ tbsp (50 g) butter
½ tsp sea salt
4 eggs
2 preserved lemons, sliced
½ tsp chili flakes

For the kale pesto
2½ oz (75 g) kale, blanched
Juice of 1 lemon
2 garlic cloves
4 tbsp olive oil
2 tbsp grated Parmesan cheese
1 tbsp pumpkin seeds

Method

01 Preheat the oven to 400°F (200°C). Add the squash slices to a roasting pan, drizzle with olive oil, and roast for 40–45 minutes.

02 Roughly chop the kale, stems and leaves together, then melt the butter in an oven-safe frying pan and add all the kale. Wilt for 3–4 minutes and season with the salt.

03 Spread the wilted kale into a bed on the base of the pan, then use the eggs to make 4 indentations in it. Crack one egg into each indentation, then top the dish with the roasted squash and preserved lemon slices. Bake in the oven for 8–10 minutes until the whites of the eggs are cooked.

04 Meanwhile, make the kale pesto. Blend all the ingredients in a food processor until you have a smooth texture.

05 Remove the pan from the oven and sprinkle with the chili flakes. Drizzle over the kale pesto and serve warm.

Kale and Roasted Fig Pizza

MAKES 4

Lacinato kale is the perfect kale for a pizza—the leaves blister into a light, chewy crunch, with a sweet, metallic taste. The juicy figs, earthy chestnuts, and creamy blue cheese work in unison, while the pesto reinforces the depth of kale running through this recipe. It takes a little planning, as you need to begin the base two days ahead, but it's worth it. This is a cold-season celebration with subtle, spicy warmth.

INGREDIENTS

2 tbsp kale pesto (see page 221)

4 lacinato kale leaves, washed and chopped

8–12 ripe figs, halved

8 cooked chestnuts, chopped

3½ oz (100 g) blue cheese

For the pizza dough

1⅓ cups (325 ml) lukewarm water

1½ tsp dried yeast

1 lb 2 oz (500 g) 00 flour, plus extra for dusting

1½ tsp sea salt

Olive oil, for greasing

2 tbsp polenta or semolina, for dusting

Method

01   Start the dough 2 days before. In a large bowl, mix the water and yeast until the yeast is absorbed. Add a couple spoonfuls of flour to make a batterlike consistency, then gradually add the remaining flour and the salt.

02   Mix, then turn out onto a floured surface. The dough will be a little sticky, so dust your hands with flour. Knead for 10–20 minutes until the dough is smooth and stretchy.

03   Put the dough in a bowl, cover with a damp kitchen towel, and leave to rest for 1 hour. Turn out onto a floured surface, gently punch down, then shape into a ball. Rub a clean bowl with olive oil using paper towel. Place the dough in the bowl and tightly cover with plastic wrap. Leave to proof in the fridge for 48 hours.

04   On baking day, divide the dough into 4 equal-sized portions and shape into balls. Leave to rest at room temperature on a floured baking sheet, covered with a kitchen towel, for about 4 hours until doubled in size.

05   Preheat the oven to 475°F (240°C) or heat a wood-fired pizza oven to 840°F (450°C). Gently stretch the dough into rounds until about 12 in (30 cm) in diameter and thin in the middle. Lay them on a pizza peel dusted with polenta (or semolina) or a lined baking sheet. Cover each with the kale pesto, kale leaves, halved figs, and chestnuts, then crumble over the blue cheese.

06   Bake in the oven for 10 minutes or in the pizza oven for 2–3 minutes, until the base is charred, then serve.

Kale Oven Chips

SERVES 2

Snacking on store-bought chips leaves me feeling a little guilty. First, there's the single-use packaging. Second, they are rarely good for you. But I love eating chips, so kale chips are a great alternative. For these, I went for a peppery seaweed vibe and dried chili for a little kick. They are light, crunchy, and devastatingly easy.

INGREDIENTS

6¼oz (180g) kale, chopped

For the seasoning

1 tbsp nori flakes (dried sea lettuce, sugar kelp, dulse, nori)

1 tsp sea salt

½ tsp chili flakes

½ tsp cracked black pepper

½ tsp pink peppercorns

Method

01   Preheat the oven to 200°F (100°C). Blanch the chopped kale for 3 minutes in boiling water, then drain and pat dry between two kitchen towels or sheets of paper towel.

02   Spread out the kale on two baking sheets and bake in the oven for 5–6 hours until light and crispy.

03   To make the seasoning, blend all the ingredients in a spice blender or crush in a pestle and mortar.

04   Once dried, remove the kale chips from the oven and sprinkle with the seasoning. Once cool, store in an airtight container and eat within 2–3 days.

Celery root

BEAUTIFUL ON THE INSIDE

EDIBLE PARTS

01 LEAVES AND STEMS

The bright, hollow stalks and serrated leaves are all edible. They are less flavorful than celery stems but still have a robust flavor and make a great addition to mirepoix and stock. They are also tasty blended into a celery root-top oil or used as a garnish for a Bloody Mary.

02 SKIN

The gnarly skin is edible but often trimmed off when preparing the bulb. You will also lose a bit of the flesh in the trimming due to deep crevices and root formations that protrude from the skin. Scrub with a vegetable brush and wash before cooking whole.

03 FLESH

Celery root flesh is bright cream or emeraldy-white but will discolor once peeled or chopped. It has a firm, nonfibrous, fine-grained texture and is less starchy than many other root vegetables. It has a pronounced celery and parsley flavor profile with savory overtones and increases in sweetness when roasted.

04 ROOT

The roots are edible. They can be washed and cooked in oil for celery root fries. They taste delicate but delicious with celery salt and cracked black pepper. Some varieties establish a more uniform system of larger tap roots that can be easily prepared.

Celery root is the unsung hero of the vegetable world. It's an alien-looking plant with brown freckles; hairy roots; and gnarly, mud-filled crevices. But beneath its furrowed visage lies the ivory flesh—clean, bright, minerally, and gentle tasting.

PLANT

Also called celeriac or knob celery, celery root is a type of umbellifer, like celery, parsnip, or parsley. The big, bulbous stem forms a knobby mass—or swollen hypocotyl, to be exact. It is not technically a root, but it can be treated as one in the kitchen. From this bulb sprouts rich green stalks and edible leaves. The plant is easy to grow and is a bit like a potato when cooked but less starchy, at only 5–6 percent, and containing more vitamin B6. Dense with nutrients such as vitamins C and K, potassium, and fiber, it can act as a useful lower-carb alternative in many recipes.

COOKING TIPS

The best way to cook celery root is to boil it with bay leaf in milk rather than water for 20 minutes or to roast it for 40 minutes until tender. It also makes a smooth, dry mash and works exceptionally well grated into a rustic gratin with dried pear, chives, and blue cheese. The flavor also pairs with herbs such as dill, rosemary, parsley, and thyme and is lovely cooked with truffle, celery salt, walnut, grapefruit, and mustard.

A simple recipe to try if you're new to celery root is to dice and roast it with other winter roots for 35–40 minutes at 400°F (200°C). Add plenty of rosemary, olive oil, and crushed garlic; season with celery salt; and you'll be blown away.

PREPARATION

Celery root takes a little effort to prepare, but don't be put off. Choose one with a firm skin and uniform color. It should feel heavy and the shoots, if still attached, should be bright green. Due to its rhino-tough skin, use a boning or paring knife to trim and peel— these allow you to access hard-to-reach crevices. Scrub well, then start by topping and tailing—store the stalks separately. Then use the same knife to slice off the rest of the skin. Try to keep your trimmings shallow. The knobby skin will hide some dirt, so I scrub again after peeling. The flesh discolors quickly, so immerse in a bowl of acidulated water once peeled or chopped.

ZERO WASTE

Store celery root bulbs and leaves in the fridge for a week or in a root cellar for 3–4 months. A no-brainer for using up the bulb is to try a simple slaw with apple and fennel and a buttermilk dressing or a classic French-inspired celery root remoulade with mustardy mayonnaise. For a zero-waste snack, roasted skin peelings can provide a twist on melba toast for spreading with nut butter or a black olive and caper tapenade. Scrub the skin well and roast with olive oil and sea salt until crispy for an intense umami hit. Alternatively, a silky, rich purée is a great way to preserve celery root. Boil for 20 minutes in milk, purée, then freeze. Use to thicken soups, enrich risotto, or serve with other veggies.

TYPES

MARBLE BALL
The best-known variety, rounded in shape, with a robust flavor. It stores well in winter and stays white when cooked.

TELLUS
Has a true celery root flavor with pronounced celery notes and a smoother skin than most. It is fast growing and retains its whitish color after boiling.

GLOBUS
A large variety, but despite this, it does not become woody like other root vegetables. It matures slowly, is harvested later in the season, and has uniform roots.

MONARCH
Has attractive foliage, smooth white skin, and succulent flesh. The deep bulb peels easily and tastes great raw or cooked.

MAIN MEAL

Celery Root Shawarma

SERVES 4

This recipe is inspired by Danish chef René Redzepi's crazy creation a few years back. He served slices of slow-roasted celery root with truffle for Noma's vegetarian tasting menu, and it blew up the internet. My version captures a late-night meaty shawarma flavor. The celery root absorbs the sweet spices and punches back with a woody depth that, when charred, makes the ultimate Turkish-inspired kebab.

INGREDIENTS

For the shawarma
2 celery root, peeled
3 pineapple slices
1 tsp smoked sea salt
4 flatbreads, to serve
Hot sauce, to serve
   (optional)

For the spice mix
1 tsp turmeric
1 tsp paprika
1 tsp ground cardamom
½ tsp ground cinnamon
½ tsp ground coriander
½ tsp ground cumin
1 tsp sea salt

For the marinade
7 tbsp (100 g) butter
¼ cup (50 ml) apple juice
2 tbsp lemon juice
2 tbsp tahini
2 tbsp date molasses
1 tbsp harissa paste
1 tbsp roasted garlic purée
1 tbsp porcini powder
3 sprigs of rosemary

For the pickles
¼ cup (50 ml) cider vinegar
1 tbsp sugar
½ tsp yellow mustard seeds
½ tsp chili flakes
1 garlic clove
Handful of celery root tops
1 red onion, finely sliced
   into rings

Method

01 Slice the celery root as thinly as you can. Combine all the ingredients for the spice mix, then sprinkle 1 tablespoon over the celery root slices. To make the shawarma, thread the celery root slices onto a skewer to form a large conical shape, then top with pineapple slices for a sweet-and-sour finish. Preheat the oven to 400°F (200°C).

02 Next, make the marinade. Melt the butter in a pan and add all the marinade ingredients. Then add in 1 tablespoon of the remaining spice mix. Warm through over a gentle heat and mix into a smooth paste. Reduce for 5–10 minutes, then start brushing the marinade onto the shawarma. Coat all of the celery root in the marinade, then stand it upright in a ceramic bowl and put in the oven. You will probably need to remove the shelves to make space. Roast for 2 hours, rotating and brushing with more marinade every 20–30 minutes.

03 Meanwhile, make the pickles. In a pan, mix the vinegar and sugar with ¼ cup (50 ml) boiling water until the sugar is dissolved. Warm the solution with the spices and garlic, then pour over the celery root tops and red onion rings in a jar while it's hot. Allow to cool, unsealed, and pickle for at least 30–40 minutes before using.

04 Remove the shawarma from the oven and season with the smoked sea salt. Grill the flatbreads for 2–3 minutes, then carve the shawarma at the table and serve with the flatbreads, pickles, and hot sauce for an extra kick.

Celery Root Fondant and Nut Roast

SERVES 2

This method is normally reserved for potatoes and is a decadent way to cook, but for celery root, it's a well-deserved chance to shine. I coat it in molten gold, and my date sauce provides a lovely sweetness served with a protein-packed nut roast.

Method

01 Preheat the oven to 425°F (220°C). To make the nut roast, heat the oil in a frying pan and add the onion to soften. Then add in the grated parsnip, sage, and spinach and cook for 5–10 minutes.

02 Blend the roasted nuts and chestnuts in a food processor into a coarse texture, then combine in a bowl with the parsnip and spinach mix and the remaining nut roast ingredients. Grease and line a loaf pan and fill with the mixture. Press down but not too firmly. Cover the top with parchment paper and bake for about 1 hour until nicely browned. Remove from the oven, then allow to cool slightly before turning out.

03 For the date sauce, combine all the ingredients in a saucepan with ½ cup (100 ml) water and cook for about 10 minutes until the dates are soft. Transfer to a food processor and blend until smooth, then reduce on the stove for 5 minutes until thick and glossy.

04 To make the fondants, heat the oil in a deep frying pan and sear the celery root disks over high heat for 4–6 minutes on each side. Add the butter, garlic cloves, and rosemary, then reduce heat and pour in the stock. Simmer for 40 minutes, turning the celery root occasionally and spooning over the hot butter and garlic. Serve when the celery root is golden and soft, with a slice of nut roast and the date sauce.

INGREDIENTS

For the nut roast
1 tbsp olive oil
1 onion, diced
1 parsnip, grated
2 tbsp chopped sage
2½ oz (75 g) cooked spinach
10 oz (300 g) roasted nuts—walnuts, hazelnuts, and Brazil nuts
5½ oz (150 g) cooked chestnuts
1¾ oz (50 g) cranberries
1¾ oz (50 g) dried dates, chopped
½ cup (50 g) panko breadcrumbs
½ cup (100 ml) sherry
1 egg, beaten
1 tsp truffle sea salt

For the fondant
1 tbsp olive oil
4 large disks of celery root
10½ tbsp (150 g) cold butter, diced
2 garlic cloves, lightly crushed in their skins
1 sprig of rosemary
½ cup (100 ml) vegetable stock

For the date sauce
5½ oz (150 g) dates
1 shallot, diced
7 tsp (50 g) date molasses
¼ cup (50 ml) apple juice
scant 2 tbsp (25 g) butter
1 tbsp tamarind paste
1 tbsp cider vinegar
1 tsp tomato paste
1 garlic clove, sliced
1 tsp grated fresh ginger root

Salt-baked Celery Root Soup

SERVES 4

This recipe takes a while to prepare, but it's worth it. The happiness derived from delving a spoon into the silken, ivory-white surface and tasting this mineral-rich, sweet-tangy soup is a fairy tale, while the garnish echoes the root's earthy depth of flavor. It requires no extra seasoning due to the salt crust, which infuses the whole bulb from the outside in.

Method

01 Preheat the oven to 350°F (180°C). Start by making the salt dough. Beat the egg whites in a clean bowl until stiff peaks form. In a separate bowl, mix the flour and salt with ½ cup (100 ml) water until it resembles wet sand. Fold the egg whites into the flour paste, then spread a small amount on a lined baking sheet, enough to cover the base of the celery root. Place the whole celery root on top, then cover it in a ½–¾ in (1–2 cm) layer of the mixture, ensuring there are no gaps. Bake for 1 hour 30 minutes until the salt crust is hard and brown.

02 Meanwhile, make the celery root oil. Blanch the celery root tops for 2 minutes, then drain and pat dry. Blend with the olive oil in a food processor, then heat in a pan until it starts to simmer. Strain through a sieve, then allow to cool.

03 When the celery root is done, start the soup base. Melt the butter in a pan and sauté the shallot over low heat. Break open and discard the salt crust and scoop the celery root flesh from its skin. Add it to the pan with the apple and cook for 5 minutes. Add the stock and milk. Bring to a boil, remove from heat, and blend in a food processor or with a hand-held mixer to a smooth purée.

04 Roast the hazelnuts and rosemary leaves in truffle oil on a baking sheet for 20–25 minutes, or fry in a pan for 4–5 minutes, and use to garnish the bowls of soup along with a drizzle of celery root oil and slices of black truffle.

INGREDIENTS

1 celery root, trimmed
3½ tbsp (50 g) butter
1 shallot, diced
1 apple, peeled, cored, and diced
1 cup (250 ml) vegetable stock
1 cup (250 ml) whole milk
2 tbsp halved hazelnuts, to garnish
1 sprig of rosemary, to garnish
2 tsp truffle oil
1 tbsp truffle slices, to garnish

For the salt dough
4 large egg whites, beaten
3¼ cups (400 g) all-purpose flour
2¼ cups (300 g) sea salt

For the celery root oil
Handful of celery root tops
½ cup (100 ml) olive oil

Sprouts

CABBAGEY BUTTONS TO LOVE OR HATE

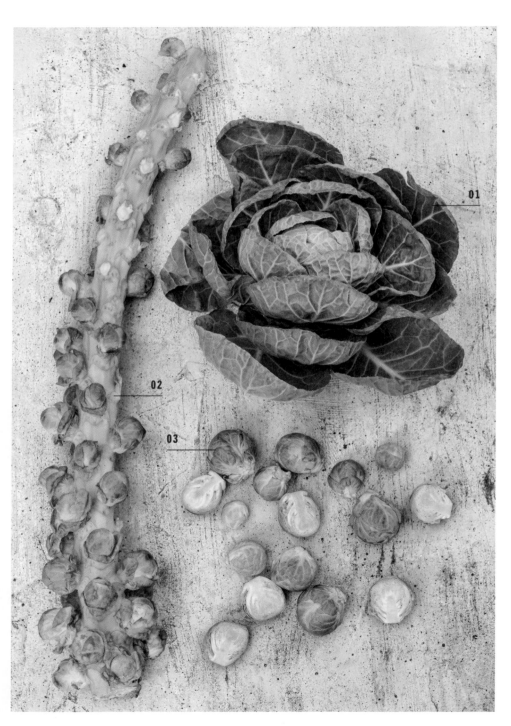

EDIBLE PARTS

01 TOPS

Not often found in supermarkets, sprout tops have flat, wide leaves, with attractive wavy edges and a thin central vein that is a paler tone of green. Wonderfully mild, tender, and sweet, they are devoid of the slightly bitter, sulfurous flavor of most cruciferous vegetables when cooked.

02 STALK

Sprouts are often sold on the stalk. The stem itself is woody and regarded as inedible but can be added to stocks for flavor or cooked for a fibrous twist on artichoke gratin. It is filled with a slightly bitter pulp. Personally, I compost rather than eating it.

03 SPROUT HEADS

The heads are entirely edible and vary in size depending on their maturity. The compact rounded leaves are tightly bound to form small spherical heads that range in color from aquamarine to dark fern or grassy green, some with purple tips.

No other vegetable is as divisive as the sprout. Studies have shown that we can be genetically predisposed to either love or hate them. But cook them with a crunch, and you will find a delicate sweetness that pairs with all sorts of exciting flavors.

PLANT

Sprouts are part of the brassica family and are a type of cultivated wild cabbage thought to have been grown in Belgium in the eighteenth century, hence the common name of Brussels sprouts. The plant grows best in cold temperatures, spiraling upward on a long, thin stalk studded with sprouts, which should ideally be harvested after the first frost—simply twist them off the stalk. They offer the bitter sweetness of cabbage, particularly the smaller ones—as they get larger, they have a more astringent quality. Like it or not, sprouts are also good for you, containing high levels of vitamins A and C and lots of fiber.

COOKING TIPS

Sprouts are quintessentially Christmassy, but cook them on more than one day a year. The most important thing is not to overcook them, as, like many cruciferous vegetables, they can release a sulfurous smell. Boil them in salted water for no longer than 5–10 minutes, until you can slide a sharp knife easily into the base, or steam for no more than 8 minutes. Roasting is the most popular method nowadays, as it retains their crunch and heightens their natural sweetness; less common is to fry them. Chestnuts, of course, go very well with sprouts, as do sage, orange, and nutmeg, but I also love them with slivered almonds, tarragon, and a squeeze of lemon.

PREPARATION

Some kitchen chores can be done at a slower pace, and prepping sprouts is one of them. Choose plump, bright green–headed sprouts that have tightly packed leaves around a paler core. Start by discarding any yellow or damaged leaves in the compost bin and trimming off any outer brown leaves, which have a much stronger flavor than the pale leaves underneath. Remove the stem and then, using a small paring knife, cut an "X" into the base where the stem has been cut away, about ¼–½ in (5–10 mm) deep. This really does help the core and the outside cook evenly and reduces the chance of overcooking.

ZERO WASTE

Keep sprouts in a cool, dark place or in the fridge for 5–7 days. They store best on the stalk. If you end up with cooked leftovers, try my bubble and squeak recipe (see page 233). Alternatively, to avoid waste, try using them raw, as well as cooked. Shred them into slaw or a salad with a sharp vinaigrette to bring them into different types of meals. You can also preserve them by blanching and then freezing or ferment sprout petals for 10–14 days in a 3 percent salt brine with dried cranberry, rosemary, and orange zest for a batch of festive kraut (see pages 284–285). Add a couple of cloves and a stick of cinnamon and serve at Christmas for a tangy sweet-and-sour garnish.

TYPES

BRUSSELS

There are many varieties of the classic Brussels sprout. A high-yielding variety is 'Wellington'. 'Trafalgar' also tastes superb—it produces medium to small, firm sprouts with a strong flavor; retains its quality during a long growing season; and provides a heavy crop.

PURPLE

These range in diameter and in color, from deep purple, to sea green, to violet or red, although they fade slightly when cooked. Purple sprouts are a difficult crop to grow but generally have a more complex flavor and are significantly sweeter than their green counterparts. The 'Red Ball' variety is delicious, while 'Falstaff' is a novelty deep-purple variety that retains its color when cooked and is becoming more widely available.

BABY

Sprouts that are picked when young and cherry-sized have a lovely sweetness on the forward part of the palate. 'Noisette' is a variety that bears smaller sprouts and is very popular in France.

KALETTES

A frilly kale-sprout hybrid with attractive purple-green leaves, also known as flower sprouts. These are increasingly popular, as they deliver outstanding sweet flavor with complex sprout notes and are very attractive on the plate—a gateway variety into the sprout world.

BRUNCH OR MAIN MEAL

Bubble and Squeak with Sprout Slaw

SERVES 2

In the UK, it's Boxing Day brunch when sprouts come into their own. Bubble and squeak is a superb zero-waste recipe but also a star dish in its own right. Here, I've served up the sprouts two ways: steamed and then fried, to bring all their sweet, bitter notes to the other roasted vegetables; and raw, in a slaw coated in aromatic truffle mayo. The dish is then garnished with crispy sage leaves.

INGREDIENTS

5½oz (150g) steamed sprouts

1lb 2oz (500g) mixed roasted vegetables (potato, rutabaga, parsnip, carrot, cabbage) and chestnuts if you have them

3 eggs

1 tbsp all-purpose flour

1 tbsp cranberry sauce

½ tsp sea salt

Vegetable oil, for frying

6–8 sage leaves

For the slaw

5½oz (150g) sprouts

Zest and juice of ½ orange

½ tsp sea salt

1 tbsp truffle mayonnaise

Method

01 Chop and then mash the steamed sprouts and roasted vegetables in a large bowl. Beat one of the eggs, then mix it into the mashed vegetables with the flour and cranberry sauce. Season to taste with the salt, then form the mixture into two large patties—it's helpful to use forming rings if you have them. Leave in the fridge for 20–30 minutes to firm up before frying.

02 Meanwhile, make the truffled slaw. Shave or shred the raw sprouts using a mandoline or knife and combine with the orange zest and juice, salt, and truffle mayo.

03 Heat a little vegetable oil in a frying pan and fry the bubble-and-squeak patties for 4–5 minutes on each side until crispy and golden but still moist in the middle.

04 Fry the 2 remaining eggs and the sage leaves in the same pan. Serve the bubble and squeak, garnished with the sage, alongside the sprout slaw and a fried egg.

MAIN MEAL

Savory Bread Pudding with Cheesy Sprouts

SERVES 4

Years ago, when I was reading a cookbook by Thomas Keller, I saw a surprisingly rustic-looking savory bread and butter pudding amid his Michelin-starred works of art. Ever since, I've been thinking of what my more artisan version could be. The result is a dish that, for me, captures winter in one rich, creamy scoop. I adore the way the mustard and Cheddar soften the bitter cruciferous note of the sprouts while accentuating their sweet profile. Cook this with yesterday's bread for added texture—and to mop up the sauce.

INGREDIENTS

3½ tbsp (50 g) butter

1 tbsp all-purpose flour

⅓ cup (75 ml) white wine

1 cup (200 ml) heavy cream

1 tsp whole-grain mustard

½ tsp ground nutmeg

½ tsp celery salt

5½ oz (150 g) mature Cheddar cheese, grated

12 oz (350 g) sprouts, halved

2 slices of sourdough, toasted

Method

01 Preheat the oven to 425°F (220°C). Melt the butter in a saucepan and stir in the flour. Mix into a basic roux base and then slacken it with the white wine.

02 Continue to stir the roux while adding in the cream, mustard, nutmeg, and celery salt, then cook over low heat for 3–4 minutes until velvety and smooth.

03 Add the cheese and allow to melt, then remove the pan from heat.

04 Steam the sprouts for 4 minutes, then add them to the cheese sauce with torn pieces of the toasted sourdough. Pour the mixture into a small casserole dish and bake in the oven for 15–20 minutes until the cheese sauce is golden and the edges have started to crisp.

SIDE

Korean Fried Sprouts
SERVES 4

Fusion cooking can sometimes feel a bit crazy, and this one is right out there, but it's very lip-smackingly sweet and sour, and a great way to convert any sprout doubter. The sprouts are reinvented by the rich Korean barbecue sauce and crispy texture, making them a world away from the soggy, boiled sprouts of yesteryear.

INGREDIENTS

2¼lb (1kg) sprouts, halved
1 tbsp Cajun spice mix
1 tbsp all-purpose flour
1 tsp smoked sea salt
Vegetable oil, for deep-frying
1 tsp sesame seeds

For the sauce
2 tbsp tomato ketchup
¼ cup (50ml) orange juice
2 tbsp maple syrup
1 tbsp mirin
1 tbsp sesame oil
1 tbsp kimchi purée
1 tbsp soy sauce
*1 tsp gochujang
   (red chili) paste*

Method

01 Preheat the oven to 300°F (150°C). Blanch the sprouts in salted boiling water for 2–3 minutes, then drain. Mix the Cajun spice mix, flour, and smoked salt. While the drained sprouts are still a little damp, dredge them in the seasoned flour to lightly coat them.

02 Heat some vegetable oil in a saucepan, about ½–¾ in (1–2cm) in depth, to 350°F (180°C) and deep-fry the coated sprouts in small batches for 4–5 minutes each until super crispy and golden brown. Remove from the oil with a slotted spoon and leave to drain on a piece of paper towel, then keep warm in the oven while you fry the remaining sprouts.

03 To make the Korean-inspired barbecue sauce, heat all ingredients in a small pan and stir until the mixture reduces slightly and thickens into a glossy, sweet, spicy, and sour sauce.

04 Serve small plates of the fried sprouts tossed in the hot sauce and sprinkled with the sesame seeds.

Onions

LAYERS OF FLAVOR

Red

02

01

03

Yellow

EDIBLE PARTS

01 SHOOTS

The long, tubular green onion tops are edible. They have a mild onion flavor and can be cooked like a spring onion—they are tender when sautéed and good in an omelet or quesadilla.

02 FLESH

Within the onion bulb lie layers of crisp, juicy flesh that range in color depending on the variety. The flesh contains a pungent oil that is full of aroma and allium flavor. It's also rich in sugar, so it often tastes sweet when cooked.

03 ROOTS

The roots are difficult to clean but delicious fried for a crispy topping to soups or salads. After removing the excess soil, try dipping them in a light tempura batter and frying as a cluster.

FLOWERS

The clusters of greenish-white flowers on one tall, leafless stem are very ornamental in the veggie patch and good for pollinating insects. They are edible and have a strong, sweet onion taste.

So much vegetable cooking begins with the humble onion, but it can also be a stellar solo performer, given the chance. I try to layer flavors like a builder laying bricks, and I trust onions to deliver essential acidity, sweetness, and pungent depth.

PLANT

The most common species of the *Allium* genus, onions can be grown from seed but are usually produced from sets that are small onions. They are easy to grow and, once harvested, store well, so they're available all year round. They are high in sugar and rich in vitamin C, calcium, potassium, and iron, but it's pyruvic acid that accounts for their pungency—this is what makes people cry when cutting them. The pyruvate scale, which measures the amount of pyruvic acid present, indicates the pungency of onions and garlic: the standard is around 8, and anything less than 5 is classed as a sweet onion.

COOKING TIPS

The versatility of onions is one of their greatest assets. I use them in chutneys, pickles, soups, and sauces, and they pair well with many flavors, particularly beer, thyme, bay, garlic, and apple. There are a few key ways to cook them. You can sweat them in oil or butter to slowly soften them—ideally at medium or low heat with the lid on to avoid coloring. Caramelized onions are also popular and very useful for an umami, sweet base to dishes. To achieve this, fry in a small amount of oil for 20–40 minutes until dark brown. Do not add salt, as that draws out moisture and prevents caramelization. Roasting also imparts a deep flavor to onions—layer in a roasting pan with garlic, root vegetables, and woody herbs.

PREPARATION

There's an old-school method of chopping an onion that has stood the test of time: start by removing the stem, then halve the bulb and remove the skin. Place the halves flat side down on the chopping board and then slice across or dice. This will make your eyes water, and people try all sorts of things to avoid this, from chilling the bulb in the freezer for 15 minutes before cutting to slicing them underwater. Wearing contact lenses or goggles seems to help. The base of the onion where the roots form holds most of the enzymes that produce pyruvic acid, so if you avoid cutting it, that could also make the task less uncomfortable.

ZERO WASTE

Store onions in a cool, dry, well-ventilated place. They need to breathe, so don't keep in plastic or sealed containers. If you have more onions than you know what to do with, try slicing them thinly and laying out in a dehydrator at 130°F (55°C) for 6–8 hours. These kibbled onions can be stored in an airtight container and added to curries and stews if there is enough excess water in the recipe to rehydrate them. To make into a powder, blend the dried onions in a spice grinder, or, for a pungent salt, blend on pulse for a minute or so and combine with sea salt flakes. Store in an airtight container and the salt will infuse with an intense onion aroma, making a great seasoning. It's also good with unsalted butter and chopped chives.

TYPES

WHITE

These have a ghostly white, tracing-paper-thin skin; crisp, firm flesh; and a globular shape. The flavor is mild and sweet, with a particularly mellow aftertaste, making them fantastic sliced raw in a grilled cheese.

YELLOW

The real workhorse of the onion world, medium to large in size and a good jack-of-all-trades. It is slightly flat in shape, with a heavy copper-yellow, papery skin. The white or cream flesh is very juicy and has a strong, pungent flavor and aroma when eaten raw. It is sweeter when cooked.

RED

This bulb is wrapped in magenta parchmentlike skin, with layers of claret and white rings beneath. Crunchy, colorful, and peppery when raw, red onions are favored for salads and garnishes. When cooked, they caramelize with pronounced umami undertones.

FRENCH SHALLOT

A pear-drop-shaped shallot with skin ranging from copper to pale pink to red and purplish flesh. It grows more like garlic as 2–3 cloves or lobes clustered together. The flavor is complex—sweet, spicy, and slightly astringent when raw, delicate and sweet when cooked—and can give subtle nuance to sauces.

DUTCH SHALLOT

This shallot has coppery-brown skin and fine-textured flesh. It has the mildest flavor of all shallots with subtle apple notes.

MAIN MEAL

Shallot Tarte Tatin
SERVES 4

This sweet tart would work as part of the cheese course instead of dessert at the end of a meal, served with some acidic goat cheese or sticky Gorgonzola. It is wonderfully sweet and salty and full of deep, pungent allium flavor.

INGREDIENTS

8–10 shallots, peeled
3½ tbsp (50 g) butter
2 tbsp soft brown sugar
2 tbsp balsamic vinegar
1 tbsp honey
8 garlic cloves, peeled
1 tsp sea salt, plus extra for seasoning
12 oz (350 g) puff pastry
1 tbsp all-purpose flour, for dusting
4 sprigs of thyme

Method

01 Preheat the oven to 475°F (240°C). Cut the shallots into fairly equal-sized rounds about 1 in (2.5 cm) long. In a large oven-safe frying pan or skillet, melt the butter and add in the sugar, vinegar, honey, and ¼ cup (50 ml) water. Heat until the mixture starts bubbling, then arrange the shallot pieces in a pattern on the base of the pan and fill in any gaps with the garlic cloves.

02 Season with the salt and cook over medium heat for 10–15 minutes. Shake the pan gently every few minutes to stop the onions from sticking. They will soften and start to caramelize; at this point, remove the pan from heat and allow to cool slightly.

03 Roll out the pastry on a floured surface into a round that is big enough to cover the shallots, plus a little extra. Carefully lay the pastry disk over the shallots, then use a wooden spoon to tuck the edges down the inside of the pan. With a small knife, make a couple of holes in the middle of the pastry for steam to escape as it bakes.

04 Bake in the oven for 35 minutes or until golden brown. Allow to cool for a few minutes once baked, then place a large plate over the pastry and confidently flip the plate and pan as one to turn it out.

05 Garnish with thyme leaves and more sea salt and serve warm or cold.

MAIN MEAL

Triple Onion and Cheese Pasty

MAKES 4–6

In Cornwall, pasties have a rich cultural history. I love them and for a few years ran an artisan company called the Posh Pasty Co., making a range of these comforting hand-held meals. This recipe uses three types of onion for a tangy, sweet, cheese-filled parcel of joy. The trick with crimping is to roll your finger toward you and tuck in the pastry so it looks like a neat rope.

INGREDIENTS

For the filling
½ yellow onion, peeled and diced
½ red onion, peeled and diced
1 shallot, peeled and diced
3½ oz (100 g) Cheddar cheese, grated
3½ oz (100 g) Red Leicester, grated
5½ oz (150 g) potato, diced
½ tsp cracked black pepper

For the pastry
9 oz (250 g) cold salted butter, diced
1 lb 2 oz (500 g) bread flour, plus extra for dusting
1 egg, beaten

Method

01 Make the pastry 1–2 hours before baking your pasties for best results. Rub the butter and flour between your fingers into a breadcrumb texture, then mix in ¾ cup (175 ml) water until it comes together to form a ball of dough. Leave to rest in the fridge for 1–2 hours.

02 Preheat the oven to 425°F (220°C). For the filling, mix all the diced onions with the grated cheeses, potato, and black pepper. Once the pastry has rested, divide it on a floured surface into 4 or 6 balls and roll them out into rounds about 8 in (20 cm) in diameter.

03 Deposit a portion of filling in the center of each pastry disk. Fold up the disk edges to meet in the middle and, with well-floured hands, roll the pasty onto its side and crimp the joined edges. I use my right thumb and index finger to fold the pastry toward me and tuck it in on itself, while my left hand guides the pastry and helps keep the crimp tight. Fold over the ends and press them down.

04 Glaze the pastry with the beaten egg and pierce the pasty with a fork or knife to allow the steam to escape.

05 Bake on a lined baking sheet for 15 minutes, then reduce the temperature to 400°F (200°C) and bake for 20 more minutes until the pastry is golden and the filling melted and hot. Eat on their own or try with some chutney, roasted vegetables, or salad.

Hot Smoked Onion Soup

SERVES 4

Growing up, I used to eat French onion soup on a weekly basis over the winter months. It's packed with immune-boosting vitamins and minerals and remains one of my absolute favorite recipes to this day. Over the years, I've tried several versions of my own and I think I've finally found a winner. This two-step recipe hot smokes the onions before caramelizing them, which adds a dark, woody, umami edge to the pungent classic.

INGREDIENTS

10–12 yellow onions, peeled and halved

1 tbsp olive oil

6 tbsp oak wood chips

3½ tbsp (50 g) butter

1 tsp golden sugar

6 smoked garlic cloves

2 sprigs of thyme

1 cup (250 ml) white wine

4½ cups (1.3 liters) vegetable stock

Sea salt and cracked black pepper

9 oz (250 g) Camembert cheese

2 sprigs of rosemary

1 baguette

Method

01 Preheat a hot smoker or kettle barbecue to 350°F (180°C) and, once the charcoal has burned down to hot embers, add the halved onions in their skins with a little olive oil rubbed across the surface. Add the wood chips to the embers, close the smoker, and hot smoke the onions for 20–30 minutes.

02 When the onions are smoked, remove from the smoker and, once cool enough to handle, remove their skins and slice.

03 Melt the butter in a saucepan and add the sliced onions and the sugar. Caramelize over medium heat for 20 minutes, then add in the smoked garlic and sprigs of thyme. Continue cooking for 10–15 more minutes until the onions are brown and sticky, then add the white wine and stock.

04 Bring to a boil, simmer for 15 minutes, then season to taste with salt and black pepper.

05 Meanwhile, stud the Camembert with the rosemary sprigs and bake on a baking sheet at 425°F (220°C) for 20 minutes. Serve alongside the soup with generous slices of baguette.

Maincrop Potatoes
SACKFULS OF NOURISHMENT

01

Red Duke of York

Maris Piper

King Edward

Alouette

Orla

EDIBLE PARTS

01 SKIN

This nutrient-dense layer is edible and, if cleaned, can make for great skin-on fries, baked potatoes, or rustic roast potatoes. If peeling, try to trim thinly and core out any black spots that have damaged the skin.

FLESH

The flesh of a potato tends to be firm, and maincrop varieties can have a waxy or floury texture. Waxy varieties can be cooked any way, as they tend to hold their shape well, while floury types tend to easily fall apart and fluff up, so they are perfect for mashed potatoes, chips, and roast potatoes. They should feel dense and are mostly creamy-yellow in color.

Around the world, this tuberous vegetable rates as one of the most eaten foods. And no wonder. It's cheap, filling, full of flavor, and beneath its rough exterior lies vast potential. If you can buy a sack of spuds, you'll be hungry no more.

PLANT

Potatoes are grown from seed potatoes, which are small tubers rather than actual seeds. They are chitted before planting to stimulate growth and, once small shoots appear, they are planted and earthed up to stop the tubers from turning green and inedible. Harvest time depends on the type, but you can have crops from May to October. Their health benefits are often overlooked, because they often get coated in fats and oil for cooking. In their unprocessed state, though, they are a good source of vitamin B6, potassium, and fiber.

COOKING TIPS

As a rule, bake potatoes for 50 minutes–1 hour 15 minutes and boil for 15–20 minutes before tossing in olive oil with lemon, salt, and pepper. To fry, make sure the oil is at least 355°F (180°C) and ideally blanch or soak the potatoes first to help reduce their water content for a crisper finish. For classic roast potatoes, parboil for 10 minutes, then drain for 10 minutes to allow moisture to evaporate and toss in a colander to rough up the edges. Heat 3–4 tablespoons of vegetable oil in a roasting pan at 400°F (200°C), then gently add the potatoes, browning each side. Roast for 20 minutes, turn, roast for 20 more minutes, turn again, and roast for a final 20 minutes. Finish with sea salt. Paprika, horseradish, chives, leeks, garlic, rosemary, truffle, and spring onions are all timeless companions for potatoes.

PREPARATION

Choose potatoes that are blemish free and avoid those with cracked or green-tinged skin. (Green skins contain a toxin called solanine and should be peeled before eating. If the whole potato is green, don't eat it.) Scrub well to remove any damp mud before storing. Peel if necessary, but think twice before you do, as there is some good nutritional content in or just under the skin. If you do peel them, try to make use of the peelings (see *Zero Waste*). In many recipes, you can swap a peeler for a firm vegetable brush to remove any dirt before cooking.

ZERO WASTE

Store potatoes in a dark, well-ventilated spot—if exposed to the light, they'll chit and sprout green shoots. I find a paper bag is the simplest option. To avoid waste, chips are a surprisingly easy snack to make at home. Slice potatoes on a mandoline for uniform thinness. Soak the slices for an hour in water to remove excess starch, then dry them on a kitchen towel and deep-fry in vegetable oil for 3–4 minutes per batch until golden brown. Remove from the oil and drain on paper towel, then season with sea salt. To preserve a bumper crop, cut into chips and blanch before freezing. The skins are also surprisingly full of flavor when fried, boiled, or roasted. Deep-fry and season with sea salt and freshly chopped herbs for delicious chips or add cleaned peel to vegetable stock for an earthy depth of flavor.

TYPES

KING EDWARD

A late maincrop variety that's great for baking and roasting. It's a large, white-skinned oval potato, with a pink tinge, a floury texture, and an excellent taste.

MARIS PIPER

These have cream-colored flesh that is dense and firm. They make great chips and wedges and are very good for roasting, with a fluffy texture when cooked.

BAKING

Larger potatoes with thicker skins such as 'Russet', 'Vivaldi', 'Melody', and 'Sante' tend to make very good baking potatoes.

RED

Crisp and waxy with a buttery flavor, these potatoes have smooth ruby-red skins. The firm flesh is pale yellow to white and smooth in texture. They are excellent for all types of cooking.

PURPLE

Small and round to oblong, this Peruvian variety is becoming more widespread. The skin is thin and the flesh deep violet. It is low in starch and will therefore crisp up well.

YELLOW

The skin is often tan to light golden and the flesh pale yellow with a waxy texture. Buttery and velvety smooth when cooked, with a reduced starch content.

FINGER

These long, oval potatoes are lovely roasted and can be used for a late-season potato salad.

BRUNCH

Potato Bread with Deviled Mushrooms

SERVES 2

It must be my Irish blood, but to me, griddled potato bread is the height of luxury—a decadent brunch that guarantees satisfaction. It's got it all: a hearty balance of buttery and meaty textures; a rich, creamy flavor; and it uses up leftover mash. I add rosemary to boost the aromatic tang in the potato farl and gently spiced mushrooms for the perfect topping.

INGREDIENTS

9 oz (250 g) potatoes
1 beaten egg
2 tbsp all-purpose flour, plus extra for dusting
Pinch of baking powder
½ tsp sea salt
1 tsp chopped rosemary
1 tbsp olive oil

For the topping
3½ tbsp (50 g) butter
7 oz (200 g) mushrooms, sliced
1 shallot, peeled and finely diced
2 garlic cloves, sliced
1 tsp paprika
½ tsp dried thyme
¼ cup (50 ml) sherry
½ cup (100 ml) heavy cream
Sea salt and cracked black pepper
2 eggs
1 tbsp cider vinegar
Handful of salad leaves
1 tbsp walnuts, chopped

Method

01 Peel and quarter the potatoes, then boil for 15–20 minutes until you can easily slide a paring knife into them. Drain well, then mash with a masher or fork. Mix the mashed potatoes with the beaten egg and flour to stiffen it slightly and stir in the baking powder, salt, and rosemary. On a floured surface, either form the mixture into one large, thin round to slice into sections after cooking or make two smaller individual cakes.

02 Preheat a griddle pan and grease it using a sheet of paper towel dipped in the olive oil for a thin, nonstick covering. Cook the potato bread for 5–6 minutes on each side until golden and firm.

03 While the bread is cooking, make the topping. Melt the butter in a frying pan and fry the mushrooms, shallot, and garlic with the paprika and thyme. After 5–6 minutes, once the mushrooms are nicely caramelized, deglaze the pan with the sherry and add in the cream, then season to taste with salt and pepper.

04 To finish, poach the eggs. Bring a saucepan of water to a boil, add the cider vinegar, then stir to create a whirlpool. Crack the eggs one by one into the center to help hold the whites together, poach on a rolling boil for 2–3 minutes, then remove with a slotted spoon. Serve the deviled mushrooms and a poached egg on top of each of the griddled potato breads. Garnish with a handful of salad leaves and a few walnuts on the side.

MAIN MEAL

Loaded Potato Skins

SERVES 2

Loaded skins are super-comforting and can be packed with flavor. These warming spiced jackets with crispy skins hold a buttery, moist filling that's rich with grilled cheese and black beans. Try your own versions with leek and mustard, three cheeses, baked beans, or a sweet potato. This is an excellent recipe for leftovers if you find yourself with spare baked potatoes.

INGREDIENTS

3–4 baking potatoes

1 tsp olive oil

4¼ oz (120 g) cooked black beans

3½ oz (100 g) grated Cheddar cheese

½ red onion, peeled and finely diced

1 tbsp chopped roasted red pepper

1 tbsp roughly chopped cilantro

1 tbsp chopped jalapeño

Sea salt and cracked black pepper

Pinch of paprika

Method

01 Preheat the oven to 425°F (220°C). Skewer the potatoes a few times and rub with a little oil. Bake in the oven for 1 hour, then remove, allow to cool slightly, and slice in half lengthwise. Keep the oven on.

02 Scoop out the potato flesh and, in a large bowl, mix half of it with the beans, cheese, onion, red pepper, cilantro, and jalapeño. Keep the remainder of the potato flesh for another recipe, such as potato bread (see page 245) or mash.

03 Season to taste with sea salt and black pepper, then add a pinch of paprika.

04 Spoon the filling back into the empty skins and return to the oven to bake for 15 more minutes. Try serving with sour cream, salsa, slaw, guacamole, and salad.

Leek and Potato Soup
SERVES 2

*There are occasions when the simple things transcend
the ordinary and turn into special foodie moments, and a
bowl of leek and potato soup with crispy, crunchy potato
croutons is one of them. This soup is simple and rustic but
velvety smooth and worth making for someone special.*

Method

01   Melt the butter in a large pan, then add the potatoes and leek. Sweat,
     stirring occasionally, for 5 minutes, then add the stock and bay leaf.
02   Bring to a boil, then simmer for 20 minutes until the potato is soft.
03   Meanwhile, make the croutons. Parboil the diced potato in salted water
     for 8–10 minutes, then drain. Heat the oil in a frying pan, add the
     potato, and fry with the salt and thyme for 10–12 minutes until crisp.
04   Finish the soup by adding the milk, horseradish sauce (if using), salt,
     and white pepper. Remove the bay leaf, then blend until smooth using
     a hand-held mixer. Serve in bowls topped with the crispy potato
     croutons and a drizzle of chive oil (if using).

INGREDIENTS

3½ tbsp (50 g) butter

*9 oz (250 g) potatoes, peeled
and diced*

1 leek, finely sliced

*4 cups (1.2 liters) vegetable
stock*

1 bay leaf

⅔ cup (150 ml) whole milk

*1 tsp prepared horseradish
sauce (optional)*

½ tsp sea salt

½ tsp ground white pepper

*Chive oil, for drizzling
(optional)*

For the croutons

1 potato, diced

2 tbsp olive oil

½ tsp sea salt

1 sprig of thyme

Parsnips
COLD CLIMATE SWEETNESS

EDIBLE PARTS

01 TAPROOT

A long root tapered at the tip with a wider crown. They can be eaten raw but are most often cooked. Larger parsnips have a woody core that is slightly darker than the pale flesh. Trim the ends before cooking.

02 SKIN

The thin beige skin is rich in nutrients, so it is best scrubbed rather than peeled before use, especially when roasted. The peel is tender on small parsnips, but as they grow larger, it becomes woody and slightly bitter in taste.

TOPS

Parsnips are relatives of cow or wild parsnip and hogweed, and like them, the green tops contain furanocoumarins. These chemical compounds can cause skin irritation and a painful rash, making parsnip tops very uncomfortable to handle. Parsnips are usually sold without the tops, but if they remain, remove them before storing. Technically, they are edible once blanched and have an herby flavor similar to parsley, but personally I avoid eating them.

Sometimes you don't need to dress up an ingredient with fancy words. The humble parsnip is pale, sweet, and unspectacular looking—but mashed, puréed, or roasted with honey and thyme until sticky, it is simply splendid.

PLANT

As part of the *Apiaceae* family, parsnips are closely related to carrots but have a stronger sweet flavor. These edible taproots have a long growing season and can reach up to 1 ft (30 cm) in length and roughly 3 in (7.5 cm) in diameter at the crown; they are one of the few vegetables that grow better the farther north you travel and tend to grow larger in colder climates, developing a mature woody flavor. The skin is always pale but varies slightly from bright white to beige-yellow. Nutritionally, parsnips are packed with vitamin C, folic acid, and potassium. They also shine as a source of fiber, which is extremely good for digestion.

COOKING TIPS

As a guide when cooking, parsnips are less starchy than potato and sweeter than carrot. They add good body to soups, provide an earthy sweetness to stews, and respond well when mashed or roasted. The trimmings are also excellent for starting off a stockpot. Its sweet profile means that parsnip is often paired with honey, maple syrup, tarragon, and thyme. I even grate it into cakes and white blondie brownies. A good way to enjoy raw parsnip is to grate a few baby parsnips; dress with lemon juice, chopped chives, and white truffle oil; then toss into a bitter radicchio salad with toasted walnuts. The raw parsnip provides a crunchy texture and surprisingly sweet flavor dimension.

PREPARATION

Choose firm, smooth specimens, avoiding those with lots of whiskers, soft or shriveled tips, and soft or dark brown patches. Once cut, parsnips quickly discolor if left to oxidize. They are best stored in cold lemon water if not using right away. The skin may need peeling, although I would recommend scrubbing instead to avoid waste. Then slice lengthwise or dice across the grain. The core is often woody and tougher than the tender root flesh, so if you are boiling to mash, you may want to start cooking it ahead of time. Alternatively, you can bone out the core, blanch, and then roast it separately—it is still tasty.

ZERO WASTE

Keep parsnips in a cool, dark, well-ventilated larder, garage, or root cellar. If kept under 50°F (10°C), they can easily be stored for 4–6 months. Avoid storing them near apples, as they emit a gas that can give the parsnips a bitter taste. Small to medium parsnips need only a gentle scrub before cooking, but with larger roots, I thinly peel and then either fry the skins in a little oil for a crouton-style topping or dehydrate them as chips. Alternatively, try blending the dried skins into a powder as a base for stocks and sauces. To preserve the root, dice, parboil, drain, and refresh, then freeze for 10–12 months. Or purée before freezing and use to add sweet, starchy body to soups.

TYPES

ALBION

This variety is evenly tapered, with broad, wedge-shaped roots and a smooth skin. The flesh is white and slow to discolor and has an excellent sweet flavor.

HOLLOW CROWN

An heirloom variety, with a crownlike shape at the base of the leaves, this requires deep soil tilling, as it can grow up to 14 in (36 cm) in length. It thrives in harsh winters and develops a sweeter flavor the colder the conditions. It mashes smoothly due to the fine-grained flesh, is good for seed saving, and has a buttery taste with good background sweetness.

THE STUDENT

An American heirloom parsnip, with long, slender roots; smooth skin; creamy flesh; and small central core. It boasts a deliciously mild flavor that increases if left in the ground beyond the first frosts.

GLADIATOR

The top of this root is broad, but then it slims down to be very long and thin. It's a high-yielding parsnip that is less sweet but has a strong, rich flavor and suits both light and heavier soils.

BABY

Tender and sweeter than the larger roots, small, young parsnips can be used whole or sliced in half. They are superb for weaning, as children love the sweet flavor and hearty texture when steamed.

MAIN MEAL

Merguez Parsnip Sausages
SERVES 2

The bulk of the filling in these sausages is grated parsnip, which means they can handle competing spices and plenty of vibrant roasted pepper. The parsnip grounds the other piquant ingredients and has a meaty texture that makes this a really lovely vegetarian banger. Ideally, this recipe requires some technical equipment to fill the casings. You can try pushing the filling through a funnel into the casings, although it is much harder than using a machine.

INGREDIENTS

3¼ ft (1 m) vegetarian
   sausage casing

1 tbsp olive oil

For the sausage filling

1 lb 2 oz (500 g) grated
   parsnip

1 roasted red pepper,
   finely chopped

4 garlic cloves, grated

1 shallot, finely diced

½ cup (50 g) breadcrumbs

1 tbsp roasted red
   pepper pesto

1 tbsp harissa paste

2 tsp smoked paprika

2 tsp dried thyme
   (preferably wild)

1 tsp cumin seeds

1 tsp fennel seeds

½ tsp chili flakes

½ tsp smoked sea salt

Method

01 Combine all the sausage filling ingredients in a large bowl and mix well, then leave to marinate for 1–2 hours while you prepare your sausage-making kit.

02 Soak the casing in cold water for 5 minutes. If using a sausage-making machine, load the wet casing onto the spout and mince the filling mixture at ¾ in (8 mm). Alternatively, blend the sausage filling in a food processor until you have a coarse texture.

03 Preheat the oven to 400°F (200°C). Steadily fill the sausage casing using either the machine or by manually pushing the mixture through a funnel, pausing halfway along to allow a small gap. Twist the sausage at the halfway point to make two long coils. Tie the ends of the sausage casings with string and cut to make two separate sausages, then hold the coils in place with a skewer for cooking.

04 Place the sausage coils in a roasting pan, brush with olive oil, then roast in the oven for 20–25 minutes until golden brown. Try serving with pickled chilies, harissa mayo, and French fries.

Spiced Parsnip Soup with Crispy Peel

SERVES 4

I couldn't leave out a humble curried parsnip soup from this book. Like leek and potato, carrot and cumin, or French onion, it is a rustic, much-loved, seasonal trump card to have in your recipe deck. My version is silky smooth and rich in spices for a warming rather than hot flavor. The crunchy nest of fried parsnip peel and red chili offers a peppy lift and another texture in the bowl without overpowering the sweet, spiced soup.

INGREDIENTS

1 lb 10 oz (750 g) parsnips

2 tbsp olive oil

1 large onion, peeled and roughly chopped

2 garlic cloves, finely chopped

1 tbsp grated fresh ginger root

1 tsp garam masala

1 tsp curry powder

1 tsp ground coriander

½ tsp ground cumin

½ tsp turmeric

½ tsp mild–medium chili powder (ideally Kashmiri yellow)

5½ cups (1.5 liters) vegetable stock

½ cup (100 ml) heavy cream (optional)

Sea salt

For the crispy peel

1 tbsp olive oil

Handful of parsnip peel

½ tsp chili flakes

Sea salt

1 red chili, seeded and thinly sliced lengthwise

Method

01 Trim and peel the larger parsnips and keep the shavings to one side, then roughly dice all the parsnips. Heat the oil in a saucepan; add the diced parsnip, chopped onion, garlic, ginger, and dry spices; and sauté for 4–5 minutes with the lid on, stirring occasionally.

02 Add the stock, then reduce the heat and simmer for 20–25 minutes. Meanwhile, make the crispy peel. Heat the olive oil in a frying pan, add the parsnip peel, and fry for 4–5 minutes until crispy. Once the peel is golden brown and crunchy, season with the chili flakes and sea salt, then mix in the raw slithers of red chili. Transfer to a sieve to avoid softening and leave to cool.

03 Test the simmering parsnips with a knife. If they are soft, use a hand-held mixer to purée the contents of the saucepan into a smooth, velvety soup. Add the heavy cream if you want to make your soup a little richer. Season to taste with the sea salt and serve in a bowl with a handful of the fried parsnip peel as a topping.

SIDE

Dirty Parsnip Fries
SERVES 2

Parsnips are the ultimate vegetable to pair with tart cranberries and creamy baked Camembert for a festive treat. This recipe might get me put on the naughty list—I'm sure some purists will think it's sacrilegious to cook a parsnip like this—but don't knock it before you try it. Frying the baby parsnips like classic oven chips and then baking them with a whole rich, mold-ripened cheese studded with rosemary is supremely decadent— but sometimes a little indulgence is well deserved.

INGREDIENTS

10–12 baby parsnips

2 tbsp olive oil

½ tsp sea salt

9 oz (250 g) Camembert cheese

2 sprigs of rosemary

2 tbsp cranberries

Method

01 Preheat the oven to 425°F (220°C). Slice the parsnips lengthwise into chip-shaped fingers. Parboil in salted water for 8–10 minutes to soften, then drain, retaining the water afterward to add to a stock or gravy later.

02 Heat the olive oil in a baking sheet. When it is sizzling hot, add the parsnips and turn to coat in the oil. Season with the sea salt, then roast for 20–25 minutes.

03 Stud the Camembert with the sprigs of rosemary, then make room for it on the baking sheet. (It should hold its shape, but it doesn't matter if it melts into the parsnips a little.) Scatter the cranberries over the parsnips and return the sheet to the oven. Bake for a 20 more minutes until the cheese is gooey, the cranberries have softened, and the parsnips are perfectly roasted, then serve.

Rutabaga

BUTTERED AND SPICED WITH ALL THINGS NICE

01

02

EDIBLE PARTS

01 LEAVES

The waxy, wavy foliage is so nutrient dense, it is often grown for fodder. The younger tops are tender and delicious sautéed in butter or oil. As they mature, they take on a stronger flavor.

02 SKIN

The purple to green to yellow skin is ridged in places and easy to peel off but very woody to eat. I personally always remove and compost it before cooking the vegetable—having tried it, I found it rather bitter and unpleasant to eat.

FLESH

The firm yellowish flesh is fine-grained and both sweet and savory when cooked, with only slight bitter cruciferous notes.

In the US they are called rutabaga; in Cornwall, turnips, but swede in the rest of England; and in Scotland, neeps. Whatever name you use, the bottom line is that a rutabaga is sweet, delicious, and large enough to provide a meal for the family.

PLANT

Based on the English name, this root vegetable likely originated in Sweden, when a Swiss botanist discovered the plant growing wild. Rutabaga is a hardy plant that grows well in cool, moist climates. It has bluish-green leaves, the younger of which are edible and taste similar to cabbage when cooked. Rutabagas are larger, denser, and sweeter than turnips. Typically, they are yellow-tan at the tip and have green-purple shoulders. They are mild tasting and only slightly bitter and are high in iron and rich in vitamins C and A. They also provide a good source of complex carbohydrates, hence the sweeter flavor compared to turnips.

COOKING TIPS

Generally I stew, boil, or braise rutabaga rather than roasting it. The fine-grained flesh can be blended to a smooth texture, while diced rutabaga is a superb flavor enhancer for soups and stews. Raw rutabaga grated for a garnish or julienned in a salad is worth trying for a sweet element. Dress with mustard, cider vinegar, honey, and olive oil to amplify the umami notes. It goes extremely well with bay, clove, nutmeg, and green peppercorns. In Scotland, tatties and neeps is a classic combination of potato and rutabaga mashed together for a traditional Burns Night supper. Some places, such as Orkney, add onion, too, and I like mashing it with carrot to accompany a Sunday roast.

PREPARATION

Select a rutabaga that feels heavy for its size and has smooth, unblemished, undamaged skin, as it will store for longer. The larger bulbs that have spent longer underground will have a sweeter flavor, while young rutabagas are more tender in texture but can be slightly bitter tasting. The skin of young, smaller rutabagas can be eaten, but if it's mature, it is unpleasant to eat, so peel and compost the skin to avoid waste. Peeling rutabagas is easy, but they are a tough vegetable to dice, so I recommend using a chef's knife or cleaver. The firm flesh can be diced small to add to a stew or kept fairly chunky if you are boiling to mash or purée.

ZERO WASTE

Store rutabagas in a cool, dark, ideally slightly damp place and they should keep for several months. Remove the leaves prior to storing to avoid them drying out and keep in the fridge. If you find yourself with a surplus of rutabaga, I suggest dicing, blanching for 5–10 minutes, then freezing it. Or try it as a seasoned purée—boil diced rutabaga for 20–30 minutes until soft. Then blend with a knob of butter into a smooth purée and freeze. You can then defrost it, ready to add to soups, mashed potatoes, or carrots. Don't discard the leaves and tops, as they are a tasty green to wilt in oil with black pepper and grated nutmeg as a side dish. They can also be added to stocks and broths like celery leaf.

TYPES

PURPLE

The most commonly available type of rutabaga that produces the heaviest crops, this variety has a nutty flavor, good sweetness, and a deeper purple top compared to other rutabagas.

GREEN

These are slower to mature and harder to find than the main variety, with a cream-colored flesh. They have green tops and an earthy flavor that works well in stews and casseroles.

BRONZE

The color of the crown is darker yellow, and in terms of flavor, it lies somewhere between the green and purple types. It has a smaller root bulb than purple rutabagas and is very good mashed with spices for a balance of sweet and savory profiles.

MAIN MEAL

Glazed Rutabaga Ham with Mustard and Cloves

SERVES 4

Boiling and then roasting a rutabaga whole like a ham is great fun and really suits its meaty texture. The intense flavor of this root works well with my sweet mustard glaze, while scoring the rutabaga with a diamond pattern and studding it with cloves infuses the heart of the vegetable with a rich, spiced aroma. You can serve with a tart relish, acidic pickles, and mature Cheddar.

INGREDIENTS

1 rutabaga, peeled
1 carrot, roughly chopped
1 celery stick, roughly chopped
½ onion, roughly chopped
1 tsp cider vinegar
2 bay leaves
1 tsp mustard seeds
1 cardamom pod
1 star anise
½ tsp black peppercorns
½ tsp sea salt
1 tbsp cloves

For the glaze
¼ cup (50 ml) orange juice
2 tbsp maple syrup
1 tsp Dijon mustard
1 tsp whole-grain mustard
½ tsp sea salt

Method

01 In a large stockpot, cover the rutabaga with water and add in all the other ingredients except the cloves. Bring to a boil and simmer for 35–40 minutes.

02 When you can insert a skewer easily into the heart of the rutabaga, carefully remove it from the pot and keep the spiced liquid for use in a vegetable stock.

03 Using a sharp knife, score the top of the rutabaga with a diamond criss-cross pattern ¼–½ in (5–10 mm) deep, then insert a clove at each intersection.

04 To make the glaze, heat the orange juice, maple syrup, mustards, and salt in a small pan. Reduce for 5–10 minutes until the mixture is thick and sticky, then brush onto the rutabaga.

05 Preheat the oven to 400°F (200°C). Place the glazed rutabaga on a baking sheet and roast in the oven for 15–20 minutes, basting again halfway through the cooking time.

06 When the rutabaga is sticky and golden, remove from the oven and allow to cool slightly. Carve into thin slices and serve with the relish, cheese, and pickles of your choice.

MAIN MEAL

Rutabaga and Root Pearl Barley Stew with Sage Biscuits

SERVES 4

Rutabaga and biscuits is a foodie memory I treasure from my childhood, but for my version, I've made the biscuits with flour, grated horseradish, and sage rather than a suet base. The stew is overflowing with sweet flavor, so I like it heavily peppered for savory background warmth. Celery root tops are the secret ingredient, adding a lingering bitterness and metallic tang.

Method

01 Get the stew started by heating the olive oil in a saucepan and sweating the onion and garlic. Then add in the pearl barley followed by the stock.

02 Bring to a boil and simmer for 45 minutes–1 hour, stirring occasionally. After the first 10 minutes, add the rutabaga, carrots, and bay leaves, then season with a pinch of salt, white pepper, and green peppercorns. A few minutes before the end of the cooking time, add the celery root tops (or celery), chives, and parsley.

03 While the stew is cooking, make the biscuits. Preheat the oven to 400°F (200°C) and rub together the cold butter and flour in a bowl until you have a crumblike texture. Mix in the herbs and grated horseradish (or horseradish sauce) and gradually pour in about 4 tablespoons of water, or more if needed, until you have a dough you can shape. Divide the dough into 12 pieces and form into round biscuits, then arrange them on a baking sheet and bake for 25 minutes or until golden.

04 Remove the bay leaves from the stew and serve with the roasted biscuits, an extra pinch of salt, and more freshly chopped chives and parsley.

INGREDIENTS

2 tbsp olive oil

1 onion, finely diced

2 garlic cloves, sliced

5½ oz (150 g) pearl barley, rinsed

5½ cups (1.5 liters) vegetable stock

1 rutabaga, peeled and diced

2 carrots, sliced

3 bay leaves

Sea salt

½ tsp ground white pepper

1 tsp crushed green peppercorns

Handful of celery root tops or 1 celery stick, finely chopped

1 tbsp chopped chives, plus extra to garnish

1 tbsp chopped curly parsley, plus extra to garnish

For the biscuits

9 tbsp (125 g) cold butter, diced

2 cups (250 g) self-rising flour

1 tsp chopped sage

1 tsp chopped rosemary

1 tsp grated horseradish or 1 tbsp horseradish sauce

Nut Roast with Spiced Mashed Rutabaga

SERVES 4

Mashed rutabaga is the magnet that pulls me back to my mom's cooking—to the taste of the weekend eating with family. It's a simple home classic that never disappoints—the buttery, sweet, steaming rutabaga with its gentle, warming spices pairs wonderfully with the crunchy nut roast and citrusy wilted tops.

Method

01 Start by making the nut roast. Preheat the oven to 400°F (200°C). Boil the diced rutabaga and carrot in salted water for 20 minutes, then drain.

02 Heat the olive oil in a pan and sauté the mushrooms, onion, and garlic for 5 minutes. Add the rosemary and paprika, stir, and remove from heat.

03 Blend the chestnuts and walnuts in a food processor to a coarse crumb texture and mix in a large bowl with the boiled rutabaga and carrots and the mushroom mixture. Combine with the cooked bulgur wheat and season to taste with half the salt, then press the mixture into a greased loaf pan.

04 Top with the seeds, the breadcrumbs, the rest of the salt, and the peppercorns and bake for 45 minutes.

05 Meanwhile, boil the rutabaga for the mash in salted water until soft—20–25 minutes, depending on the size of the dice. Remove from heat and drain.

06 Melt the butter in a saucepan, add the boiled rutabaga, then mash. Season with the white pepper, salt, and nutmeg, then add the cream and mash again until fluffy.

07 For the rutabaga tops, melt the butter in a pan, add the tops, and cook for 4–5 minutes until wilted. Season to taste with salt, add the lemon juice, then serve with the nut roast and mash.

INGREDIENTS

For the nut roast
½ rutabaga, peeled and diced
1 carrot, diced
2 tbsp olive oil
3½ oz (100 g) mushrooms, finely chopped
1 small onion, finely chopped
2 garlic cloves, finely chopped
1 tsp chopped rosemary
1 tsp paprika
1¾ oz (50 g) cooked chestnuts
1¾ oz (50 g) walnuts
3½ oz (100 g) cooked bulgur wheat
1 tsp sea salt
2 tbsp sunflower seeds

1 tbsp pumpkin seeds
½ cup (50 g) breadcrumbs
1 tsp cracked pink peppercorns

For the mash
1 small rutabaga, peeled
3½ tbsp (50 g) butter
½ tsp ground white pepper
1 tsp sea salt
½ tsp grated nutmeg
¼ cup (50 ml) heavy cream

For the rutabaga tops
3½ tbsp (50 g) butter
Large bunch of rutabaga tops, roughly chopped
Sea salt
1 tbsp lemon juice

"

Seasonal vegetables are fleeting and precious—to be treasured and appreciated—so make sure you store, preserve, and cook them well.

"

WAYS WITH VEGGIES

From bin to Michelin

My culinary mission is to help cooks avoid food waste, to bring new ideas to the world of vegetable cooking, and to inspire you to create your own delicious food. There are so many negative repercussions from the huge amounts of food that get thrown away. It causes untold damage to the planet and contributes to global food shortages. The problem doesn't just cost the earth; our weekly shopping expenditure could also be reduced if we managed our food better and adopted a zero-waste approach. I don't want to write a manifesto or provide a set of rules. At heart, I'm a kitchen rebel and I hate being told what to do—especially in my own kitchen. So instead of criticizing the way things are, I hope to encourage you in this section to prepare vegetables with a fresh perspective and a renewed enthusiasm. By accepting the challenge to waste less and save more, we are forcing ourselves to rip up the old rulebook and cook in new ways.

The core methods we can employ for reducing vegetable food waste at home include better storage, a greater understanding of basic cooking techniques, and learning how to preserve vegetables. My other key piece of advice is to treat your food with respect and to be excited by the potential you have to push the boundaries and reimagine something you've taken for granted all your life.

One of the biggest problems we face is still the simple challenge of extending the "shelf life" of fresh produce. Eating seasonally is rising in popularity, but we can often be presented with lots of one type of vegetable all at once. Learning how to store food and at what temperature; knowing what parts of a plant to trim off; and, most importantly, starting to build meal planning into your weekly routine can all help keep control over your food. Personally, I shop for my vegetables based on a weekly plan, but there are still times when our vegetable box arrives and there are four extra zucchini or a lovely bunch of fresh chard that I wasn't expecting. It's then time to adapt, plan, and make sure that everything is in its right place—ready to cook or preserve.

The basic techniques that I want to cover in this section have been used in many of the vegetable recipes, but I want to discuss them a little more fully to hopefully help you cook dishes without recipes. Devising your own meals once you understand the cooking principles can be fun and is essential if you want to be a zero-waste cook. Knowing the basic skills of braising, steaming, grilling, or roasting remove anxiety from the kitchen, while preserving ideas not only help you use up a surplus, they also help you fill your cabinets with delicious snacks, seasonings, and condiments. With the right tool kit and a little know-how, you can transform any vegetable into a delicious meal.

If you aim, like me, for zero waste at home, then you will quickly find yourself becoming a fridge forager. The odds and ends that once upon a time you might have thrown in the compost bin can become brand-new creations. This shift in mindset is the key to change. The forgotten cuts, roots, shoots, peel, and cores are no longer an afterthought to be discarded. Instead, these leftovers can become your star ingredients—from bin to Michelin.

Essentials
STORING

To extend the shelf life of your veggies, the best advice is to get organized and store them in the place that suits them best. Some prefer the cold of a fridge, while others prefer a cool, dark paper bag. By treating each one differently, you can keep it fresh for longer and reduce waste, too.

STORAGE TIPS

Get into the habit of trimming, wrapping, and storing your veggies as soon as they come into the house. Keep root veggies on the same rack every week and nominate a shelf in the fridge for salad leaves or tender greens.

FRIDGE

A well-packed fridge uses less energy to keep cool. However, it's important to allow some room for air circulation, particularly with vegetables such as mushrooms, cauliflower, and eggplant. Generally, lots of vegetables like high humidity, so I wrap them in damp paper towel, then seal in an airtight container to stop them from drying out. Invest in a combination of beeswax wraps and sealable containers and reuse paper and plastic bags to wrap your veggies. Clean your fridge every week, being careful not to lose or forget things that are hidden. Rotate new vegetables to the back and bring older ones forward when you put away your groceries. Also keep an eye on delicate greens in your salad trays—don't squash them, or the leaves can wilt early.

PAPER BAGS

Old fashioned but still very useful, paper bags allow air to circulate, prevent sunlight from getting in, and can be easily labeled.

CLAMPS

Consider packing beets or carrots in a sealed box with slightly damp sand so they don't dry out. Then leave in the garage, shed, or basement. It minimizes sugar loss and prevents light from getting to the vegetables.

RACKS

Tiered racks are useful for storing veggies in a cool pantry. They need air circulation and should be on the north-facing side of your kitchen for less temperature fluctuation.

VEGETABLE	WHERE TO STORE	STORAGE LIFE	QUICK TIPS
Artichoke	Fridge	4–5 days	Store in a porous paper bag.
Asparagus	Fridge	5–7 days	Wrap in damp paper towel.
Beans	Fridge	1 week	Also consider blanching and freezing.
Beets	Larder/cold cupboard	1–2 months	Trim off leaves and keep the greens in the fridge.
Broccoli	Fridge	1 week	Keep in a sealed container to extend life.
Brussels sprouts	Fridge	1 week	Remove from stalk and don't remove outer leaves.
Cabbage	Fridge	1 week	Keep outer leaves on for protection.
Carrots	Fridge	1 month	Separate leafy tops and store them with salad.
Cauliflower	Fridge	1 week	Leave unwashed before storing.
Celery root	Larder/cold cupboard	1–2 months	Remove tops and store greens in the fridge.
Chard	Fridge	5–7 days	Trim leaves from stalks and store both in a sealed container.
Chili	Fridge	2 weeks	Store in an airtight container. Also easy to air-dry.
Cucumber	Fridge	1 week	Wrap in damp paper towel and store in a sealed container.
Eggplant	Fridge	1 week	Allow good ventilation and avoid bruising.
Fava beans	Fridge	1 week	Pod, shell, and blanch before storing to conserve space.
Fennel	Fridge	1 week	Remove fronds and store separately.
Garlic	Larder/cold cupboard	2–3 months	Keep in a brown paper bag away from sunlight.
Kale	Fridge	5–7 days	Wrap in a damp towel to retain moisture.
Leeks	Fridge	2 weeks	Don't trim or wash before storing.
Lettuce	Fridge	1 week	Keep in a sealed humid bag in a cold part of the fridge.
Mushrooms	Fridge	1 week	Store in a porous paper bag.
Napa cabbages	Fridge	1 week	These keep well in a storage bag.
Onions	Larder/cold cupboard	2–3 months	Consider netting and hang in a cool, dark, dry place.
Parsnips	Larder/cold cupboard	2–3 months	Store in a cool, dark place—in a garage or basement is best.
Peas	Fridge	1 week	Allow air to circulate in a perforated bag or unsealed container.
Potatoes	Larder/cold cupboard	2–3 months	Avoid storing near onions. Keep in a dark, cool place in a paper bag.
Rutabaga	Larder/cold cupboard	2–3 months	Chop off any tops before storing and remove damp soil.
Spinach	Fridge	1 week	Store in a sealed container wrapped in dry paper towel.
Sweet corn	Fridge	2–3 days	Store unhusked loose in the fridge or husked in a sealed bag.
Tomatoes	Fridge	1 week	If underripe, leave on a sunny windowsill before refrigerating.
Watercress	Fridge	2–3 days	Keep roots standing upright in a glass of water in the fridge.
Zucchini	Fridge	1 week	Store flowers in damp paper towel and use within 1–2 days.

PRINCIPLES

Before refrigeration, many people stored perishable food in a larder, root cellar, or pantry. Today, most homes lack such storage rooms, but understanding the principles associated with them will help make your space work for you.

Ventilation: Allow airflow for balanced humidity when storing veggies. For good ventilation, don't pack things too closely together.

Temperature: Try to maintain a consistent cool temperature, as veggies may start sprouting or rotting if exposed to warmth. If you don't have a larder, dedicate a small cupboard to veggies in the coldest part of the house—ideally in a dark, well-ventilated room. Also, try to avoid fridge burn—when veggies starts to freeze if it is too cold. I try to keep mine safely above 32°F (0°C) at a comfortable 41°F (5°C).

Butchery: Leave the mud on root veggies to protect the skin, but trim off leafy shoots before storing, as these draw moisture from the root and dry it out. Delicate shoots and flowers should be stored in the fridge. Remember to label and store your various cuts in their favored conditions, and always compost any rotten or moldy food so that it doesn't contaminate your other fresh produce.

Cooking Techniques

STOCKS AND BROTHS

Making your own stock builds a solid foundation for all your cooking. It's an excellent way to use up any vegetable scraps, and the result can form a tasty and nutritious base for soups, stews, and sauces. There is a vast range of flavors to play with, which you can extract using these basic skills.

PRINCIPLES

The basic method for stocks is to sweat chopped vegetables, simmer them in water with seasoning and aromatics, then strain. They can have diverse, complex flavors and bold colors, depending on the ingredients you choose to include.

Equipment: It's worth investing in a large stainless-steel stockpot, a skimmer, and a conical strainer for making your own stocks.

Sweat: All vegetable stocks begin with sweating diced vegetables to soften them before simmered in water to release their flavor.

Simmer: Vegetable stock requires less simmering time than protein stocks—under 1 hour—as cellulose breaks down more quickly. Aim for a steady simmer at around 180°F (82°C), as vitamin loss is a consequence of a rapid boil.

Aromatics: Add a bouquet garni to give depth to stocks. Bay, thyme, and parsley stalks tied

together will work with most stocks, or try aromatic spices for more complex back notes.

Skim: Regularly skim off the scum that floats to the top of your stock. This removes impurities; the clarity of the finished broth can be largely determined by this process.

Strain: Use a conical strainer, double-mesh strainer, or muslin-lined sieve to strain your stock for a smooth, clear broth. After straining, vegetable stock has a 2–3-day shelf life for maximum flavor.

Salt: Seasoning is essential for a strong stock. Use sea salt rather than table salt, as it's naturally lower in sodium and contains over 60 sea minerals.

Thicken: There are no proteins in vegetable stock to bind the molecules, so it will be thin. Add agar-agar or vegetarian gelatin for more viscosity, or seaweed is a great addition for more body.

Figure a.

Figure b.

POSSIBILITIES

Use the basic method to create distinctive stocks with different vegetables and aromatics.

Mirepoix: Sharp onion, bitter celery, and sweet carrot combine to form a white stock that adds depth to a risotto or forms a poaching liquid or braising liquor. The key is not to make it with roasted veggies. Soften chopped veggies in butter or oil for 25–30 minutes on medium-low heat to avoid caramelization, then add just enough water to cover the veggies. Add 1 teaspoon of salt for every 2 cups (1 liter) of water, plus aromatics such as bay, parsley, and thyme. Simmer for 15–20 minutes, skimming regularly, until the color diffuses from the veggies into the stock, then strain (see *opposite*). Use right away, store in the fridge in a sealed container for 2–3 days, or freeze.

Brown broth: Roast butternut squash peel, celery root skin, and onion in a little oil at 400°F (200°C) for 15–20 minutes **(fig. a)**.

Then add the roasted veggies to a mirepoix base, add water, and simmer for 15–20 minutes, skimming and straining as usual. The roasted flavors form a dark, silken stock with a rich umami flavor and caramelized notes, great for enriching soups, deglazing vegetables, and braising.

Green stock: Green stock has a delicate complexity and a subtle grassy flavor. Soften diced onion, broccoli stalks, celery, leek, and other green vegetables in oil, then simmer with fennel seeds, yellow mustard, green peppercorns, and herb stalks for 30–45 minutes. Try adding cauliflower stalks and cabbage cores for the last 5–10 minutes of simmering, then strain.

Dashi: For an umami powerhouse, use seaweed and dried mushroom for a vegetarian twist on a dashi **(fig. b)**. I use 1 tablespoon each of kelp, dulse, sea spaghetti, and sea lettuce. They add salty seasoning, savory depth, and velvety

thickness to the stock. You can either add these to a mirepoix base or make a pure seaweed stock. Add soy or tamari to intensify the flavor, and simmer for 15 minutes.

Mushroom stock: Mushroom makes a wonderful woody broth. Dried or fresh, simmer the mushrooms until you have a rich dark brown broth that goes very well with white miso.

Sweet corn stock: This makes an excellent base for chowders and can be reduced to glaze squash and baste carrots. Follow the mirepoix method, but add a mixture of leftover corn cobs and juicy kernels for a milky, bright yellow stock with a delicious sweetness.

Tomato stock: Try adding fire-roasted tomatoes to a mirepoix for a real earthy tone, or strain juiced raw tomatoes for a clean tomato broth. Green tomato also works well with garlic and green chili for a tart, gently spiced stock.

Cooking Techniques
STEAMING AND BOILING

Steaming is perfect for young spring vegetables, to avoid overcooking and help retain nutrients, a firm bite, and delicate freshness. Boiling, on the other hand, is a great way to cook tougher root vegetables if you want to soften them for roasting or for making mash and purées.

STEAMING

The principles of steaming are simple: suspend delicate veggies of a uniform size above water at a rolling boil for just a few minutes and cover so the evaporating steam cooks them. This leaves the produce with a clean, intensified taste, while its *al dente* texture is retained along with most of its nutrients, as they don't leach out into the water. My preferred veggies to steam include asparagus, beans, and spinach for 3–5 minutes; spring greens, kale, and chard for 5–7 minutes; and baby carrots and cauliflower for 8–10 minutes. Skewer the veggie with a knife or snap it to check if it's done. A sieve or colander with a saucepan lid on top can act as a steamer, or you can use a classic stainless-steel basket or bamboo steamer, which is traditionally used in a wok and can be stacked to steam several items at once. Alternatively, try cooking *en papillote.* This involves wrapping food in a parcel made of parchment paper or foil. You can also use banana leaves, grape leaves, or corn husks. This is then baked to steam the ingredients inside. I add herbs, butter or oil, and often a splash of wine or slices of citrus for extra flavor. Fennel, thinly sliced potato, and asparagus all work well using this method.

BOILING

It pays to understand how a hard boil differs from simmering. A gentle simmer will keep veggies *al dente*, while a rolling boil breaks down veggies ready to mash. I salt the water and stir to dissolve, as it hastens the breakdown of the veggie's fibrous structure; raises the boiling temperature of the water; and helps preserve some of the colors, especially for green veggies. I often cover veggies in cold water, then bring the water to a boil so they cook through evenly. Boil root veggies such as parsnip, potato, and rutabaga for 15–20 minutes. For cruciferous vegetables like sprouts, broccoli, and cauliflower, boil for no longer than 8–10 minutes.

Cooking Techniques
GRILLING AND GRIDDLING

Cooking with fire or intense direct heat is all about control. Grilling and griddling are fast methods that lock in freshness and nutrients and have a transformative effect on flavor. The smoky sweetness of caramelized vegetables packs a powerful punch in record time.

GRILLING

Cooking under an oven grill or on a barbecue allows you to have one direct heat source that cooks vegetables quickly and caramelizes them effectively. Skewers of veggie kebabs work extremely well grilled by a fierce heat—although it's essential to turn them for even cooking. A wet marinade can make all the difference. Try combining oil with freshly cut herbs, garlic, and spices. A marinade protects the vegetables and provides some fat to laminate the layers between onions, baste corn kernels, or coat the flesh of a pepper. Remember when grilling kebabs to soak wooden skewers before cooking to prevent them from burning. The most popular vegetables for grilling include peppers, mushrooms, onions, eggplant, and zucchini.

GRIDDLING

I love my ridged griddle pan (or skillet) and find griddling an easy cooking method for a whole range of veggies. It's important to preheat the griddle before you start. If you don't, the vegetables will slowly steam rather than sear and can end up being soggy. Test it is hot enough by splashing a few drops of water from your fingertips—the water should sizzle and evaporate instantly rather than pool on the surface. Season the pan in between use by rubbing oil into the surface and baking in an oven 340°F (170°C) for 20 minutes. When cooking, never oil the pan; instead, lightly oil the food. I often dry griddle for a clean char and then marinate or dress the veggies in oil after cooking. Cook thinly sliced veggies for 3–4 minutes on each side until softened and charred. The best veggies to griddle are zucchini, sweet corn, eggplant, peas in their pods, peppers, mushrooms, lettuce, fennel, and asparagus.

Cooking Techniques

FRYING AND BRAISING

Frying provides theater in the kitchen. To sauté, stir-fry, or braise a vegetable immediately transforms its texture and flavor, but it also carries the risk of burning. This is a make-or-break moment for your food, so it takes focus and attention to detail to get it right.

SAUTÉING

Sautéing is lightly frying vegetables in a little fat for just a few minutes over a relatively high heat. It's a term that comes from the French to jump or bounce and refers to tossing the contents of the pan while cooking. The movement allows you to cook at a high temperature without burning the food. Vegetables are usually thinly sliced or diced to provide a larger surface area so they cook evenly while remaining moist and full of flavor. Onions, garlic, peppers, and mushrooms are the most common choice of vegetable for this method, but diced root vegetables can also be sautéed.

I sauté with a small amount of olive oil over medium to high heat. I tend to sauté with the lid off the pan, but by reducing the temperature and closing the pan with a lid, you can sweat the vegetables, which steams them as they fry. This tends to avoid caramelizing and browning them.

Equipment: A sauté pan or sautoir is an extremely versatile piece of equipment. They tend to be sturdy constructions, with a solid base, a straight edge, and a lid, and are at least 12 in (30 cm) wide and deeper than a frying pan. Good pans do not have hot spots but rather distribute the heat evenly.

Deglaze: After sautéing, I always deglaze the pan to remove the flavorful browned fats and sugars from the bottom and make an umami-rich sauce from them. This can be done with a splash of wine, cider, stock, or citrus juice.

Flambé: Another effective way to deglaze a pan and then burn off the alcohol to infuse the sautéed vegetables with intense flavor is flambéing. Try adding brandy, rum, or whisky to the hot pan, then carefully light the liquor with a match or blowtorch. If you're more confident and are cooking on gas, tilt the pan slowly until the naked flame lights the alcohol.

Figure a.

Figure b.

FRYING

Fried food has a bad reputation, but there are many ways to fry veggies without them tasting greasy. Try a range of vegetable oils for subtle nuances in flavor. Sesame oil is great for stir-frying, sunflower oil for deep-frying, and canola oil has a high frying temperature, which makes it useful for shallow-frying. For me, you still can't beat olive oil for confit, but experiment and see what works for you.

Shallow-frying: Larger, portion-sized vegetables, patties, or fritters are cooked in a little oil until browned, then drained on paper towel to remove excess oil.

Stir-frying: This is a fantastic way to cook quickly with a little oil over high heat. The food is kept in constant motion to sear the edges but prevent it from burning, which helps retain some bite and captures the flavor of the oil. A curved wok allows vegetables to move easily and transfers heat quickly through the metal and into the food.

Deep-frying: Ideal for chips, tempura, bhajis, fries, and croquettes, this method is similar to shallow-frying but uses more oil. Vegetables are submerged in very hot oil at around 355°F (180°C) **(fig. a)** and are usually protected from the fierce heat by a batter or breadcrumb coating. The surface becomes crisp and golden, while the inside stays moist. Fry in small batches so the temperature of the oil isn't lowered and drain on paper towel afterward to remove excess oil.

Confit: Food is submerged in oil, often with aromatics, then slow-cooked at 199–210°F (93–99°C) for 1–2 hours or until tender. Strain once cooked and either store in the oil once cool in sterilized jars or eat and keep the oil for dressings or cooking. This is a good way to preserve vegetables such as garlic, chili, and onions.

BRAISING

Braising is a combined approach that uses both dry heat and wet steaming to build flavor while retaining moisture. The two-stage method starts with searing the vegetable in hot oil, which creates a base of deep umami, caramelized flavors. You then add liquid to the pan and cover with a lid to stew and tenderize the vegetable, which keeps it soft and succulent, with an intense, enhanced flavor. You can sear on the stove and then braise in the oven or do the whole process in a casserole dish on the stove—it should take 20–40 minutes. The braising liquid can be a rich stock; juice; or alcohol such as wine, cider, vermouth, or beer—all of which lend vegetables a concentrated flavor as the liquid reduces. Try braised cabbage **(fig. b)**, spring greens, rutabaga, beets, or carrots. Bold spices such as star anise, juniper, cinnamon, or peppercorns and fruit such as dates and dried apricots also work well braised with vegetables for added flavor.

Cooking Techniques
ROASTING AND BAKING

The oven is the greatest culinary invention ever. Though slower than frying or grilling, oven cooking is the best way to bring out the natural sweetness of vegetables. I have a deep love of roasted root vegetables, as well as baked vegetables wrapped in anything from pastry to salt dough.

ROASTING

I always use the fan to assist with circulating the heat when oven roasting, and there are a few default settings I use: 325°F (170°C) for a low-and-slow roast, which might be vegetables in a casserole dish or a deep tray of mixed vegetables covered with foil. I add some stock or liquid when cooking at this lower temperature to allow the veggies to steam as they roast. Then it's up to 400°F (200°C) for an all-in-one tray roast or to 425°F (220°C) or 475°F (240°C) for blazing heat that can sear vegetables and crisp up the edges.

PAN

A well-seasoned roasting pan shouldn't need to be lined if the veggies are generously coated in oil first. This also prevents them from drying out while the skin browns. I always preheat my roasting pan to speed up the cooking process—this means it doesn't suck all the heat energy out as soon as you start cooking—and I also chop all the veggies to a similar size so that they roast evenly. Try adding thyme, rosemary, and garlic for extra flavor or lemon slices, figs, or dried fruit for sweetness. Season well with salt and parboil root veggies before roasting. Generally, they will roast in 40–45 minutes. Hasselbacking—partially cutting into layers (see pages 23, 159, and 164)—is a useful way to prepare potatoes, sweet potatoes, squash, parsnips, and beets for roasting, as it increases their surface area and creates an extra-crisp texture while keeping the inside soft.

TRIVET

When roasting whole vegetables, try placing them on a wire rack or trivet to allow hot air to circulate around them. I often make an edible trivet using scraps of veggies. It's also handy to add aromatics under a whole squash or cauliflower to infuse them as they cook.

Figure a.

Figure b.

BAKING

I bake vegetables on their own and in pies and pasties, but I also love to bake them wrapped in salt dough, hay, or foil. The idea is to protect them from intense direct heat while the warmth cooks them within. It's a good method for trapping moisture and keeping the vegetable succulent.

OVEN BAKING

A baked potato is the perfect example of simply baking a vegetable whole. I skewer the skin and rub it with oil, then bake for 60–70 minutes at 425°F (220°C) until the middle is fluffy and the jacket is crisp. You can also bake sweet potatoes, squash, or beets this way.

Also try making gratins (see page 128), which traditionally involve baking thinly sliced vegetables in a shallow dish with not too much liquid—often cream, milk, or stock—and are sometimes topped with cheese or breadcrumbs **(fig. a)**. Bake for 35–40 minutes at 400°F (200°C). When preparing vegetables for a gratin, try grating them for a consistent texture that will cook evenly. Alternatively, use a Japanese mandoline to slice thinly. A gratin is a superb opportunity to use yesterday's bread to make a breadcrumb topping. I prefer to store my breadcrumbs already baked for a longer shelf life and added crunch. I bake torn chunks for 20–30 minutes at 275°F (140°C) until they turn golden, then blend. Try combining with pumpkin and sunflower seeds for more protein. Alternatively, *pangrattato*—"poor man's Parmesan"—is breadcrumbs tossed with olive oil and toasted garlic, which makes a delicious vegan topping for all sorts of dishes.

PASTRY BAKING

If baking pies (see page 152), tarts (see pages 61 and 239), pasties (see pages 183 and 240), or Wellingtons (see page 171), be mindful of the high moisture content of most vegetables and the effect this will have on the pastry. You'll end up with a soggy bottom if you don't add holes to allow the steam to escape or blind bake first.

SALT BAKING

A salt dough can be made by mixing either egg whites or all-purpose flour with salt and water (see page 229). It covers the vegetable entirely, forming an inedible crust that roasts, steams, and seasons the veggie beneath while it cooks **(fig. b)**. The best candidates are celery root, carrots, beets, and squash. Also try mixing herbs or hay into your salt dough for a fragrant roast. Usually, you need to bake a salt crust for at least 1 hour at 400°F (200°C), or you can bake it low and slow at 350°F (180°C) for 2–3 hours for a tender whole pumpkin or other larger vegetables.

Cooking Techniques

ALFRESCO

Cooking outdoors encourages timid vegetables to step out of their skins and take a moment to shine. Glowing embers, hot coals, and wood smoke transform vegetables with a down-to-earth sweetness and umami char. You can spend a lifetime trying to recreate these magical flavors indoors.

WOOD-FIRED OVEN

Wood-fired ovens come in all shapes and sizes, but the best designs have good thermodynamic properties. They should be well insulated, enabling them to retain heat that is radiated from the wood fire and conduct it into the food through the stone oven floor, while the hot air currents cook the food evenly via convection.

Pizza oven: The temperatures in a classic Italian-style domed pizza oven far exceed a domestic oven for fast, intense cooking. I tend to cook my pizzas at 840°F (450°C) for just 4–5 minutes. This gives a better crust, with a crispy texture that's not brittle and dry. It also ensures perfectly melted cheese. This kind of oven is excellent for cooking much more than just pizza though. I often use mine for roasting, cooking dirty on the embers, and baking bread as well.

Barbecue oven: A kettle barbecue can double as an oven when the lid is closed if you can build up a good temperature inside. Consider a drum-shaped or ceramic egg-shaped barbecue as a hybrid for grilling, roasting, and hot smoking.

Underground oven: To try making an underground oven, dig a hole in the earth and line the base with stones, then build a wood fire on the stone base. Allow the logs to burn down to hot embers, then spread them out and add your vegetables wrapped in foil, parchment paper, or hay. Cover with at least 12 in (30 cm) of soil and leave to slow-roast for 2–3 hours. The stored heat in the hot stones will radiate back out and cook the vegetables perfectly.

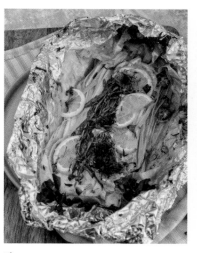

Figure a.

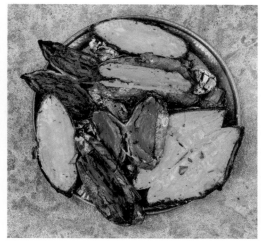

Figure b.

CAMPFIRE

I've cooked on campfires all around the world. It's a wonderful way to reconnect with nature and removes all the fuss and stress from cooking. Go foraging for some kindling in the woods or collect driftwood from a beach, build a small fire, then slow down to feed the fire and nurture your soul while cooking a simple meal.

Kotlich: This Hungarian-style enamel cooking pot can easily be suspended above a fire using a tripod. It is perfect for soups, vegetable stews, pearl barely risotto, or curries. It's a great introductory piece of equipment for outdoor cooking.

Rocket stove: The technology of a rocket stove involves creating a chimney effect to increase draw, which makes it a highly efficient outdoor cooker. These little stoves really suit cooking with frying pans and skillets on top and can be a good way of quickly firing up a meal in the garden or campsite.

BARBECUE

I'm a massive fan of barbecues, but I've always struggled with the excessively meaty culture that goes with them. Vegetables are also excellent grilled, smoked, or cooked dirty on the coals and often only need a salsa or herby butter to bring out their flavor.

Grilling: I love cooking kebabs, corn, and whole peppers or eggplant over charcoal. Remember to baste regularly with oil or butter to keep the food moist, and avoid flame-grilling, as this can taint the vegetable.

Parcels: Wrapping veggies in foil and then baking on embers is a superb way to cook with no fuss. I love leeks and butter with a little lemon wrapped in foil and thrown near the fire **(fig. a)**. Cook for 15–20 minutes until tender and steaming. Also try sliced fennel, buttered new potatoes, diced sweet potato, and even baby sprouts.

Smoking: A kettle or drum barbecue can double as a hot smoker if you add wood chips or some oak offcuts to the coals. Try smoking vegetables like onions, tomatoes, mushrooms, and potatoes with hardwood and fruit trees. Some of my favorites include apple, cherry, oak, and maple. Herbs also deliver aromatic smoke from their volatile flavor compounds, so throw rosemary, thyme, or sage on the coals, too.

Dirty: This type of cooking is incredibly easy. All you need to do is place veggies directly onto hot coals or embers. Turn every 15 minutes with tongs and, once the skin is blackened and the vegetable feels soft in the middle, it's done. Try cooking onions, potatoes, sweet potatoes, and beets this way for the best dirty veggies **(fig. b)**. Peel off the blackened skin and discard to enjoy the wood-infused, soft flesh inside with some butter and a pinch of sea salt.

Preserving Techniques
FREEZING

A freezer is the single most useful piece of equipment to reduce food waste. Vegetables freeze extremely well, retaining the majority of their flavor and nutrients if frozen the correct way, as do many soups, stews, and purées.

BLANCHING

This is the process of cooking or parboiling veggies before you freeze them, which helps keep their vibrant color and texture.

Enzymes: Blanching in boiling water slows or stops the enzymes that cause vegetables to lose flavor and color. This enzymatic activity will decay the veggies if not blanched for long enough, as they can survive the freezing process. Blanching also kills unwanted bacteria, making it safe to store frozen veggies for up to 12 months.

Timing: This varies from 2–3 minutes to 6–8, but rarely extends beyond that. The aim is not to completely cook the veggie, just to stop it from deteriorating when frozen. Heat the water to a rolling boil, then submerge clean, cut-up vegetables for their allocated time (see *below*). Avoid overcrowding the pan so the temperature doesn't drop, and time the process from when the water returns to boiling point. Remove the veggies from the boiling water and refresh or shock in ice water (see *right*).

VEGETABLE	TIME	NOTES
Spinach/greens/shelled peas	*1–2 minutes*	*Squeeze out excess water from spinach and greens after refreshing and before freezing.*
Asparagus/beans/pea pods/broccoli/peppers	*2–3 minutes*	*Store in sealed bags or containers.*
Sprouts/cauliflower/ onions	*3–5 minutes*	*Freeze spread out on a tray to avoid clumping when you pack them.*
Artichoke/carrots/corn/ rutabaga/squash	*5–8 minutes*	*Remember to refresh for at least the same time, if not longer, in cold water before freezing.*
Mushrooms	*Don't blanch*	*Better to just shock in ice water before freezing.*

Figure a.

Figure b.

REFRESHING

This is the act of halting the cooking process of blanching as quickly as possible by submerging the blanched veggies in a large bowl of ice water or under a cold running tap to remove the heat from them. This speedy method of cooling is known as "refreshing" or "shocking" the veggies. As a guide, you should do this for the same time, if not slightly longer, than you blanched them for, although there are exceptions. With corn, you should refresh for twice as long as it was blanched. Once drained and dried, the vegetable is ready to be stored, then frozen.

STORAGE

There are various tips and tricks for storing in the freezer. I tend to reuse a selection of old plastic zipper-lock bags to freeze many of my vegetables. I also try to reuse rather than recycle other freezer-proof containers, which I wash out thoroughly beforehand.

Tray freezing: Before storing, I often freeze blanched and shocked veggies such as peas, sliced peppers, cauliflower florets, and fava beans on a tray to avoid clumping. Spread them out in a single layer and, once they've frozen solid, you can pack them more closely. This means you can pull out a single portion at a time.

Labeling: It's really important to label your frozen veggies so that it doesn't end up getting lost in the freezer and you can keep track of how long it's been in there. I'd also suggest a vertical freezer with shelves or drawers that you can label rather than a chest freezer, which is harder to navigate.

Ice trays: Ice cube trays or silicone molds are very useful for freezing portion-sized quantities of stock, pesto, and purées **(fig. a)**. They can then easily be added to stews, curries, or soups without defrosting a whole batch.

Purées: It saves lots of space if you make a purée to freeze rather than storing bulky root vegetables. A carrot purée **(fig. b)**, for example, can be defrosted and added to a soup or curry sauce to enhance the flavor. Try making carrot, tomato, squash, or garlic purée, then freeze in a silicone mold. A typical method is to melt some butter in a large saucepan and add finely diced shallot and garlic. Add the diced vegetables and soften for 5–10 minutes, stirring regularly. Try not to color the veggies. Add in enough stock to submerge the veggies, then simmer for 5 minutes. Blend with a hand-held mixer until smooth, then add a splash of cream and blend until smooth and silky. Finally, season to taste.

Preserving Techniques

UNDER OIL

Chefs are masters at making food appear complicated, but there are certain techniques that are so simple, they can be carried out with an almost Zen-like calm. Preserving with oil is just this type of technique. The oil does all the hard work, while the vegetable waits for service under a golden coat.

PESTO

A classic pesto is made with basil, pine nuts, and Parmesan cheese, but there are many variations on this theme using other herbs. Sage, arugula, cilantro, or pea shoots all work well, and personally, I love vegetable pestos; they have bold, aromatic notes and make great dressings or bases for sauces. Generally, I make pesto blending 1 part nuts (such as pine nuts, hazelnuts, or pumpkin seeds), 2 parts olive oil, 2 parts grated cheese (normally Parmesan, mature Gouda, or pecorino), and 6 parts fresh herbs or veggies. If you want to make a vegan version by removing the cheese, I would recommend increasing the proportion of nuts or seeds. The key is to pack the pesto tightly into an airtight container to remove any air pockets and then cover with a layer of oil before sealing. Store fresh pesto in the fridge and use within 1 week.

Kale: Lacinato makes a wonderful pesto with walnuts, lemon zest, and walnut oil. Season with sea salt and blend until you have a coarse pesto. I use raw kale for this pesto, so it only takes a few minutes to make and retains all the vegetable's nutrients.

Carrot top: Rather than wasting vegetable tops and shoots, try blending them into a pesto for a zero-waste pasta sauce. Carrot tops are delicious with garlic, lemon, and olive oil. They taste very similar to parsley, so have a good herbaceous profile.

Arugula: For a peppery variation, try wild arugula pesto with pumpkin seeds, lemon juice, garlic, and olive oil. I love the heat you get from this; it's delicious on a pizza base or in a grilled sandwich with goat cheese.

Figure a.

Figure b.

UNDER OIL

Oil provides a protective barrier, which prevents harmful bacteria and the oxygen they need to survive from reaching your vegetables. If you place cooked or dried veggies in a sterilized jar and submerge them in olive oil, you can keep them in a cabinet for 2–3 weeks, or longer in the fridge.

Griddled vegetables: Cook zucchini, garlic, and peppers in a ridged griddle pan or skillet or under the grill (see page 269) and then mix with preserved lemons, capers, oregano, and sea salt. Submerge under oil **(fig. a)** and use on bruschetta or add to roasted vegetables for a salad.

Dehydrated vegetables: Drying vegetables first preserves them for even longer when stored under oil. It also makes them great to cook with, as they are already coated in a rich flavored oil—sun-dried tomatoes are a prime example. Semidried vegetables are particularly fantastic under oil, as the process of semidrying concentrates their natural sugars and intensifies their flavors. Dry them for half the recommended time in an oven or dehydrator (see page 281) and, once cool, transfer to a sterilized jar and cover with oil. They will rehydrate more quickly when you are cooking and retain a lovely chewy texture.

CONFIT

This method involves covering sliced vegetables with fat or oil in a dish and then cooking them low and slow in the oven. I use olive oil mostly, but coconut oil or clarified butter also work very well.

Garlic: My favorite confit recipe is garlic with chili **(fig. b)**. Peel the garlic cloves and cover with olive oil, then cook at 203–210°F (95–99°C) for 2–3 hours until they are soft and slightly browned in color. Allow to cool, then store in a jar and use within 1–2 weeks. The oil and garlic are superb added to hummus or pesto or even spread on toast with fresh tomatoes.

Root vegetables: The confit technique works for all sorts of starchy or sugary vegetables, such as potatoes, onions, squash, or carrots. It doesn't work so well with spring greens or salad leaves, but it is amazing with cherry tomatoes for a rich, slowly cooked garnish or base for a sauce.

Preserving Techniques

DEHYDRATING

Drying is a superb way to preserve vegetables and avoid food waste. It intensifies flavor, reduces storage space, and retains most of the valuable nutrients. Dehydrated vegetables are easy and convenient to use in your cooking. For me, it's the best way to store a surplus.

PRINCIPLES

Vegetables are exposed to gentle heat or fresh air for a relatively long period to draw out their moisture. Use only the best specimens—so no damaged or bruised produce.

Temperature and time: You can dry veggies relatively quickly in an oven at 200°F (95°C), but for me the best temperature is 165°F (75°C). It takes a little longer, but you retain more flavor. Dry for 4–6 hours or until leathery and light to hold.

Surface area: Slice larger veggies into equal-sized pieces before drying. The thinner the slices, the greater the surface area, so the quicker they'll dry. Cherry tomatoes should be halved and mushrooms can often be dried whole. All pieces should be the same size so they dry evenly at the same rate.

Blanching: Many veggies are better blanched first to destroy any enzymes that could cause the food to deteriorate. With carrots, peas,

kale, and leafy greens, it also helps retain their color and flavor. Pat dry after blanching, then dehydrate.

Storage: Store in an airtight container in a cool, dark place for up to a year. Rehydrate in warm water for at least 15–20 minutes.

AIR-DRYING

This is the most basic method of dehydrating and involves hanging the produce to dry naturally. Hang veggies in a sunny, well-ventilated spot with low humidity and prevent it from touching others if possible, so air can circulate on all sides.

I often dry chilies in the greenhouse, but indoors works well, too. Tie or thread the stems together for a chili ristra, then dry for 2–3 weeks, depending on the climate. Also try this with rosemary, bay, thyme, and sage to preserve them, though not leafy herbs such as parsley, cilantro, and basil— these work better dried in a dehydrator, used in pesto, or frozen.

Figure a.

Figure b.

DEHYDRATOR

Investing in a dehydrator is worthwhile if you want to preserve vegetables on a regular basis. It's a simple piece of equipment but really efficient, as there are several racks, allowing you to dry lots at once, and the temperature can be adjusted from 86–167°F (30–75°C) via a thermostat. Lots of vegetables dry well in a dehydrator, including mushrooms and tomatoes, and drying at lower temperatures preserves more of their nutrients, almost as if they were raw, making this a particularly healthy method.

OVEN-DRYING

Oven heat works well as a dehydrator. If using this method, keep the door slightly ajar or open it regularly to keep the air inside from getting too humid. Aim for the minimum temperature setting, which is normally 200–210°F (95–100°C). For about 30 minutes of energy-saving drying time, use the residual oven heat after cooking.

POSSIBILITIES

Dehydrating veggies is a really fun way to lock in fresh flavor for lightweight snacks on the go and versatile ingredients in the larder.

Powders: Lay chopped mushrooms (or whole, if small enough) on a dehydrator rack at 131°F (55°C) and dry for 8 hours or longer, then blend into a mushroom powder (**fig. a**), which can be used to season a mushroom risotto, add an umami note to veggie burgers, or give greater depth of flavor to a buckwheat pancake batter. You can also dry vegetables used for making stocks and blend them into powders for bouillon or an umami-rich replacement to reduce salt when seasoning. Or try fermented powders after making kimchi or kraut for a sweet-sour topping for salads, chips, and roasted vegetables.

Root chips: Try making some colorful root chips (**fig. b**) in the oven. Thinly slice vegetables such as carrots, beets, and sweet potatoes with a mandoline. Spread out in a single layer on a baking sheet, then bake for 2–3 hours at 250°F (120°C) until light and crispy. Season with smoked sea salt and paprika.

Sun-dried tomatoes: I love making my own version of sun-dried tomatoes. Chop tomatoes into slices or segments and dip in lemon juice to retain their bright color. Then arrange them, evenly spaced, on a dehydrator rack. Dry for 6–8 hours at 131°F (55°C), then store submerged in oil (see page 279) or in an airtight container in the fridge.

Preserving Techniques

FERMENTING

Enhancing the flavor of your vegetables while extending their shelf life is the biggest benefit of fermentation. In the right conditions, the lacto-bacteria in the veggies can transform them into a complex vintage of tangy sourness, with a distinctive bitter-sweet profile full of probiotic goodness.

PRINCIPLES

Lacto-fermentation is an anaerobic process in which the beneficial lactobacillus bacteria that are present in all vegetables reproduce and break down their natural sugars, converting them into lactic acid and gases, which inhibit the growth of harmful bacteria. The result is fermented food with a distinctive, powerful, tangy flavor. Lacto-fermentation can be unpredictable, but with patience and practice, you will learn to manipulate this living process to produce a whole new world of vegetable flavors.

Lacto-bacteria: These are the gut-friendly microbes that occur naturally on the surface of most vegetables and thrive in an anaerobic environment. Lacto-bacteria inhibit other "bad" bacteria and molds from growing and impart a delicious sourness to ferments as they reproduce and create an acidic environment that preserves vegetables for many

months. Lacto-fermentation also boosts your body's gut flora, which has been proven to boost general health and well-being.

Salt: Osmosis is one of the key processes that enables fermentation to preserve vegetables. Salt is either massaged into the vegetables, so that it breaks down the cellulose and draws water out of the permeable barrier of the cells to create its own brine covering; or, if the vegetable doesn't generate enough liquid to create a covering, as with whole carrots (see *left*), it is submerged in a premade brine. The salt helps to kill off harmful bacteria and dissolves back into the vegetable, lending it built-in seasoning. I use sea salt for all my fermentation; it has no additives or anticaking agents and amplifies flavor with its unique profile of sea minerals.

Figure a.

Figure b.

Temperature: A warm environment will help speed up the process to allow full fermentation within 7–10 days. However, if you ferment at a slightly lower temperature for 10–14 days, the flavors will be deeper and have less of a sour tang. Personally, I prefer the taste of a good winter ferment, even though it's much slower than fermenting in the summer, as it boasts an earthier bitterness and more body.

Anaerobic environment: Preventing air from reaching the vegetables is vital for fermentation to work, so tightly packing the vegetables down in their jar to remove air bubbles is essential. The liquid covering provided by the brine then creates a protective anaerobic environment for the veggies. A fermentation weight is also a very handy tool for weighing down the veggies so that it doesn't come into contact with the air. You can make your own using a small zipper-lock bag filled with water to keep the ferment below the surface level of the brine, but I recommend buying a few fermentation weights **(fig. a),** as they are super useful and last a lifetime.

Timing: It takes practice and precise timekeeping to judge when the ferment has reached the ideal level of sourness for your palate— I vary mine from 7–14 days. Sometimes I even ferment veggies for just a few days to begin the transformation of their flavor before cooking. You are looking for a level of sourness that enhances rather than overwhelms the flavor of the vegetable.

Flavorings: I often add spices to my ferments to build complexity and color. For example, I will add grated turmeric to my sauerkraut and use a combination of mild chili, ginger, and garlic to achieve that Korean chili flavor for my homemade kimchi **(fig. b).** Even fermented cucumbers benefit from aromatics such as dill, mustard seeds, chili, and peppercorns added to the fermentation process.

Storage: Halt fermentation by transferring the jars to a freezer— the pickling process will continue in the fridge, albeit at a much-reduced rate, but freezing kills off the lacto-bacteria. However, doing this negates the health benefits of the fermentation process.

RECIPE

Sauerkraut

MAKES 1 × 1¾-PINT (1-LITER) JAR

If you want to start with one of the classics, learning to make your own sauerkraut has to be your first ferment. This simple method can also be adapted to include a whole host of different vegetables, including red cabbage, fennel, celery root, and carrot. For a bit of extra flavor, add juniper berries, ginger, or dill.

INGREDIENTS

1 small cabbage
½ cucumber
Fine sea salt
1 tsp caraway seeds

Method

01 Finely slice the cabbage and cucumber, then weigh both and measure out 3 percent of the total weight in salt. Place the cabbage and cucumber in two separate bowls, then evenly cover both with the salt and caraway seeds. Massage the salt into the cabbage with your hands to break down the cellulose and encourage osmosis. The cucumber won't need massaging in the same way.

02 Leave the salted vegetables overnight, then use a pestle or rolling pin to ram them both into a sterilized jar. Ensure that you squeeze out the air pockets and allow the cabbage and cucumber to be completely submerged in their own brine. Press them beneath the surface of the brine with a fermentation weight or a small disk of parchment paper to provide an anaerobic environment.

03 Leave the jar lid loose enough to allow air to escape while the kraut ferments. Keep it at room temperature (warmer if you want a fast ferment, or cooler if you want it to ferment more slowly) and allow to ferment for 10–14 days.

04 Seal once fermentation has slowed and leave until you want to serve. Once opened, keep refrigerated and use within a week.

Figure a.

Figure b.

POSSIBILITIES

The world of sour-vegetable ferments is vast, so once you've mastered the basics, experiment with unusual vegetables, blends of root veggies, or combining veggies with fruit. Also try including strongly flavored spices and herbs in the ferment to build complexity.

Sauerkraut with a twist: Try making sauerkraut with Savoy, red, or white cabbage; Chinese cabbage; or other brassicas for your own variations on the classic. Add fennel seeds, cumin, caraway, or dill for a fresh balance of aromatic flavor.

Whole vegetables: Carrots, squash, beets, and potatoes are all excellent fermented whole. Serve torched or grilled for a contrasting sweet tang and woody char.

Blending: Blend vegetables in a food processor before fermenting them for a lower-effort ferment that's a fast track to flavor. This allows a greater surface area for the bacteria to work their magic on, resulting in a strong, rounded flavor and a quicker ferment. Use a rough paste mixed well with 2–3 percent salt to ferment garlic or chili peppers in bulk—it saves lots of time compared to chopping veggies by hand. The purée can be used as a component in kimchi or curries.

Juice: The juice drawn out of veggies during fermentation makes a fantastic salad dressing—try fermented carrot juice with a cashew and golden beet salad for zing **(fig. a)**. It also makes a great smoothie shot to kick-start your day either blended with carrots or added to other smoothies.

Dehydrate: Try drying your ferments in a dehydrator or on a baking sheet in a low oven, no hotter than 160°F (70°C). Slowly dehydrate until the texture is dry enough to crumble or blend the veggies in a spice blender. Use these complex umami powders to season dishes.

Spice it up: Tinker with a plain ferment by adding your own herbs and spices to enhance the flavor. Retain crunch for cucumber and softer vegetables with tannin-rich herbs and spices such as bay, tarragon, clove, and cinnamon—tannins inhibit the action of enzymes that break down cell walls.

Kimchi: This is a world-renowned type of vegetable ferment that is delicious with stir-fries, ramen, barbecue dishes, and eggs. It's made with cabbage, carrot, ginger, and chili—I sometimes add spring onions, chard, or kale for a twist. It has a really sweet and spicy sourness and makes an amazing pantry staple.

Colorful ferments: If you want to create a really bright ferment, add in a pinch of saffron or use root turmeric or grated beets with your veggies. A small amount will stain the whole ferment yellow or purple, and the mix of flavors makes a really interesting sour pickle **(fig. b)**.

Preserving Techniques
PICKLING

Pickling in a zingy vinegar solution is the quickest way to preserve vegetables. The benefit in the kitchen is a tart ingredient with high notes of flavor and often enhanced color. And, of course, the great win is that you can extend the shelf life of vegetables by at least a couple of weeks.

PRINCIPLES

Making your own pickles is easy. It involves submerging vegetables in a solution of vinegar and water, which is normally spiced and can be salted and sweetened, too. Once sealed in a sterilized jar, pickles can keep for up to a month in the fridge. The acid in the vinegar kills off harmful organisms, while the solution itself creates an anaerobic environment, where bacteria can't survive. Veggies with a high moisture content should be salted first to draw out excess liquid before pickling; otherwise, it will leach out in the jar and dilute the acidity of the solution. I always use a little sugar in my pickling vinegar to provide a sweet-and-sour tang; it helps preserve the veggies for longer. I also tend to use hot vinegar unless I'm pickling something delicate like flowers or baby veggies, as it softens the veggies while retaining its crunch.

Pickling vinegar: There are a few good options when considering which type of vinegar to use for pickling. For a strong acidic base, use a cheap, astringent, distilled condiment vinegar that would be unpleasant in a dressing but has a complex depth of spice and sweetness. Alternatively, use cider vinegar or white wine vinegar. I use red wine vinegar for pickling beets or red cabbage, malt vinegar for pickled onions, and mirin for radishes.

Spices: You can buy pickling spices, but I make my own blends to complement each veggie profile. My standard combination includes coriander seeds, black peppercorns, cloves, allspice, star anise, and mustard seeds. Other strong contenders are cumin seeds, dried chili, cardamom pods, juniper berries, and cinnamon sticks. Gather the spices into a muslin bag **(fig. a)**, add to the vinegar, then bring to a boil and simmer for 5 minutes. Remove the infused vinegar from heat and leave to cool, then remove the spice bag before pickling the veggies. Reuse it a couple times before discarding.

Figure a.

Figure b.

POSSIBILITIES

As soon as you start pickling vegetables to accompany your meals, you are very likely to become addicted like me. It's such a superb way to serve a vegetable garnish and takes surprisingly little effort, so start experimenting.

Flavored vinegar: To really add some depth to your pickles, try flavoring your vinegar before pickling by infusing it with fruit, such as raspberries, sloes, or strawberries, or herbs and flowers. I love using elderflower vinegar with a chargrilled tomato, tarragon vinegar with a pea pesto, or black garlic vinegar when I want to really experiment with an umami pickle dressing. To flavor, simply place your chosen ingredient in a bottle of vinegar and leave to infuse for 2 weeks. Shake daily for the first week and use within 1–2 months.

Beer pickles: The combination of beer and vinegar makes a delicious pickle and is a great way to add a hoppy depth to shallots. Heat the beer and vinegar solution with a little sugar at a ratio of 3:2:1, with a few sprigs of thyme and some juniper berries (**fig. b**). Slice the shallots in half, then submerge in the hot vinegar and leave to cool. Seal, then transfer to the fridge and use within 2–3 weeks. Beer onions are best enjoyed after 48 hours, once the flavors have had time to infuse.

Whole vegetables: It's super easy to pickle whole vegetables if they are thin enough for the vinegar to penetrate. Try thinly sliced carrots, artichoke hearts, or asparagus spears (**fig. b**) in a white wine or cider vinegar solution fortified with peppercorns and chili. Sliced or smaller veggies usually take 1–2 days to pickle, but I tend to leave whole vegetables for 5–7 days before eating—this allows more time for the pickling solution to work its way into the veggies.

Pretty in pink: Red onions (**fig. b**) are utterly transformed when submerged in a heated solution of cider vinegar, water, and sugar at a 2:2:1 ratio. They become a vibrant pink color and take on a tart sweetness that plays with their pungent profile perfectly. The weak acidity in the solution means these are not well preserved; keep in the fridge for 1 week as a tasty garnish.

Root and fruit: Combine fresh and dried fruit in your pickles to bridge the flavor trail from an earthy root vegetable to a tart pickling vinegar. Classic combinations to try include beets and cranberry, carrot and raisin, and turnip with citrus.

Scraps: Try pickling your veggie scraps for a zero-waste garnish. Thinly sliced broccoli or cauliflower stalks, carrot tops, peelings, and other offcuts destined for the compost bin can be given a fresh lease on life preserved under pickling vinegar.

Preserving Techniques

CHUTNEY

There is something truly exciting about the transformation that vinegar, sugar, and time can bring to a humble pan of chopped veggies. Chutney is a great way to preserve in bulk and an opportunity to experiment with fresh combinations of spices or dried fruit to add to the tangy vegetables.

PRINCIPLES

Chutney is one of the few vegetable recipes that can fulfill every single taste sense in one jar: salty, sweet, sour, bitter, and umami all work in harmony. The basic method is to cook diced fruit and vegetables in a large pan with vinegar, sugar, and spices until the sugar dissolves and the contents reduce in volume. The long, slow cooking evaporates much of the moisture from the ingredients and provides an acidic environment, both of which help preserve the chutney. Once you've mastered the ratios (they differ depending on the ingredients, but as a general rule, use 5 parts fruit and veggies to 2 parts vinegar to 1 part sugar) and the cooking process, you can then make your own chutneys with a wide range of vegetables. Making chutney has a transformative magic, changing the color and texture of fresh fruit and veggies beyond recognition, and will fill your kitchen with aromatics and an intense vinegar tang.

Preserving: To prevent the growth of bacteria or molds in the veggies, chutney needs a high acidity level, because these organisms cannot survive in an acid environment. This is achieved by adding plenty of vinegar. The sugar in chutney also helps preserve the ingredients; as a result of osmosis, the micro-organisms denature when placed in a concentrated sugar solution, helping the veggies last for months.

Spice it up: There are several key aromatic spices that I use for chutney making, chosen for their robust warming flavor, which cuts through the sweet-sour base of the sugar and vinegar. If you are stuck for a seasonal recipe, try my fruit and spice combination guide (see *table opposite*). These ideas are mostly interchangeable but could provide some helpful chutney inspiration if you have a surplus.

VEGETABLE	SPICE AND HERBS	FRUIT	NOTES
Beet	*Horseradish, dill, juniper berries, fennel seeds, chili, cinnamon, star anise*	*Dates, raspberries, cranberries, oranges*	*Use red wine vinegar to enhance the natural sweetness.*
Broccoli/Cauliflower	*Turmeric, mustard seeds, green chili, garlic, coriander, galangal*	*Apricot, golden sultanas, mango*	*Try making piccalilli with green beans and pickled onions.*
Carrot	*Cardamom, ginger, thyme, coriander, saffron, tamarind*	*Mango, figs, apple*	*Grated carrot cooks more quickly and is a faster chutney to make.*
Eggplant	*Nigella seeds, ginger, garlic, chili, cloves*	*Lime pickle, raisins*	*Smoked eggplant makes a great base for this chutney.*
Fennel	*Fennel seeds, dill, chervil, red chili, mustard seeds, mint, cardamom, pink peppercorns*	*Preserved lemon, apple, orange*	*Fantastic light chutney with fruity notes.*
Green beans	*Garlic, ginger, turmeric, black peppercorns, black mustard seeds, fermented red chili*	*Raisins, apple*	*A green bean, whole-grain mustard, and spiced apple chutney works really well.*
Mushroom	*Truffle, rosemary, cloves, bay, thyme, fermented garlic, juniper berries*	*Coconut, apple, blueberries, prune*	*Enrich with pungent red onion and lots of garlic.*
Onion	*Mustard seeds, black peppercorns, paprika, cloves, smoked garlic*	*Apple, raisins, figs*	*Sweet and sticky like a marmalade, a red onion chutney can work well with smoked flavors.*
Parsnip	*Cardamom, cinnamon, star anise, kashmiri chili, makrut lime leaves*	*Pear, cherries*	*Add cider during the cooking process for a sweet edge.*
Pepper	*Jalapeño, coriander, cayenne pepper, paprika, ginger*	*Peach, apple, apricot, pineapple*	*Try making with chargrilled peppers for more depth of flavor.*
Squash	*Ras el hanout, cinnamon, harissa, coriander, cumin*	*Apple, raisins, pomegranate*	*Roast the squash in advance to soften the skins and add a deeper flavor to the chutney.*
Sweet corn	*Coriander, pepper flakes, chipotle chili*	*Lime, pineapple*	*Combine with red onion and peppers for a sweet corn relish.*
Tomato	*Garlic, paprika, allspice, garam masala*	*Apple, raisins, dates, plum*	*Cook for long enough to evaporate some of the moisture from the fruit.*
Zucchini	*Fenugreek, cumin, coriander, red chili, ginger, chimichurri*	*Apple, raisins*	*Try making a marrow chutney with pollen to use up large zucchini.*

Cooking: All the chutneys I plan to preserve for the winter months are slow-cooked for long periods of time, usually 2–3 hours, in a thick-bottomed, stainless-steel pan, until they are thick enough to stick to the spoon and pour slowly. This prolonged cooking is another element of the process that helps kill off unwanted micro-organisms—through the application of heat and by lowering the available moisture content. Make sure you stir the mixture regularly, especially as it thickens, scraping the base of the pan to prevent it from burning and tainting the flavor.

Storage: Always use sterilized glass jars that have had heat of above 175°F (80°C) applied for more than 15 minutes to make sure there's no contamination before you start. Also fill the jar near to the top to minimize the amount of oxygen in the container. For preserves, you want as little oxygen as possible and less than 10 percent water present, as the oxidization of the veggies leads to spoilage. The high acidity level in chutney should make it safe for long-term storage of up to 12 months. Once opened, keep in the fridge and consume within 2 weeks.

Hot Red Tomato Chutney

MAKES 3½ PINTS (2 LITERS)

This recipe has everything you want from a good chutney: sweetness, acidity, spice, and that slow-cooked umami depth. It's inspired by a classic tomato chutney with chili, ginger, and garlic for background heat. This warmth makes it perfect with cheese or served on the side of a curry.

INGREDIENTS

1 tbsp olive oil

2 red onions, finely diced

8 garlic cloves, finely chopped

1 tbsp grated fresh ginger root

2 red chilies, seeded and finely sliced

1 tbsp mixed spice

1 tbsp paprika

1 tsp ground ginger

1 tsp chili flakes

1 tsp coriander seeds

1 tsp ground cinnamon

4½ lb (2 kg) red tomatoes, roughly chopped

2 Granny Smith or Bramley apples, peeled, cored, and sliced

3½ oz (100 g) raisins

3½ cups (1 liter) cider vinegar

2¼ lb (1 kg) golden sugar

1 tsp sea salt

Method

01 Heat the olive oil in a large saucepan; add the onions, garlic, ginger, chilies, and spices; then fry on low heat until softened. Before the onions brown, add in the tomatoes, apples, and raisins.

02 Simmer on low heat for 45 minutes, stirring every 5 minutes or so, until the apples and tomatoes are nicely cooked. Remember to stir the mixture at the bottom of the pan, not just the top, to stop it from sticking on the base.

03 Next, add the vinegar and cook for 1 more hour, remembering to stir occasionally at first and then more attentively as the liquid reduces to keep the mixture from burning on the bottom of the pan.

04 Add the sugar and stir until dissolved. Cook for 15–20 minutes on medium-high heat until it has reduced to the right consistency—you should be able to draw your spoon across the bottom of the pan and leave a trail for a few seconds. Finally, season to taste with the salt—it's best to do this near the end of cooking, because you'll be better able to judge the final flavor.

05 Spoon the chutney into sterilized jars, then seal and label. It will keep for 6–12 months.

Figure a.

Figure b.

POSSIBILITIES

Using similar cooking methods to chutney, you can experiment with smooth ketchups and dips. The process may differ slightly, but making your own condiments allows you to include exciting spices and to build strong flavors to preserve vegetables for longer.

KETCHUP

When making your own ketchup, don't try to match your favorite brand. Instead, have fun making your own proud creation.

Tomato: Soften onion, celery, and garlic in oil, then add tomatoes and spices—try coriander, cinnamon, paprika, cayenne pepper, celery salt, and allspice. Cook for 10–15 minutes, then add cider vinegar and light brown sugar. Cook for at least 45 minutes, then blend and strain. Reduce further until it reaches your consistency of choice.

Mushroom: Sauté mushrooms with shallot, garlic, mustard, allspice, cloves, and nutmeg. For herbs, try rosemary or thyme. Cook until rich and darkly colored **(fig. a)**. Add dates or prunes for sweetness, then blend.

VEGETABLE HUMMUS

I grew up eating a rainbow of colorful vegetable hummus. They add depth to the classic dip and use up roasted vegetables.

Beet: Blend cooked beet with garlic, orange juice, olive oil, and tahini. Try adding some dried apricots and cumin seeds to the blender and garnish with dill. This is fantastic with tortilla chips or crudités or with pita bread and feta cheese **(fig. b)**.

Squash: Roasted squash works really well blended with smoked garlic, olive oil, lemon, and a pinch of paprika. Garnish it with pumpkin seed dukkah and lots of chili oil.

Fava bean: Fava bean hummus with mint, lemon, pine nuts, and Parmesan cheese is a bit like a chunky pesto. Add lima beans and lots of olive oil to give it more body.

Index

Acknowledgments

This book was written and produced almost entirely in a lockdown environment. So the challenge was to produce all of the recipes and photographs from home without turning the house into a complete workplace. For this, I'd like to say a very special thank you to my wife, Holly, who helped with endless encouragement, vegetable growing in the garden, patiently reviewing my batches of photography, and sharing our living space with me while continuing to do a fantastic job of home-educating our children. Holly, you made this book possible and I'm hugely grateful.

Thank you to my children, Indy, Pippin, and Arrietty, for your taste-testing and understanding that Daddy had to spend a lot of time in the studio this year (even on weekends!) and that I needed lots of reminding when the oven timer was beeping inside. To my mom, Brigit Strawbridge-Howard, and her husband, Rob—you both read through most of this book to offer expert gardening advice, and I loved sending you pages for your feedback and input each week. To my mother-in-law, Jan, too—thank you for coming down to share so many of the meals with us and for your encouragement.

My agent, Julian, from Soho Agency, has again been an absolute pleasure to work with, and all of the DK team have made this book a wonderful experience to be a part of. Special mention to Alastair; Harriet; Christine; Abi; Ruth; and my amazing editor, Holly. A big thank you to Simon Burt for taking the photos of me in this book, Oli at Ollo Fruit, and Tia and Richard from Botelet for sharing your space on location—as always, a pleasure working with you all. The team at Veggies & More, the weekly Riverford vegetable box, and all the suppliers and producers I work with—thanks for your support and great ingredients.

Cheers, and happy cooking!
James x

About the Author

James Strawbridge is a Cornish chef, food photographer, and writer. As a chef, James creates recipes and develops new products for food brands. As a photographer, he shoots and styles the recipes he's developed for social media, websites, and his books. James works with a range of food clients across Southwest England, delivering innovative content from his home studio. He is passionate about cooking seasonally with local produce.

On television, James co-presented ITV's *The Hungry Sailors* and the BBC's *It's Not Easy Being Green*, and also makes appearances on Channel 4's *Escape to the Chateau*. When not cooking or taking photos, James can be found gig rowing, gardening, or painting.

www.strawbridgekitchen.com

@jgstrawbridge

@eco_boy